advanced

coursebook

Innovations

a course in natural English

Hugh Dellar and Andrew Walkley

THOMSON™

United Kingdom • United States • Australia • Canada • Mexico • Singapore • Spain

THOMSON

Innovations Advanced Coursebook

Dellar/Walkley

Publisher: *Christopher Wenger*
Series Editor: *Jimmie Hill*
Project Manager: *Howard Middle/HM ELT Services*
Director of Product Development: *Anita Raducanu*
Director of Product Marketing: *Amy Mabley*
International Marketing Manager: *Ian Martin*
Editors: *Liz Driscoll & Madeleine Williamson*
Development Editor: *Sarah O'Driscoll*

Sr. Print Buyer: *Mary Beth Hennebury*
Production Development: *Oxford Designers & Illustrators*
Illustrators: *Mark Duffin, Melvyn Evans, Ed McLachlan*
Photo Researcher: *Suzanne Williams/Pictureresearch.co.uk*
Cover/Text Designer: *Studio Image & Photographic Art (www.studio-image.com)*
Printer: *G. Canale & C S.p.A-Borgaro T.se (TO) -Italy*

Cover Images: Kandinsky: © *2003 Artists Rights Society (ARS), New York/ADAGP, Paris;* Da Vinci: © *Bettmann/CORBIS;* Guggenheim Museum: *Tim Hursley/SuperStock*

Printed in Italy.
1 2 3 4 5 6 7 8 9 10 _ 10 09 08 07 06

For more information, contact Thomson ELT,
High Holborn House, 50–51 Bedford Row, London WC1R 4LR,
United Kingdom.
You can visit our website at elt.thomson.com

ISBN: 1-4130-2184-0
(Coursebook)

Illustrations

Mark Duffin pp 31bl, 61r, 122tr & br; Melvyn Evans p 55; Ed McLachlan pp 14, 15
p85 Taken from "Conflict Stages" by Eric Brahm. In *Beyond Intractability*. Available at http://www.beyondintractability.org/m/conflict_stages.jsp

Photo credits

The publishers would like to thank the following sources for permission to reproduce their copyright protected photographs:

Alamy pp 11b (Bill Varie), 13l (Brian Harris), 21 (Gerald Nowak), 23 (Sylvia Cordaiy Photo Library Ltd), 25l (James Cheadle), 37 (Network Photographers), 39l (Pacific Press Service), 39r (Adams Picture Library), 51 (Shout), 56tl (David R. Frazier Photolibrary, Inc.), 56tr (WoodyStock), 56bl (David Hoffman Photo Library), 56br (Wally Bauman), 68 (Vincent MacNamara), 71 (Jeff Greenberg), 75 (Cut and Deal Ltd), 91b (Adrian Sherratt), 93 (Issac Rose), 104t (Manor Photography), 104c (Frances M. Roberts), 104b (Mark Sykes), 136tl (Homer Sykes), 141 (Dennis MacDonald); **Capital Pictures** p 119; **Cartoonbank.com** p 18 © The New Yorker Collection 1989 Eric Teitelbaum from cartoonbank.com. All rights reserved, p 52 © The New Yorker Collection 1977 Joseph Mirachi from cartoonbank.com. All rights reserved, p 62 © The New Yorker Collection 2004 Mick Stevens from cartoonbank.com. All rights reserved, p 97 © The New Yorker Collection 1992 Ed Fisher from cartoonbank.com. All rights reserved, p 101 © The New Yorker Collection 2002 Alex Gregory from cartoonbank.com. All rights reserved, p 107 © The New Yorker Collection 1998 Christohper Weyant from cartoonbank.com. All rights reserved, p 121 © The New Yorker Collection 1989 Arnie Levin from cartoonbank.com. All rights reserved, p 140 © 2006 Ted Goff from cartoonbank.com. All rights reserved ; **Corbis** pp 11tr (Chris Carroll), 31tr (Reuters), 34 (Tito Guzman), 58 (Jamil Bittar/Reuters), 69 (Architecture Studio/Vincent Kessler/Reuters), 82 (Laszlo Balogh/Reuters), 91t (Ajay Verma/Reuters), 102 (Anthony Redpath), 125l (Sygma), 125r (Reuters); **Empics** pp 16r (Michael Regan), 59 (Phil Noble/PA), 88 (Associated Press), 94 (Associated Press), 114l (Amy Sancetta/AP), 114cl (Martin Rickett/PA); **Getty Images** pp 20 (Robert Harding World Imagery), 36 (Julia Fullerton-Batten), 63 (Kelvin Murray), 65 (Angela Wyant), 83 (Carlo Allegri), 105 (Scott Barbour), 112 (Ross Kinnaird), 114cr (Stuart Franklin), 117 (Christopher Bissell), 126 (Jennifer Leigh Sauer), 136tr (Romeo Gacad), 137 (Luke Frazza); **John Birdsall Social Issues Photo Library** p 16l; **The Kobal Collection** pp 42 (New Line /Saul Zaentz /Wing Nut /Pierre Vinet), 99tr (Touchstone/Caravan); **Motoring Picture Library** p 122l; **Punchstock** pp 11tl (Digital Vision), 12l (Digital Vision), 13r (Matthias Tunger/Digital Vision), 25r (Dynamic Graphics Group/Creatas), 27 (Brand X Pictures), 47 (Corbis royalty-free), 61bl (Dan Dalton), 66 (Photodisc Red), 129 (Photodisc Green), 133 (Dana Neely), 139 (Digital Vision); **Rex Features** pp 12r (Jonathan Hordle), 22 (Page (PGE), 45l (Sipa Press), 45r (Tess Peni), 48 (JEV), 78 (Everett Collection), 99tl (Peter Brooker), 99b (London Weekend Television/LWT/KMK), 100 (Everett Collection/EVT), 114r (Ron C Angle / BEI), 134 (Alex Segre), 136bl (Sipa Press), 136br (Ilpo Musto); **Science Photo Library** p 79 (Jim Reed)

To the student

Reaching an advanced level of English is a real achievement and it can be difficult to make the next step up in competence. **Innovations Advanced** will provide the spur to reach that new level of fluency through its unique mixture of focused language tasks and stimulating skills work.

Innovations Advanced contains:

- 24 compact units covering a wide range of topics people talk about in their day-to-day lives, each one packed with the natural language English speakers use when discussing them.
- 12 units focusing on different kinds of writing, providing models and useful analysis of core structural and lexical items that occur within specific genres.
- naturally contextualised grammar practice that helps you brush up on areas you've studied already and which will stretch you by looking at new grammar patterns in speech and writing.
- challenging reading and listening texts that spark discussion and debate or which bring up personal anecdotes to share in the classroom.
- a focus on both idiomatic and more formal language to broaden the range of your English.

We hope you find **Innovations Advanced** as fun and interesting to learn from as we did to write!

Acknowledgements

Hugh Dellar has taught EFL, ESP and EAP in Indonesia and Britain, where he is now a teacher and teacher-trainer at the University of Westminster, London. He trains both native-speaker and non-native speaker teachers. He also gives papers and teacher development workshops all over the world.

Hugh would like to thank the following people for their love, encouragement, support and guidance over the years: Lisa, his mum and dad, Julian Savage, Andy Fairhurst, Andrew Walkley, Darryl Hocking, Scott Thornbury, Michael Lewis, Michael Hoey, Sally Dalzell, Maud Dunkeld and Ivor Timmis.

He would also like to thank the following for providing inspiration, joy and a world away from writing and teaching: Robin Van Persie, Manfred Krug, Peter Guralnick, Bob Dylan, Cesc Fabregas, the Vinyl Vultures, Dan Abbott, Phil Marriott, Steve Marriott, Priscilla and the peerless Thierry Henry!

Andrew Walkley has taught English since 1990. He has mainly taught in Spain and Britain, and over recent years has taught and run teacher training courses at the University of Westminster. In addition, he has given talks and workshops in various other countries.

He would like to thank the continued forbearance and love of Macu, Rebeca and Yago. He'd also like to thank the family and friends who he's seen less of because of writing, but who are no less important to him for all that. In particular, Mum, Dad, Simon, Matthew, Ben and Ruth.

Hugh and Andrew would both like to thank:
Jimmie Hill, Chris Wenger, Nick Broom, Ian Martin, Howard Middle, Stuart Tipping, Stefanie Walters, Sarah O'Driscoll, Liz Driscoll, Madeleine Williamson, David Baker for their good work and encouragement. To Nick Barrett, Rose Nicols, Rebecca Sewell – thanks for support and shared beers, coffees and laughs. We would also like to thank the University of Westminster for work, wages and other support in our writing.

Finally, mention should be made of the influence and impact our former CELTA trainees and former students have had on us. Similarly, a big hello should go to the fine people we've met on our travels around the world, the staff at The Social, London W1 and finally to Mr. Tetley and Mr. Kipling!

The authors and publishers would like to thank the following teachers for their invaluable input on this material during production:
Kerry Davis, Euro Language Consultants; Lynda Edwards; Kirsten Holt; Violeta Karastateva, The Technical University of Varna; Yordan Kosturkov, The University of Plovdiv; Amanda Lloyd, Embassy CES; Kathryn McNicoll, Chilterns English Swan; Brendan Ó Sé, University College, Cork; Giles Perry, Lingua Viva; Maria-Magdalena Pławecka, Gimnazjum no.1; Nicky Seth, British Study Centres.

Contents

He used to pick on me because I wore glasses. • It was quite a weird bunch of people. • I couldn't get a word in edgeways. • He was rambling on about something or other. • Stop fiddling! • You're going to drive me nuts! • He thinks he's God's gift to women. • Mmm, that's gorgeous! • You slob! • She's constantly sticking her nose in. • He never lifts a finger round the house. • The guy's a complete egomaniac. • Stop whingeing and do something about it! • He's very in touch with his feminine side. • Some of my best friends are black. • He's a right yuppie. • He's so smug. • You haven't heard it? It's the latest buzzword! • Can't you bend the rules just this once? • I don't like to be pigeonholed.

1 Describing people

Conversation

1 Speaking

Discuss these questions with a partner.

1. How long have you been studying English?
2. What was your last English course like? How did you get on with the other students?
3. Have you tried learning any other languages? How did you find it?
4. Who's the best language teacher you've ever had? Who's the worst?

2 Talking about language learning

Complete the sentences with the words in the box.

alive	day-to-day	her favourites	praise
around	deadly	hit it off	rambled
bully	disparate	on and off	tricky

1. She knew how to bring the subject ....
2. All the language we learnt was very relevant to our .... lives.
3. He was a bit of a .... He used to pick on people if he didn't like them.
4. She had .... who she'd speak to all the time and then she'd ignore everyone else.
5. She was very encouraging. She gave people lots of ....
6. The grammar and pronunciation is very ....
7. Ages. It must be about ten or eleven years now – ....
8. It was just .... dull. I dropped out after a few weeks.
9. He just .... on and on about grammar.
10. All we did was sit .... and chat.
11. It was quite a weird bunch of people. We were all from very .... backgrounds.
12. We got on really well. We all just .... immediately.

With a partner, decide which question in Activity 1 each sentence is an answer to.

Change partners and discuss the questions in Activity 1 again. Do any of the sentences apply to you?

3 Listening

Listen to a conversation between two people – Patrick and Zoë – talking in the break of their French class. As you listen, try to answer these questions.

1. What was their last class like?
2. What's the new class like? Do they get on with the other students?
3. What other things do they talk about?

4 Listen again

With a partner, match the verbs with the words they went with in the conversation.

1. watch	☐	a.	everybody else
2. stick	☐	b.	about grammar
3. ramble on	☐	c.	a word in edgeways
4. get	☐	d.	you in the eye
5. correct	☐	e.	my weight
6. be stuck	☐	f.	to a diet
7. look	☐	g.	next to that guy

Now match these verbs with the words they went with.

8. mumble	☐	h.	you up and down
9. fiddle	☐	i.	me the creeps
10. fancy	☐	j.	it up to you
11. eye	☐	k.	with his pens
12. give	☐	l.	to himself
13. wind	☐	m.	him
14. make	☐	n.	you up

Can you remember who or what the speakers were talking about in each case? Listen again and check your answers.

5 Speaking

Discuss these questions with a partner.

1. Patrick says, 'Life's too short to be worrying about your weight all the time.' Can you think of any other things that life's too short to be doing?
2. Do you agree that there's no harm in looking at other women/men when you're married?
3. Does anyone you know give you the creeps?

6 Using grammar: modifying nouns and adjectives

Choose the correct words in each sentence.

1. She's so / such a slob.
2. She's really / a real bitchy.
3. She's really / a right pain in the arse.
4. She's a bit / a bit of a bully.
5. She's so / such a selfish.
6. She's completely / a complete nerd.
7. She's a bit / a bit of a weird.
8. She's really / a real busybody.
9. She's so / such a hypocritical.
10. She's so / such a dizzy.

All the sentences above could be used to describe men as well as women. Do you think any of them are more common with one sex?

Now match these follow-up comments with the sentences above.

a. She's always talking behind your back. She can just be quite nasty.
b. She's always complaining about something or other and wasting my time.
c. She's forever pushing people around and telling them what to do.
d. She's constantly sticking her nose into other people's business.
e. She's constantly losing things and she can just be a bit stupid sometimes.
f. All she does is sit in front of her computer all day.
g. All she does is lie around all day, smoking and watching telly. She just never lifts a finger round the house.
h. All she thinks about is herself.
i. She just never really talks to anyone and she looks a bit strange as well.
j. She'll tell you off for something and then she'll go and do exactly the same thing herself.

Work with a partner and test each other.
Student A: Close your book.
Student B: Read out the follow-up comments.
Student A: Say the matching sentences.

Do you know anyone like the people above?

For more information on modifying nouns and adjectives, see G1.

Real English: bitchy

Saying someone is a bitch is very rude. However, if you say someone is a bit bitchy or that they make bitchy comments, it is not rude. It just means they say unkind or unpleasant things about people. The meaning has nothing to do with sex! We can also bitch about or have a bitch about people or things when we complain about them.

When the boss isn't there, we usually sit around and bitch about him!

I went out with Julie last night and had a good bitch about work.

7 Ways of adding emphasis

Did you notice these patterns for emphasising frequency?

- He's always / constantly / forever ... -ing
- He just never ...
- All he (ever) ... is ...

Choose some of these words to describe people you know. Use the patterns above to add follow-up comments.

an egomaniac	a loser	a party animal
a know-all	macho	tight-fisted
a ladies' man	moody	a whinger
laid-back	obsessed with	a workaholic

Tell some other students about these people.

Reading

1 Before you read

In Britain, it's common to categorise people in lots of different ways. People may be pigeonholed depending on the newspaper they read, the city they grew up in, what social class they are, what kind of lifestyle they lead, how they dress, their age, and so on.

Discuss these questions with a partner.

1. Do you stereotype people in similar ways in your country?
2. Do you have special names for any particular type of person?
3. Do you think any of the stereotypes are fair/unfair? Why?

2 While you read

Read the humorous text about British social types on the opposite page. As you read, decide if any of the social types are similar to the ones you have in your country.

3 Comprehension

Which of the social types might say these things?

1. Rather than spending all that money on weapons, they should improve hospitals.
2. My taxes have gone up, but the country's going downhill.
3. I can't remember how I got home last night, but it was a great night!
4. Just because I look after myself and I'm into clothes, it doesn't mean I'm gay!
5. Children are just so time-consuming, not to mention expensive!
6. If you stick together and can laugh about things that go wrong, you can get through anything.
7. You mean some people actually clean their own houses? Doesn't everyone have a maid, then? How ghastly!

4 Speaking

Discuss these questions with a partner.

1. Do any of these social types exist in your country?
2. Do people see these types as negative, positive, or just neutral?
3. Do you fall into any social group? Do people ever stereotype you? Do you mind?

5 Word check: collocations

Below are different groups of collocations. Find the missing words from the text.

Compound adjectives

1. fashion- / environmentally / health- / politically ....
2. university- / highly / privately / well- ....
3. community- / bloody- / open- / politically ....

Adjective + noun

4. privileged / deprived / religious / working-class ....
5. extravagant / acquired / eclectic / strange ....

Verb + noun

6. develop / damage / have / live up to ....
7. bend / flout / follow / stick to ....
8. pursue / boost / end / ruin ....

Can you find any other examples of these types of collocations in the text?

Try to use some of the collocations to talk about:

- yourself.
- your country's leader.
- people from your town/city.

Typical!

Buzzwords come and buzzwords go. In 1980s Britain, we had **yuppies** – young urban professionals – living in their converted warehouses, driving BMWs, drinking in expensive wine bars and making loads of money. Following hot on their heels were the **Buppies** – black urban professionals! Then came **the lad** and his female equivalent **the ladette** – binge-drinking, chain-smoking and swearing their way through the 90s. A few years later, David Beckham introduced **the metrosexual** – fashion-conscious straight men in touch with their feminine sides, and very keen on shopping and hair and beauty products!

Here, we explore some of Britain's other social types, some of which have stood the test of time and moved from buzzword to institution, some of which may well be here today – and gone tomorrow!

Typical Guardian readers

The Guardian – a popular broadsheet newspaper – is the bible of left-wing voters. Stereotypically, *Guardian* readers are middle-aged, middle-class and university-educated. They like to think of themselves as open-minded, but others think they're simply smug and self-satisfied! They tend to be pro-public spending on health care and education, pro-political correctness and pro-immigration – although some cynics say that's only because they don't live close to any of the poorer immigrants! By and large, they're anti-war, anti-hunting and anti-*Daily Mail*!

Typical Daily Mail readers

The Daily Mail is a paper that likes to think of itself as serious, but that actually seems to be full of 'My husband left me for another woman' articles, puzzles, quizzes and lifestyle questionnaires. If you asked a typical *Guardian* reader, they'd probably tell you that *The Mail* is aimed at frightened, paranoid white right-wingers who like to imagine they are now an oppressed minority. *Daily Mail* readers always seem to be whingeing about one thing or another. Stereotypically, they often preface their opinions with 'I'm not racist, but ...' and constantly remind us that 'Things aren't what they used to be'.

Scousers

Scousers are people from Liverpool, a port on the north-west coast of England with a large Catholic community and strong links to Ireland. It was also the home of The Beatles. Liverpool is traditionally a working-class city that has gone through a lot of ups and downs, and its people have developed a reputation for being survivors – even if that may sometimes have meant bending a few rules. Scousers are also believed to be natural comedians who are very proud of their city and their football clubs, and very community-minded.

Sloanes

Sloanes (also known as Sloane Rangers) are named after Sloane Square, an incredibly posh area in west London. Princess Diana was regularly described in the newspapers as a Sloane before she became a Princess. Sloanes come from very privileged backgrounds and spend half their lives going to lavish parties and the other half in their big country houses hunting, shooting and fishing. Sloanes have extravagant tastes in almost everything and seem utterly uninterested in anything outside of their narrow little world – hence their reputation for not exactly being Einsteins!

Dinkie couples

DINKIE stands for Double Income No Kids and Dinkie couples are a growing social trend. Not only are couples getting married later and later nowadays – if they bother to tie the knot at all – but many are also choosing not to have kids, and to pursue their careers and enjoy the wealth it brings instead. They holiday in the sun twice a year, own two decent cars and possibly even have a second home in the countryside – much to the horror of *Daily Mail* readers, who think they are selfish, self-centred and contributing to the downfall of society! ■

I like to delegate. • I feel totally out of my depth. • I get very irate about all their time-wasting. • I'll draw up the contract and have it sent to you. • Don't hassle me! I've got a lot on my plate at the moment. • That was a bit insensitive, wasn't it? • There's no need to snap. • He seems to think I'm Superwoman. • I'm absolutely knackered by Friday. • They're having a crackdown on stealing office stationery. • I find manual work slightly demeaning. • Teaching is emotionally very demanding. • He's a very conscientious worker. • I find the job immensely rewarding. • I've got some very tough sales targets to meet. • When's the deadline for this work? • I refuse to feel guilty about it.

2 Work and office politics

Conversation

1 Talking about what your job involves

Complete the expressions below with the verbs in the box.

deal with	do	draw up	keep in touch	make

1. .... research into the causes of Alzheimer's / my tax return
2. .... the marketing side of things / irate customers
3. .... ads and promos / travel arrangements for the boss
4. .... with our branches overseas / with clients around the country
5. .... a contract / a new policy

Now complete these expressions with the verbs in the box.

delegate	liaise	organise	oversee	negotiate

6. .... prices with our suppliers / contracts with the unions
7. .... with the police / between different departments
8. .... spending / the launch of our new range of clothing
9. .... international conferences / weddings and events like that
10. .... a lot of work to my assistant / responsibility to some of the juniors

2 Speaking

Discuss these questions with a partner.

1. Are you working at the moment?
2. If yes, doing what? What exactly does your job involve?
3. Have you always done this kind of thing?
4. How do you get on with the people you work with?
5. If you're not working, have you got any idea what you'd like to do in the future?

3 Work idioms

Match the idioms with the meanings.

1. I've got a lot on my plate at work at the moment.
2. My boss is a real slave-driver.
3. I'm still finding my feet.
4. They just threw me in at the deep end.
5. I'm totally out of my depth.
6. She's not pulling her weight.
7. I don't want to rock the boat.
8. She's supposed to be showing me the ropes.

a. not doing her fair share of the work
b. showing me what to do and how everything works
c. getting used to things
d. force people to change the way they do things
e. I'm very busy with things.
f. I can't cope. The work is too demanding.
g. very demanding and bossy, dictatorial
h. didn't give me any support when I first started

Spend two minutes trying to memorise the idioms. Then work with a partner. Cover the idioms. Use the meanings to help you recall the idioms.

My boss is a real slave-driver.

She's not pulling her weight.

4 Role play

Choose two of the idioms in Activity 3. Imagine you have these problems at work. Spend two minutes thinking about the circumstances.

Now work with a partner and role-play a conversation between two friends about work. One of you should explain your problems. The other should sympathise. Begin like this:

- So how're things at work?

5 Listening

You're going to listen to two friends – Rachel and Lynn – talking on the phone. Lynn has recently started working as a PA. Before you listen, discuss what you think being a PA involves. Do you think it's a good job or not? Why?

Now listen and decide how things are going for Lynn and why.

Real English: He seems to think ...

We use seems to talk about things we feel are true, things that appear true to us.
He seems to think I'm some kind of idiot!
All I seem to do all day is just make the tea for everyone!
I can't seem to find my keys. Have you seen them?

Find three more examples of seem in the tapescript at the back of the book.

I've got a lot on my plate at work at the moment.

I'm totally out of my depth.

6 Describing people you work with

Complete the sentences with the words in the box.

accessible	dictatorial	inflexible	moody
ambitious	direct	insensitive	reliable
conscientious	even-handed		

1. My boss is really domineering and he never listens to a word anyone else ever says. He's so .... !
2. I'll say one thing for her. She's very .... She doesn't mince her words. She always tells you exactly what's on her mind.
3. He probably doesn't mean to be, but he can be really .... sometimes. Some of the things he says are very hurtful.
4. She's a great boss – very .... She treats all of us exactly the same, she doesn't have any favourites or anything.
5. He's quite .... , quite up-and-down. He loses his temper really easily!
6. He seems frighteningly .... I don't think I've ever met anybody quite so keen to climb the career ladder.
7. She's a very .... worker. She always pays a lot of attention to detail and makes sure everything is done properly.
8. He's a very .... worker. If he says he'll do something, he does it.
9. She can be a bit .... at times. She's kind of stuck in her own way of doing things.
10. She's a great boss, very .... Her door's always open to everyone and she's really easy to talk to.

Can you use any of these sentences to talk about people you know? Tell a partner.

7 Role play

You are going to do the role play in Activity 4 again. First, look at the tapescript at the back of the book and underline any expressions you want to use this time.

Now find a new partner and do the role play again – this time, on the phone!

Reading

1 Vocabulary and listening

Read the six newspaper headlines. Then discuss with a partner what you think happened in each case.

1. Woman wins £22,000 in sexual harassment case
2. Mother wins posthumous racial discrimination claim
3. New legislation outlaws age discrimination in the workplace
4. Tribunal upholds mother's right to work part-time
5. Government crackdown on bullying in the workplace
6. Unfair dismissal verdict upheld in landmark case for the disabled

Listen to a short extract from a news programme. Which of the stories above do the two reports talk about? What happened in each case? How did the company respond?

2 Listen again

Listen and complete the first report.

The family of a black man who committed suicide after being subjected to (1) .... bullying have agreed an (2) .... settlement from his employers. Julian Smith hanged himself at his family home two years ago and his mother (3) .... the company for racial discrimination on behalf of her son.
The company conducted a (4) .... investigation, which revealed that white colleagues had (5) .... Julian in his work and ostracised him following an (6) .... he had made to management about abuse and name-calling.
In a statement the company expressed (7) .... at its handling of the affair and stated that it was instigating (8) .... to ensure that all discrimination is stamped out.

3 Speaking

Discuss these questions with a partner.

1. Have you heard of any cases of unfair dismissal or discrimination in the workplace? What happened?
2. Have you heard of anyone ever suing a company? Why? Did they win?
3. Do you think workers have too many rights or too few?

4 Describing jobs

Make sure you know what the jobs in the box on the left are. Then discuss with a partner which of the expressions in the box on the right you could use to describe the jobs. Use each expression as many times as you want.

a care assistant	challenging
a football manager	emotionally demanding
a GP	financially rewarding
a history academic	highly stressful
a househusband	high-powered
a housewife	immensely rewarding
a journalist	incredibly competitive
a labourer	incredibly tedious
a management consultant	not very fulfilling
a marketing manager	physically demanding
a plumber	slightly demeaning
a psychiatrist	very varied
a refuse collector	
a social worker	
a stockbroker	
a street cleaner	

Change partners. Tell your new partner which of the jobs you would/wouldn't like to do. Why / why not? Do you know anyone who does any of these jobs? What do they think of their job?

5 While you read

You're going to read an article about a woman who made a change in her work life. Read the article and answer these questions.

1. What change did she make? Why?
2. Do you think she made the right decision? Why / why not?

Reclaiming my life

It's 10.30 and I'm just settling down to my mid-morning coffee break. I open the paper and two articles leap out at me. The first – *Overworked Britons feel ill and too tired for love* – reports the findings of a survey which found that over half the working population are so tired by the time they get home that their sex lives are suffering. The other article – *Unpaid overtime tops £23bn mark* – reports that research conducted by a trade union reveals that businesses increasingly rely on staff putting in extra hours without extra pay, and that the average person would have each earned £4,650 for their efforts if they had received a wage.

I love reading the newspaper, because it is always full of articles like these, which just confirm to me that I have made the right choice: I am a stay-at-home mum.

I was not the most obvious candidate for being a stay-at-home mum. My own mother always worked – she was a teacher – and when I became pregnant, my intention was always to continue my successful career in marketing after my first child, Naomi, was born. In fact, I did go back to work after my six months of maternity leave. I left Naomi at a childminder's at eight o'clock in the morning and collected her at six o'clock in the evening. This worked for a while, but as she grew and started to walk and talk, she got increasingly upset when I left her in the mornings. I had incredible pangs of guilt. I still enjoyed my job, but whereas before it had been everything to me, now it seemed somehow more trivial. What was more important – promoting toiletries or raising a happy child? However, the pressures of work hadn't changed – there were still sales targets to meet, new products to be pushed – and I was frequently home late. There were some days when my husband Alan picked Naomi up when I wouldn't see Naomi awake all day and, yes, I was too knackered to speak to my husband, let alone make love.

The crunch came one day when I was on my way home from work. The rush hour was just beginning and the underground train was particularly packed. I just about squeezed on and found myself pressed up against the sweaty armpit of a guy holding up *Computer Weekly* to his face to read. I got off at Victoria to catch my train out of the city, only to find the place was in chaos. The main station had been evacuated because of a security alert. Nobody knew when it would reopen. There were hundreds of people getting increasingly agitated.

I rang my childminder to warn her I'd be late. We had a rather terse conversation – it wasn't the first time, but as it turned out, it was the last. I told her I'd see if I could get Alan to pick up Naomi. I rang him, but as soon as he picked up the phone, I knew I shouldn't have. I could hear the stress and anxiety in his voice. He'd told me he had to work late – a tight deadline to meet. 'How the hell am I going to get it done with you phoning me all the time?' he snapped. When I pointed out that phoning him once is hardly 'all the time', he just slammed down the phone on me.

I understood his situation, but it didn't stop me from feeling angry and resentful, until I really thought about who or rather what was to blame – work. There and then I took out my laptop and typed my letter of resignation.

That was seven years ago now and I've hardly looked back. Of course, when people ask me 'what do you do?', there are some who look on me as some kind of lesser being when I say I'm a homemaker, but that's their problem, not mine. I see it as working with children and that can be as rewarding, fulfilling and challenging as any other job.

From a personal point of view, I think it's probably saved our marriage. Of course, the lack of money places a bit of a strain on things every once in a while, but sacrificing a new car or a second holiday for a better home life seems the sensible option. And of course, I no longer feel too ill or too tired, which is perhaps why I'm expecting my third child.

6 Speaking

Which of these statements about the article do you agree with?

1. I don't like her. She's a bit smug.
2. I like her. She knows her own mind.
3. She's just kidding herself she's happy.
4. Her husband is just taking her for granted.
5. Her mother created unrealistic expectations for her.
6. She had no reason to feel guilty about being a working mum.
7. Not everyone can afford to make the decision she's made.
8. Companies aren't interested in their employees as people.

7 Vocabulary check

Complete the sentences with words from the article.

1. I'm hoping to publish the .... of my research next year.
2. Recent research has blamed the increase in divorce on the mounting .... of work.
3. The government has set some tough .... for reducing crime. The question is, can they meet them?
4. She's a nice person, but if it came to the .... , I just don't think I could rely on her to pull her weight.
5. The shop had to be .... because of a security ....
6. We're working to a very .... deadline for this project and we'll be penalised if we miss it.
7. I'm sorry I .... at you. I shouldn't have spoken to you like that.
8. When I got sacked, it put an enormous .... on our marriage.

Writing: An introduction

1 Speaking

Discuss these questions with a partner.

1. Do you write much in your own language? What kinds of things?
2. Do you enjoy writing in your own language?
3. In English, do you think you are better at speaking or writing? Why?
4. What kinds of things do you write in English? Why?

2 Listening

You're going to hear a brief talk by one of the authors of this coursebook about why students may be better at writing than speaking, or vice versa.

Listen and answer these questions:

1. What are the reasons the author gives?
2. What examples does he give of the differences between spoken and written English?
3. What two comparisons does he make near the end of the talk?

Is there anything you heard that you disagree with? Can you think of any other reasons why someone's writing might not be very good?

3 Spoken and written English

Choose the words in red which are more appropriate for the context.

1. Cross it out / Delete where applicable.
2. I'm sorry, but I bought this yesterday and there's something wrong with it / there is a defect in the appliance.
3. Applicants should affix / stick a recent photograph to the form.
4. This timetable is subject to alteration / change.
5. I hope you read all the small print on the back / reverse of the form before you signed it.
6. Apparently, you've got to have / be in possession of a driving licence or some other ID to get in.
7. He charges £100 a week in rent and then on top of that / in addition I have to pay all the bills.
8. Attractive arty Irish guy, 36, laid-back, into cinema, theatre, music, exhibitions seeks / looks for similar 25–40 F.

What would you write if you put a personal ad in the paper?

4 Spelling and punctuation

In each line, there is one spelling or punctuation mistake. Correct the mistakes. For example:

1 *interviews*

Make your writing look neat and organised

They say that in job ~~interveiws~~ and meetings, people make their minds up about a person within the first ten seconds. appearances are important and the same is true of a piece of writen work. A teacher, or more importantly an examiner picking up an essay which has scrawled handwriting or sloping lines, will immediately be predisposed to giveing that essay a bad mark – irrespective of the actuall content. If you can't write legibly in joined-up writing, it's best not to try. However, don't write in capitol letters as it's harder to see where sentences begin and end. Similarly it's important to organise you're writing into paragraphs. An essay written in one block, gives a bad impression because it looks as if the writer has'nt considered what's important and what's not – where one part of a story or essay stops and another begins. Paragraphing brakes up a piece of writing and makes it easier to follow an arguement. Weather your paragraphs are well constructed or not, making sure you have them gives the impression of an organised mind! Finally remember that writing, which has a lot of spelling mistakes is seen by many readers as a sign of a lack of intelligence. Always check your writing thoroughly, even if you have spell checked it on your computer. Keep a record of the mistakes you make and practice spelling them, correctly.

This text should be paragraphed. How would you divide it into paragraphs?

5 Speaking

Rank these pieces of advice on improving your writing from 1 (the most important) to 8 (the least important).

a. Make your writing look neat.
b. Organise your writing in paragraphs.
c. Read good models of writing.
d. Notice and copy chunks of language.
e. Plan what you're going to write.
f. Re-write what you've written.
g. Keep records of language you learn and mistakes you make.
h. Practise regularly.

Compare your ideas with a partner. Explain your decisions.

6 Reading: noticing, copying and plagiarism

In Activity 5, did you think the idea of copying was good or bad? Why? Read this short text and decide if the writer agrees with you.

On the whole, I think copying is essential when learning to write in any language, but especially in a foreign language. However, isn't copying cheating? Surely students should write in their own words and give their own ideas? Well, yes and no. In a sense, it depends on the kind of text you're writing. Many formal letters are very formulaic and use chunks of language – even whole sentences – over and over again. For example:

Please do not hesitate to contact me should you require any further information.

In fact, many companies have templates for staff to copy with some minor adaptations. Obviously, for a foreign student who has to write a letter like this under exam conditions, then peering over someone's shoulder and copying is wrong. However, the initial copying of the formulaic chunks is not – it's normal. You just have to remember them for the exam!

Although copying formulaic sentences is acceptable, copying from books when writing essays for school or university is very much frowned upon. Copying someone else's writing and ideas, and pretending it is your original work is known as plagiarism and is illegal! At worst, people can be sued in the civil courts and, at best, would be failed for an assignment. However, the key here from a language learner's perspective is the word *original*. Many pieces of academic writing also contain a large number of semi-fixed chunks or sentence frames which you can copy. In these cases, noticing and copying whole chunks of language does not necessarily mean you always have to convey the same message. A sentence like the example below could be 'copied', but adapted in many ways especially if you keep a record of other useful collocations.

In conclusion, I feel that the death penalty offers a lasting solution to the problem of violent crime.

Has the text changed your mind about copying or ways of improving your writing?

7 Making use of sentence frames

Complete the sentences with the words in the box.

congestion	fails	partial
doesn't	goes	radical

1. In conclusion, I feel that the death penalty largely .... to offer a lasting solution to the problem of violent crime.
2. In conclusion, I feel that the death penalty .... offer any kind of solution to the problem of violent crime.
3. In conclusion, I feel that the death penalty .... some way to offering a lasting solution to the problem of violent crime.
4. In conclusion, I feel that the death penalty only offers a .... solution to the problem of violent crime.
5. In conclusion, I feel that enforced therapy offers a more .... solution to the problem of violent crime.
6. In conclusion, I feel that road pricing offers a lasting solution to the problem of ....

Write three sentences of your own based on the same sentence frame.

8 Collocations: *problem* and *solution*

Many essays require you to focus on problems and solutions. Having a good range of collocates that go with these key words can help develop your writing. There are many exercises in this book and in the Workbook which focus on collocation. You may also find books like *Key Words for Fluency Upper-Intermediate* useful.

Complete the collocations with the word *problem(s)* or *solution(s)*. In some gaps, both the singular and plural forms are possible.

1. It is an intractable ....
2. We need to start addressing the ....
3. It is a very drastic ....
4. A number of .... have been put forward, but they were all rejected.
5. It's a long-standing ....
6. We need to get to the root of the ....
7. It will only exacerbate the ....
8. The .... proved unworkable.
9. We should try and find a diplomatic ....
10. It's a .... which is fraught with ....

Choose five of these collocations and give examples of how you could use them to talk about problems in the world today.

It's a city steeped in history. • You can look out across the skyline from the hotel bar. • They're a bit provincial there. • It's right off the beaten track. • It didn't really live up to the hype. • He's always jetting off somewhere or other. • We didn't really venture out of the hotel. • Really? It sounds like my idea of hell. • It's nowhere near as big as Istanbul. • It's the Chinese equivalent of Liverpool. • I'm a bit worn out after all that sightseeing. • Town twinning? What a joke! • It's caused a huge row. • It's just a complete eyesore. • They're trying to foster better relations. • We have strong links with Glasgow. • It's been a major source of corruption. • They exploit the system to line their own pockets.

3 Describing places

Conversation

1 Describing places

Complete the sentences with the words in the box.

ancient	no-go	skyline	compact
remote	skyscrapers	deprived	residential
sleepy	ghost town	shanty towns	sprawling

1. It's an .... city. It was founded over 2000 years ago.
2. It's a seaside resort, but we stayed there in the off-season, so it was more like a .... It was absolutely dead!
3. What I like about Amsterdam is how .... it is. I mean, you can walk round it very easily.
4. It's a huge .... city – it goes on for miles and miles!
5. She's from some place called Batagal, in a really .... part of Siberia.
6. All round the outskirts of Johannesburg are these huge sprawling .... They're really rough. They're like complete .... areas for the police!
7. When we had kids, we decided to move to a more .... area – it was just quieter with less traffic.
8. It's a nice enough place. It's just a .... little provincial town where nothing much ever really happens.
9. As you come across the Brooklyn Bridge, the Manhattan .... is just incredible – all those .... everywhere! It's really exciting.
10. It's a very poor area – one of the most run-down, ... areas of the city.

Which of the sentences can you use to talk about places you know? Tell a partner as much as you can about these places.

2 Listening

Listen to three short conversations. As you listen, try to answer these questions.

1. What kind of places are the people talking about?
2. Why are the places being discussed?

3 After you listen

Discuss with a partner whether you think these sentences are true or false. Try to justify your decisions.

1a. Ruth's job in Sierra Leone was financially rewarding.
1b. The students in Sierra Leone weren't keen on learning English.
2a. Neil and Becca are a bit tired at the moment.
2b. Their new flat is fairly central.
3a. Jane Peel found the food in Tallinn quite heavy.
3b. She thought the Estonians were pretty cold, miserable people.

Listen again and check your answers. Try to note down the exact words that tell you why each sentence is true or false.

Real English: hype

Jane Peel said that the hype about the Baltics seems to be true. Hype is advertising and other kinds of publicity that tries to get everybody talking about how good something is. Sometimes things don't live up to the hype and are a real let-down. You can then tell people Don't believe the hype! The media sometimes hypes things up and makes them sound better than they are.

4 Speaking

Discuss these questions with a partner.

1. Do you know anyone who's ever done any volunteer work?
2. Have you ever done any D-I-Y? Are you any good at it?
3. You heard that living out in the commuter belt 'sounds like my idea of hell'. What's YOUR idea of hell?
4. Which holiday destinations are being hyped at the moment? Have you been to any of them? Is anything else being hyped up?

5 Holiday activities

Match the sentence beginnings with the endings.

1. We didn't really venture
2. We saw
3. We just spent the whole time lazing around
4. We hitch-hiked
5. We camped out
6. The people there party

a. by the pool.
b. in the mountains for a few days.
c. out of our hotel very much.
d. all the sights.
e. like there's no tomorrow.
f. all round the country.

Now match these sentence beginnings with the endings.

7. We went out and hit
8. You're always jetting off
9. I usually try and stay
10. We spent ten days trekking
11. John and Ben just spent the whole time hanging out
12. It was really nice just being able to let

g. round the pool with all the other kids!
h. my hair down for a change.
i. for the weekend to some foreign city or other.
j. off the beaten track.
k. through the rainforest.
l. the town every night.

6 Role play

Work with a partner. Role-play a conversation between two friends who have recently returned from their holidays.

Student A: You're an adventurous holidaymaker.
Student B: You're a dull and predictable holidaymaker!

Spend three minutes deciding where you went, who you went with and what you did each day. Decide which of the expressions in Activity 5 you want to use. Try to remember them. Begin the conversation like this:

A: Hi, how're you? How was your holiday?
B: Oh, not too bad, thanks. Didn't do very much, you know.
A: Oh, right. So where did you go again?

7 Using grammar: comparing places

Choose the correct form in each sentence.

1. Their economy is nowhere / nothing near as strong as ours at the moment. Inflation is out of control over there.
2. The food here is miles / metres better, I can tell you! Everything there was really stodgy and it's very limited too.
3. The transport system there is a million fold / times better than the rusty, worn-out mess we've got here!
4. I like it here, but it's not even similar / close to being as romantic or charming as Paris. Paris is just such a seductive city.
5. I suppose Mar del Plata is the Argentinian equal / equivalent of somewhere like Bournemouth or Torquay – a classic seaside holiday resort.
6. The standard of living here is nowhere / nothing like as good as it is there. They've got it all figured out over there, you know!
7. I think there are definite comparisons / parallels between the two countries. We've both lost empires, we're both on a bit of a downward spiral and we're both very proud.
8. There's no comparing / comparison! I much prefer it here. It's out in the middle of nowhere there and it's totally dead at night.
9. I like my hometown, but it's not in the same league / competition as the capital.
10. Bangkok is amazing! I found the rest of the country a bit dull by / when comparison, to be honest.

For more information on making comparisons like this, see G2.

8 Practice

Think of five towns, cities or countries that you know well. Spend a few minutes thinking about how they compare with the place you're studying in. Decide which of the comparison forms in Activity 7 you want to use. Then tell a partner.

Reading

1 Before you read

Towns or cities often sign an official agreement with a town or city in another country to establish a social or economic connection. This is called town twinning.

Do you know if the place you live in is twinned with anywhere? Do you think twinning is a good idea? Why / why not?

2 While you read

Read the article and find out if the author thinks twinning is a good idea. Why / why not?

3 Comprehension

Discuss these questions with a partner.

1. Why do you think people in Belper were insulted by the gift? Would you have been?
2. Why do you think Wincanton and Preston wanted to twin with the towns mentioned? Why do you think they were stopped? Who do you agree with?
3. Which of the examples of bad publicity are the most serious? Why?
4. What kind of insights do you think students gain from exchanges? Do you agree with Tom Clark that they couldn't get them otherwise?

Twin Trouble?

A ROW HAS erupted between the twin towns of Belper in Derbyshire (UK) and Pawtucket, Rhode Island (USA). At the centre of the row is a £6,000 seven-foot-tall Mr Potato Head figure which was given to the people of Belper as a sign of friendship and respect from their American cousins. Mr Potato Head is a game produced by the toy company Hasbro, which is based in Pawtucket.

Unfortunately, the 'gift' has largely been taken as an insult by the people of Belper, who have condemned it as 'tacky' and 'an eyesore', and have started a campaign to have the fibreglass statue returned. The campaign has, in turn, caused upset in Rhode Island, where they perceive the reaction to their 'warm gesture of friendship' as rather snobbish. Both town councils are now looking for a compromise which may see the figure rehoused in a local theme park.

The incident is in fact just the latest in a long line of controversies that has dogged the twinning movement. Last year, the government stopped Ankh-Morpork from being put on road signs in Wincanton in south west England, despite the towns having been successfully twinned the year before. They explained that the fictional Ankh-Morpork, which features in the books of best-selling author Terry Pratchett, did not qualify, as all towns featured on road signs needed to actually exist. In 2003, there was a public outcry over a proposed link between the northern town of Preston and the Palestinian town of Nablus. The idea was seen as inappropriate, given the reputation of Nablus as a source of suicide bombers, and the proposal was eventually rejected.

The following year, Glasgow provoked controversy when it entered into an agreement with Karachi in Pakistan. Apart from the huge differences in culture and climate, the agreement attracted attention because Glasgow was already twinned with eight other towns and cities. It was seen as excessive and a potential source of corruption.

And certainly there have been instances of malpractice in other towns. Two councillors were recently condemned for using twinning links as an excuse to take part in a German beer festival, a visit to the

Mr Potato Head, Pawtucket

home of Elvis, and a flight in a hot-air balloon over a French valley – all at taxpayers' expense.

Yet perhaps all this bad publicity is exaggerated and unfairly detracts from the true value of town twinning. Tom Clark, a twinning representative, says that in fact 'councillors are generally very wary of using twinning links for freebies, because they are aware that it can be a vote loser'. He prefers to highlight the economic and social benefits of town twinning: 'Although the first twinning took place back in the twenties, the movement really took off in the fifties as a way of fostering good relations between nations and repairing the damage done by the war. I think the twin town movement has helped in no small way to maintain peace in Europe. Just think of all the student-exchange programmes twinning has facilitated. Millions of British children have visited families in foreign countries over the years and in doing so have gained insights into other cultures that they wouldn't have got otherwise. And of course twinning has led to many beneficial links between companies and often attracts inward investment.'

If Belper is anything to go by, Tom Clark is right. Despite the misunderstanding over Mr Potato Head, the relationship has led to the creation of a new tourist visitor centre. A Rhode Island company has also opened a factory in Belper creating 500 new jobs. And as for student exchanges – I had my first kiss on one! Not the kind of insight Clark had in mind perhaps, but a valuable insight nonetheless! ■

4 Vocabulary check

When you read, it's important to notice combinations of words. It's often useful to start with a noun and notice the adjectives, verbs and other nouns that they collocate with. Also notice grammatical features – does the noun go in front of the verb or after it? Is the noun plural or singular? Does it go with *a*, *the* or is there no article?

Below are ten nouns from the text. Make a list of the collocations for each noun that were used in the text.

row	movement	agreement	relations
campaign	outcry	benefits	damage
controversies	source		

Compare your list with a partner. Which combinations did you know already? Of the new ones, which do you think are the most useful to remember?

5 Speaking

Discuss these questions with a partner.

1. Do you have any of these movements in your country?
   Are they big? Do they have much influence? Do you support any of them?

animal rights movement
anti-globalisation movement
feminist movement
home-schooling movement
human rights movement
peace movement
separatist movement
trade union movement

2. Has there been a public outcry over anything recently? What? What do you think about it?

6 Word building

In the article, the writer says, 'there was a public outcry over the proposed link' and later says 'the proposal was eventually rejected'. This kind of change of form is quite common in written English because writers often like to avoid a lot of repetition.

Complete the sentences with the correct forms of the words given.

1. **vary**
   The nightlife in the town is very .... There's everything from football to opera as well as a huge .... of restaurants.
2. **pressure**
   Hatton Council has bowed to public .... and agreed not to demolish the historic church of St John the Baptist. The council had claimed the building was unsafe and it could not afford to repair it, but demonstrations and petitions by local people have .... the council into reversing its decision.
3. **apply, regenerate**
   Liverpool is .... for European funding to .... the inner city area of Toxteth. Toxteth is one of the most deprived areas in Europe.
   If the .... is successful the .... work will start early next year.
4. **critic, succeed**
   A number of people have .... the poor organisation of the city's arts festival following problems with ticketing and publicity. However, the organisers have rejected the ....
   They claim that, while there was always room for improvement, the festival had been hugely ....
   They pointed to the large attendances at most events as a sign of this ....

Find words in the sentences above based on the verbs in the box.

demonstrate	fund	organise	improve
decide	deprive	publicise	attend

7 Pronunciation

Sometimes the word stress changes as words change form. How does the word stress change in these pairs of words?

anxious	anxiety
controversy	controversial
export (n)	export (v)
finance	financial

insulting	insult
photography	photogenic
publicity	publicise
responsible	responsibilities

Listen and repeat the sentences.

He got off lightly. • He took a plea bargain. • It was an awful miscarriage of justice. • They just turn a blind eye to it. • It's bound to cause problems. • They've made spamming an offence. • They've taken out an injunction against the paper. • They billed me £50 – just for writing a letter! • That's outrageous! • We had our car towed away. • It's all jargon. • I couldn't make head or tail of it. • He's a bit dodgy, if you ask me. • He's involved in a pretty nasty custody battle. • You should've kicked up a fuss. • That's such a sick joke. • There's been a spate of burglaries round our way. • The police should launch a crackdown. • Did they manage to recover the car? • I feel like my home's been violated. • Apparently, I'm liable for damages. • My car got towed away. • He got off on a technicality. • What a drag.

4 The law

Conversation

1 Speaking

Discuss these questions with a partner.

1. Are there any laws in your country which the police don't strictly enforce?
2. Are there any laws which you think should be changed?
3. Are there any new laws which the government is planning to introduce at the moment?
4. Have you heard of any miscarriages of justice in your country?

2 Talking about aspects of the law

Complete the sentences with the words in the box.

a blind eye	convicted	obey	toughen
breakdown	having	an offence	overturned
a caution	hands	tightening	updating

1. As a rule, people .... the law now as much as they ever did.
2. In some places, there's just been a total .... in law and order.
3. The police often know drug-dealing is going on, but they just turn .... to it.
4. The police often let offenders off with ....
5. Because the police don't always deal with their problems, people sometimes take the law into their own ....
6. They're thinking of .... the divorce laws. Some of them are really antiquated.
7. They're talking of .... the rules governing immigration. They want to make it more difficult to get into the country.
8. Apparently, they're going to make sending junk e-mails ....
9. They're thinking of .... a crackdown on speeding. They want to .... the law so that you can lose your licence after your first offence.
10. They were wrongly .... of an offence they didn't commit and spent ten years in prison before the conviction was ....

Use some of the expressions to talk about the questions in Activity 1.

3 Listening (1)

You are going to listen to two women – Saroj and Natalie – talking on the phone. They talk about Saroj's holiday and some changes to the law. Look at the words below. They are in the order you will hear them. Try to decide what happened.

security	boarding gate	terrorist attacks
tweezers	hassle	evidence
stab	fingerprints	Catch 22

Now listen and find out what actually happened. Retell what happened using the words to help you.

Have you ever had a similar experience to Saroj? Do you agree with Natalie that anti-terror laws go too far? Why/why not?

4 Using grammar: modal verbs

Complete each sentence from the conversation with one of the modal verbs in the box. In some cases, you will need to add *'ve* or *be*.

bound to	could	must	shouldn't	would
can	could	must	won't	

1. It's such a palaver – they .... searched my bag about ten times.
2. They said they .... used as an offensive weapon.
3. They said they were too sharp – I .... stab someone with them.
4. Honestly, you .... been furious. I .... kicked up a right fuss.
5. They .... make things really awkward for you.
6. I .... go into the whole story.
7. It's .... lead to miscarriages of justice.
8. Strictly speaking, I .... using this phone for personal calls.

Listen again and check your answers.

Complete this sentence in as many true ways as you can. Who has the most sentences?

- Strictly speaking, I shouldn't ... , but ... .

For more information on using modal verbs like this, see G3.

4 Speaking

Discuss these questions with a partner.

1. Is compensation culture a growing problem in your country or is the trend towards litigation a good thing?
2. Can you think of any trials where the defendants were expected to be found guilty, but then got off?
3. Do you find it easy to understand legal jargon in your own language?
4. Have you ever had to read any legal documents?
5. Are there any professions you personally dislike? Why?

5 Dealing with lawyers

Complete the sentences with the words in the box.

bankruptcy	compensation	injunction	purchase
battle	contract	liable	will
bust	custody	maintenance	

1. When my parents got divorced, they were involved in this lengthy legal .... about who was going to get the kids and in the end, my mum was awarded .... of us both.
2. After they got divorced, she had to take her ex-husband to court to force him to pay ....
3. I really should go and see my lawyer and get a .... drawn up. You never know. I could die in an accident tomorrow!
4. My old landlord was horrible! He threatened to take us to court for breach of .... – and all because we had a party!
5. The company he set up went .... and he had to file for ....
6. My lawyer really helped me with the .... of my house. She read through all the contracts and sorted out all the payments I had to make and everything.
7. I was injured at work and I decided to make a claim for .... because my lawyer told me my employers were ....
8. A friend of mine took out an .... against her ex, stopping him from coming round to her house!

Now discuss these questions with a partner.

a. Have you ever had any dealings with lawyers?
b. Have any of your friends or relatives?
c. Have there been any divorce cases, custody battles or paternity suits in your country recently that involved famous people?

6 Lawyer jokes

Have you ever heard any lawyer jokes? Tell them to a partner. Then read the jokes below. What do you think the punchlines will be?

1. How can you tell when a lawyer is lying?
2. What's the difference between a lawyer and a vampire?
3. What do lawyers use for birth control?
4. What's the difference between a lawyer and God?
5. What do lawyers have in common with rhinos?
6. How do you stop a lawyer from drowning?

Listen and see if you were right.

Do you think any of these jokes are spot-on? Are any of them sick? Are any a bit much?

7 Speaking

Can you think of any examples of these different kinds of lawyers?

1. a crusading human-rights lawyer
2. a famous criminal lawyer
3. a controversial lawyer
4. a fictional lawyer from a book, film or TV series

Tell a partner what you know about each person – and what you think of them.

Writing: Job application letters

1 Trying to find a job

Complete the sentences with the words in the box.

advertised	post
applied	refuse
apprenticeship	short-listed
headhunted	work experience
messed up	

1. I saw it .... on the web and I .... for it online.
2. This guy from an agency .... me. They made me an offer I just couldn't ....
3. I did some .... there when I was at college. Then they offered me a full-time ....
4. I did a one-year .... with them. At the end of it, they took me on full-time, which was great.
5. I got as far as being .... , but I really .... the second interview, I'm afraid.

Have any of these things ever happened to you – or to anyone you know?

2 Before you write

Read the job advertisement. Spend three to four minutes deciding what information you would include in the covering letter that accompanies your CV – and what order you would put it in. Then compare your ideas with a partner.

We are a UK trading company looking for a full-time

OFFICE ADMINISTRATOR

We require:

- very good spoken English.
- office administration, including good IT skills.
- import/export experience – desirable, but not essential.
- strong communication and inter-personal skills.
- desire and ability to work hard and face challenges.

Please fax your CV and covering letter in English to: (815) 332-07212 or email duncan@shotmail.com

3 The covering letter

First read the letter and decide if you would give Terry an interview. Why / why not? Then, complete the letter with the words in the box.

benefited	enclosed	interview	references	response
challenges	further	invaluable	relevant	suitable

549 Shaftesbury Road
Finsbury Park
London N6 4ST

20 February 2006

Ms Angela Cartwright
Personnel Department
Speed Software Development
150–154 The Avenue
Croydon CR2 0QU

Dear Sir / Madam,

I am writing in (1) .... to your recent advertisement for an office administrator. Please find (2) .... my current CV.

I feel I would be (3) .... for the post for a number of reasons. Firstly, I speak excellent English, having recently passed the Cambridge First Certificate exam with a C grade. Secondly, I feel I possess the (4) .... import / export experience, having previously spent a fortnight working in the canteen of a French company trading in lingerie. During this time, I gained (5) .... experience. I also feel my social skills and ability to communicate (6) .... from dealing with customer complaints in my workplace. I am now looking to put these new skills into practice.

On top of all this, I am a dedicated, motivated worker, able to act both independently and also as part of a team. In my last job, I was responsible for establishing a new system for the collection and cleaning of trays, for which I received an Employee of the Month award. I enjoy new (7) .... and never give less than my all.

I am available for (8) .... at any time and would be happy to provide (9) ...., should you require them.

Please do not hesitate to contact me should you require any (10) .... information.

I look forward to hearing from you soon,

Yours faithfully,

Terry S Durham

Terry S Durham

4 Starting and ending formal letters

Discuss these questions with a partner.

1. Where do you usually place your name and address in formal letters in your own language? And in English?
2. Where do you usually place the name and address of the person you're writing to in formal letters in English?
3. If you start a letter *Dear Sir/Madam*, how should you sign off?
4. If you start *Dear Mr Jones*, how should you sign off?
5. If you are writing to Sue Jenkins, what's the best way to write her name?
6. What's the difference between starting *Dear Sir/Madam* and starting *To whom it may concern*?

5 Using grammar: ... *-ing* clauses

Discuss with a partner the meanings of these different forms. Then compare your ideas with the explanation.

a. I possess the relevant experience, having previously spent a year working in a German company trading in industrial furnishings.

b. I feel I am suitably qualified for the post, having both a degree and a Master's in relevant subjects.

In formal writing, we often use *-ing* clauses to add explanations. In sentence a. above the meaning is *because/as I have previously spent*. In b. the meaning is *because/as I have*.

Complete the sentences with the correct form of the verbs in the box.

be	complete	deal with	have	pass	spend

1. I have considerable experience in this line of work, ... over 20 years in the field.
2. I feel well-suited to this particular position, ... a highly-qualified practitioner with a range of previous experience.
3. I feel confident of my English abilities, ... recently .... the Cambridge First Certificate.
4. I feel confident of my computing skills, ... recently .... a six-month IT course.
5. I am sure I would be able to meet tight deadlines, ... similar pressures in my previous job.
6. I feel I possess the appropriate qualifications for this post, ... a degree in modern languages and a Master's in translation.

For more information on using *-ing* clauses see G4.

6 Using grammar: *should*

In formal writing, should is often used to mean *if*. For example:

- Please do not hesitate to contact me, should you require any further information.

Use the words in brackets to report these formal sentences as if you were talking.

1. Should you require any further information, please do not hesitate to contact me.

   I told them that ....
   (need / more / get in touch)
2. Should payment not be immediately forthcoming, further action may well be taken against you.

   They told me that ....
   (pay / take / court)
3. Should you find our products available cheaper elsewhere, we would be happy to reimburse you the difference in cost.

   They say in their publicity that ....
   (find / cheaper / else / pay back / difference)

Now write the formal sentences being reported here.

4. He told me to make an appointment with his PA if I wanted to talk about it anymore.

   ....
   (wish / discuss / further / please / appointment)
5. I asked them to get in touch with me straightaway if any jobs come up.

   ....
   (vacancies / available / contact / earliest possible opportunity)

Compare your ideas with a partner.

7 Writing a covering letter

Read the job advertisement. Then work with a partner and spend three minutes deciding what information you would include in the covering letter and what order you would put it in.

Modify search | New search | Next >>

Position: Technical Training Engineer
Location: Liverpool, England
Responsibilities:
- Deliver technical training courses to overseas customers.
- Write or edit technical training documentation.

Requirements:
- Excellent English – mother tongue or second language.
- Good telecom or computer background.
- Wide teaching experience preferred.
- Telecom equipment maintenance background preferred.
- Responsible, cooperative and enthusiastic.
- No limits on nationality.

Underline or make a list of the expressions from this unit that you'd like to use in your letter. Cover the expressions and write your first draft. Then check that you used the expressions correctly and write a second draft.

Is that your stomach rumbling? • I'm a bit peckish. • Keep stirring. • What's the secret ingredient? • I just add a splash of chilli sauce. • Was that coriander it had in it? • Bananas make me constipated. • Spare me the details! • Squirrel? I'd rather eat my cat! • Personally, I'd draw the line at brains! • I just associate macaroni with school. • You're so unadventurous. • Sprinkle each side with pepper. • I can't stand the texture. • No wonder he's so fat! • It's not in season. • It's treated with so many pesticides. • Mind you, it is very convenient. • It wasn't exactly filling. • My whole face swelled up like a balloon. • I left it to marinate overnight. • It's gorgeous. • You must give me the recipe. • I forgot to grease the tin. • You should've soaked them longer. • Just sprinkle some grated cheese on top.

5 Food

Reading

1 Explaining how to cook things

Complete the sentences with the words in the box.

bring	grease	simmer	stir-fry
chop	roast	sprinkle	toss

1. You .... all the vegetables up into little pieces and then .... everything in a wok, adding a bit of soy sauce if you need to.
2. Make sure you .... the baking tray before you put the cake mixture in it. Otherwise, everything will stick.
3. First, you have to .... the soup to the boil and then let it .... for about ten minutes.
4. You pour the dressing over the top and then .... the salad and it's ready to go.
5. You basically just leave the meat to .... in the oven for three or four hours. Oh, and make sure you .... some chopped rosemary or thyme on it about an hour before it's done.

Now complete these sentences with the words in the box.

bake	grate	marinate	steam
drain	leave	serve	whisk

6. After the dough has risen, you leave it to .... in the oven for between thirty and forty minutes.
7. Boil some water and then just .... the fish for about twenty minutes. You then .... it with rice and chilli sauce.
8. .... the cream until it's light and fluffy.
9. Once the pasta is ready, ... off all the water, then just .... a bit of parmesan cheese over the top – and it's ready to serve.
10. I usually .... the meat in lime juice, olive oil, cumin or coriander and a bit of oregano. You can add a splash of vodka to it, too, if you want. It's best to .... it in the fridge overnight.

Do you ever do any of the things above? When? With what kind of food?

Can you think of four other cooking verbs? Compare your ideas with a partner.

2 Speaking

Discuss these questions with a partner.

1. What's the best dish you can cook?
2. Do you ever cook for other people? How often?
3. Who's the best cook you know?
4. Do you eat out much? Do you have a favourite restaurant?
5. What was the last place you went to? What did you have?

3 Reading

The class should divide into three groups. You are going to read three different recipes from around the world.

Group A: Read the recipe on page 31.
Group B: Read the recipe on page 173.
Group C: Read the recipe on page 176.

When you have finished reading, compare what you remember with someone else who read the same recipe as you. Make sure you both understood the recipe. Act out how you'd cook your recipe.

Now work in groups of three with students who have read the other two recipes. Tell each other how to cook the dishes you read about. Use the lists of ingredients to help you.

When you have all finished, discuss these questions.

a. Which recipes do you like the sound of?
b. Which could you cook yourself?
c. Is there anything in any of them you can't eat?

4 Listening

You are going to listen to two people discussing the three recipes. As you listen, complete this chart by deciding if each person really likes (✓✓), quite likes (✓) or doesn't like (✗) the sound of each recipe. Then compare what you heard with a partner.

	Robin	Sharon
Mexican chicken mole		
West Beach diet spinach salad		
Spicy Asian chicken livers		

A

Mexican chicken mole

Serves 4–6 people.

Ingredients

MOLE SAUCE
400g can chopped tomatoes
100g can chopped green chillies
1/2 cup whole almonds
1 clove garlic
1/2 small onion, roughly chopped
1 tablespoon chilli powder
1 teaspoon ground cumin
1 teaspoon ground coriander
1 teaspoon salt
1/2 teaspoon sugar
1/2 teaspoon ground cinnamon

1 tablespoon olive oil
1.5 kg skinless chicken parts
15g unsweetened chocolate, chopped up

Directions

1. To make the mole sauce: In a blender or food processor, blend all the ingredients except the oil, chocolate and chicken until smooth. Set aside.
2. In a large frying pan, heat the oil, add the chicken pieces and cook for 2–3 minutes or until browned on the outside. Set the chicken to one side.
3. To the same pan, add the mole sauce, the chopped chocolate and a quarter of a cup of water. Cook and stir continuously until the chocolate is melted.
4. Add the chicken back into the pan and bring to the boil. Reduce the heat, cover and leave to simmer for thirty to forty minutes. The juices in the chicken should run clear when the chicken is pierced and the mole sauce should be nice and thick.

almonds

cinnamon

shallots

ginger

blender

5 Speaking

Discuss these questions with a partner.

1. Do you like contrasting flavours in dishes? What kind?
2. Have you ever heard of the Atkins diet? Do you know any other famous diets? What do they involve?
3. Have you ever been on a diet? Did it work?
4. Are there any foods you hate the texture of? Why?

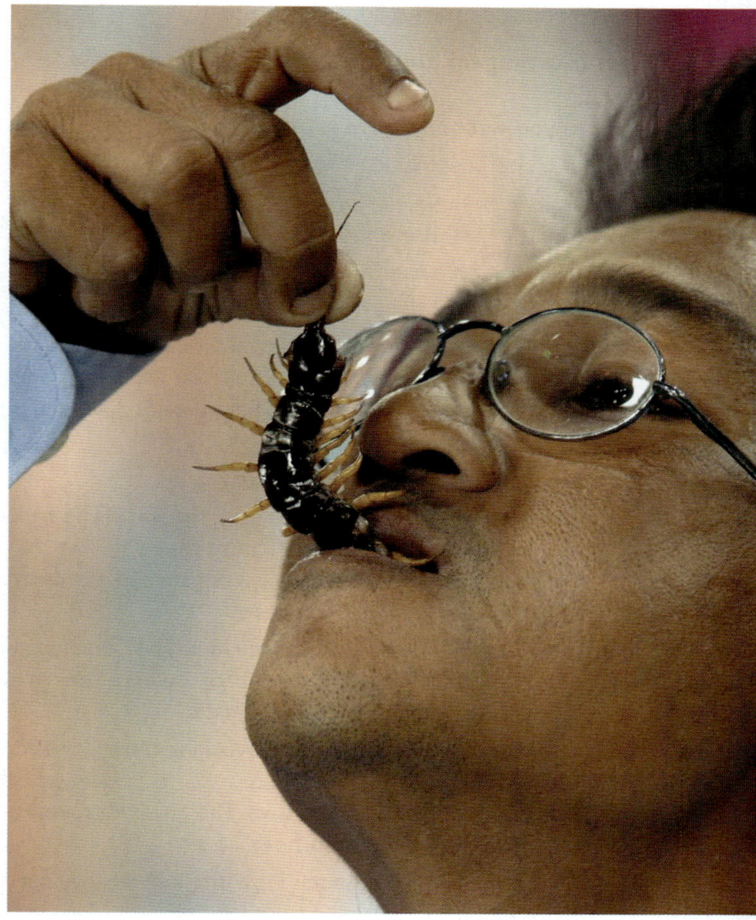

Look at the words in the box. How do you feel about eating these things?

avocado	dog	horse	mussels	snake
brains	figs	insects	raw garlic	tofu
celery	frogs' legs	kidneys	shark fin	tripe

Tell your partner how you feel, using these structures.

- I'd have no problems whatsoever eating horse.
- I'd be OK with tripe, but I'd draw the line at brains!
- I must admit, I'd be a bit reluctant to eat dog.
- I wouldn't eat snake if you paid me!

Now look at the tapescript at the back of the book and find three more expressions you'd like to use in this discussion.

Think of three more things you'd have problems eating. Then work with a new partner and tell each other how you feel about all of these things.

Conversation

1 Listening

You are going to listen to two couples – Nigel and Stef, Mena and Larry – having dinner together. Cover the conversation below. As you listen, try to answer these questions.

1. What do they say about basil and tomatoes?
2. Why do they start talking about them?

Now listen again and complete the conversation.

N: Do you want any more salad?

M: No, that's fine, thanks. It was great. Was that fresh basil (1) .... ?

N: Yeah, they sell it in the shop round the corner.

M: Really? Isn't it expensive?

N: No, not really. I think it's about 50p (2) ....

M: 50p? That's really good. I never buy it in the supermarket because it's just too expensive and you hardly get any.

S: I know. I don't know why people buy fruit and vegetables in the supermarket. (3) .... , especially herbs and things.

L: Absolutely. And they're never really that nice. The fruit's never really ripe. I think it's because they (4) .... from abroad, rather than selling it when it's in season here.

N: Yeah, it's awful. There was an article in *The Guardian* about it recently, about all these places abroad where they grow tomatoes all year round under plastic.

M: Yeah, I saw that. I can't imagine working there. It sounded awful! The heat (5) .... And the other thing is it's so exploitative. The guys who work there earn about three euros an hour.

S: Three euros! That's peanuts! How the hell do they survive?

M: I don't know.

L: That's why tomatoes don't taste as good (6) ....

N: What? Because they exploit workers?

L: No! Because they're all artificially ripened rather than (7) .... by the sun.

N: Oh right. I wouldn't know. I never really eat tomatoes.

M: Never?

N: No. My mum made me eat one once when I was younger, and I (8) .... her best dress.

M: My God! So are you allergic to them or something?

N: I don't know. I don't think so. I think I just did it (9) .... my mother, because she made me eat one. Anyway, now I just associate tomatoes with pools of vomit, so...

M: OK! OK! (10) .... !

N: What?

S: Take no notice. He does it on purpose.

N: What?

2 Speaking

Discuss these questions with a partner.

1. Where do you shop for food – a supermarket? Your local shops? A market? Why?
2. Do you know when different foods are in season? What's in season at the moment? Do you ever buy food out of season? Why / why not?
3. Have you ever done anything just to spite your parents, brothers, sisters or someone else you know?

3 Pronunciation: sounding surprised

When we are surprised by what someone has told us, we often respond by repeating what surprised us and then adding an extra comment and/or a question. For example:

M: The guys who work there earn about three euros an hour.

S: Three euros! That's peanuts. How the hell do they survive?

Listen to the intonation and practise.

With a partner, write similar responses to the statements below. Remember to first include the information that surprises you.

1. A: I made frogs' legs soup for the starter.
   B: ....
2. A: I think we had eight different courses in the end.
   B: ....
3. A: He's a bit overweight.
   B: ....
4. A: I'm going to Siberia for my holidays.
   B: ....
5. A: When I graduate, I'd like to become a tax inspector.
   B: ....
6. A: They got thrashed 8-0.
   B: ....
7. A: He smokes 20 cigars a day.
   B: ....
8. A: She's dating four different guys.
   B: ....

Try to remember your responses. Change partners and practise the conversations. Continue each conversation.

Have you seen or heard anything recently that has really surprised you?

4 Food and dietary problems

Complete the sentences with the words in the box.

agree	diarrhoea	rumbling	threw up
allergy	heartburn	stuffed	ulcer
constipated	obese	swell up	wind

1. Whenever I travel, I always get really .... It takes me several days before I can go to the toilet.
2. I keep getting this really bad rash. I don't know what's causing it. Maybe I've developed some kind of ....
3. I .... about six times last night. I must've eaten something that was off.
4. He's incredibly allergic to nuts. If he eats anything with even a trace of them, his whole face and throat .... so he can't breathe properly.
5. I shouldn't have drunk the tap water. I had dreadful .... for about two days. I was constantly in and out of the toilet.
6. Have you got any indigestion tablets? I shouldn't have eaten that curry. Spicy food always gives me ....
7. I'm not really allergic to onions. They just don't really .... with me.
8. A: Oh, I'm sorry. I've got terrible .... today.
   B: Yes, I know what you mean. It must be the beans from last night.
9. A: Is that your stomach .... ?
   B: Yeah, I'm starving. I missed lunch.
10. I've got a really annoying mouth .... on the inside of my cheek.
11. We absolutely .... ourselves. I couldn't move afterwards. I had to loosen my belt before I could stand up.
12. Honestly, he's .... He must weigh about 140 kilos. He's going to end up with serious health problems if he doesn't do something about it now. I mean, he's only 19.

Do you know anyone who has – or has had – any of these problems? What causes them?

> **Real English: wind**
>
> Some people feel embarrassed about bodily functions. An informal way (only with friends) of talking about having wind is to say He keeps farting.

5 Listening

You are going to listen to a continuation of the conversation from Activity 1. As you listen, try to answer these questions.

1. Which of the food and dietary problems mentioned in Activity 4 do the four people talk about?
2. What caused these problems?

6 Speaking: developing arguments

When we agree, we usually say something extra. Sometimes we say the same thing as the first person, but in a different way – or we give an example or a comment.

Match the statements with the agreeing responses.

1. The food you get in supermarkets is really expensive. ☐
2. There are too many additives in food these days. ☐
3. I don't know why parents let their children eat so much crap! ☐
4. School dinners used to be much better. ☐
5. We shouldn't import so much food. ☐
6. It must be awful being a farmer these days. ☐

a. I know. It's awful – and it's treated with so many pesticides and chemicals while it's being grown.
b. I know. They give in to their demands too quickly.
c. I know what you mean. It must be terrible.
d. Absolutely. We were never served all that processed food they get now.
e. I know. The other day I saw they were charging £5 for a kilo of oranges!
f. Absolutely. I mean, there's plenty of fresh produce you can buy locally. You don't have to get it from overseas.

In each response above, replace the comment with your own idea. Then practise the conversations in pairs.

Now have each conversation as many times as you can, adding a different comment each time.

> **Real English: Mind you**
>
> We often contrast or give an exception to an argument by starting Mind you. For example:
>
> A: *The food in supermarkets is so expensive.*
> B: *I know. It's terrible. Mind you, it is very convenient.*
>
> A: *Kids eat so much rubbish these days.*
> B: *I know. And they don't do enough exercise.*
> A: *Mind you, it's difficult finding the time to cook fresh food.*
>
> Think of some Mind you statements to respond to the ideas in 1–6 above.

The village was destroyed in a landslide. • They've suffered a two-year drought. • Were you affected by the flooding? • We just had to sit tight and wait for it to blow over. • There was sheer panic. • People were running around like headless chickens. • I heard an almighty bang. • It must've been started deliberately. • Thousands are still buried beneath the rubble. • Over a hundred are feared dead. • I work for an NGO. • He just flatly refused to discuss it. • The government's condemned the strike. • It hasn't attracted much media attention. • It's a charitable organisation. • We're lobbying the government to change the law. • Please give generously. • One million pounds is a mere drop in the ocean. • They've been accused of financial mismanagement. • It's gone up in absolute terms, not in real terms.

6 Disasters

Conversation

1 Speaking

Make sure you understand the words in the box. Then discuss the questions with a partner.

avalanche	flood	landslide	tsunami
earthquake	forest fire	tornado	volcano
drought	hurricane		

1. Have any of these natural disasters ever happened in your country? When? How serious were they?
2. Have you heard any news stories about them happening anywhere else in the world?
3. Which of the disasters do you think are unavoidable 'acts of God'? Which are sometimes the result of human actions?

2 Role play

Imagine you live in a place which has been affected by one of the disasters in Activity 1. A friend is going to call you to see how you are. You're going to tell them what's happened. Before you start, think of five questions you expect them to ask you about the situation.

Now role play the conversation. When you have finished, change roles and have another similar conversation.

3 The effects of disasters

Complete the short conversations with the words in the boxes.

Conversation 1

flash recede stranded submerged

A: So did all the flooding last year affect you?

B: Yes, it was awful. It was (1) .... flooding, so the river went up 15, 16 feet overnight. By the time we woke up, the ground floor was totally (2) .... and everything was ruined. We were (3) .... upstairs and we just had to sit tight and wait for the waters to (4) ....

A: Really? That must've been awful.

Conversation 2

control deliberately evacuated flames ground

A: So were your parents affected by all the forest fires?

B: Yeah, they were. Their village was (1) .... and they had to go and stay with my uncle for a few days until the firefighters got everything under (2) .... The next village along from them was pretty much burnt to the (3) .... , though. Everything just went up in (4) .... My mum was telling me they now think it might all have been started (5) ....

A: Really? What kind of person would do that?

Conversation 3

almighty	fleeing	sheer	terrifying
eruption	lit up	terrified	tremors

A: So was the area you were staying in affected by the volcano?

B: Yeah, totally! It was (1) .... , it really was. Apparently, they'd been feeling (2) .... for a few weeks and then the night before the (3) .... , all these strange lights (4) .... the night sky. Then at around 5 in the morning, there was an (5) .... bang – like a huge explosion – and all these enormous clouds of ash and smoke started pouring out. People started (6) .... their homes to escape the lava. There was just (7) .... panic everywhere!

A: God! You must've been absolutely (8) .... !

Work with a partner, and have the conversations. Try to continue them for as long as you can.

4 Listening

Listen to three short texts. As you listen, take notes about:

a. what each disaster was
b. where each one happened
c. how much damage was done
d. the number of casualties

Compare what you heard with a partner. Then listen again and read the tapescript at the back of the book as you do so. Try to guess the meaning of the words in red.

5 Speaking

Discuss these questions with a partner.

1. Would you feel comfortable going on holiday somewhere that had been affected by a disaster? Why / why not?
2. How many different examples of a national tragedy can you think of?
3. Have any of the countries near you suffered a national tragedy recently?

Real English: feared dead

In the third extract you heard that at least fifteen thousand people are feared dead. This means the authorities think these people are dead. Passive structures like this are common in news reports and newspapers. Here are some more examples.

Many people are believed to be buried under the rubble.
Her injuries are not thought to be life-threatening.
The decision is not expected to be made until after Easter.
The President is alleged to have been involved in the scandal.
The explosion is reported to have occurred at 3.36 in the morning.

Reporting verbs such as *allege*, *believe*, *expect*, *report* and *think* are useful in journalism as they imply uncertainty – the writer is not absolutely sure the information is accurate.

6 Writing

Work with a partner. Choose two disasters from Activity 1 and write similar conversations to those in Activity 3. Use a dictionary for help if you need it – or ask your teacher.

7 Using grammar: reporting speech

In the third text you listened to, you heard that President Khatami of Iran *urged all Iranians to help* the victims of the earthquake.

Complete the sentences with the correct form of the reporting verbs in the box.

accuse	condemn	nag
persuade	suggest	warn

1. I'll phone him later and see if I can .... him to change his mind.
2. My mum's been .... me for weeks to clean the car, so I guess I should really do it this weekend.
3. She actually .... me of trying to take it without paying! I couldn't believe it!
4. I'm glad the union has come out and .... the new management pay offer. It was outrageously low, wasn't it?
5. Don't moan to me about how bad you feel! I did .... you not to eat so much earlier, didn't I?
6. You might want to .... to the others that they meet us in the café after lunch.

Now complete these sentences with the correct form of the reporting verbs.

beg	deny	moan	reassure	refuse	reject

7. I spoke to Sandra yesterday. She spent about an hour .... about how much she hates her new job!
8. They asked him about all the allegations earlier, but he .... to comment.
9. I put forward a couple of proposals, but the board flatly .... them!
10. The kids had been .... me to get a rabbit for ages and in the end I just gave in and bought them one.
11. If I were you, I'd just .... any knowledge of ever having met her!
12. I was quite worried about the lump, to be honest, but the doctor was great. He .... me that it's perfectly normal.

Underline the patterns that the reporting verbs above take. The first one has been done for you.

With a partner, discuss exactly what you think each person said / will say in the cases above. For example:

1. Are you really sure? Is there no way I can talk you out of it?

For more information on how to use reporting verbs, see G5.

Reading

1 Vocabulary and speaking

Make sure you understand the words in red. Then discuss the questions in small groups.

1. How many national newspapers are there in your country?
2. Are any of them pro-government, anti-government, right-wing, left-wing, or gutter press?
3. Which has the biggest circulation? Which is the most influential?
4. Which paper do you read? Why?
5. Which of these parts of the papers do you usually read? What do you read first?

the business pages	the national news
the comment pages and editorials	the obituaries
the foreign news	the reviews
the front page	the sports pages
the letters pages	the travel section
the magazine	the TV listings

Real English: gutter press

The gutter is the side of the road where water drains away. The gutter press is a negative name for tabloid newspapers that contain a lot of stories about crime, sex and celebrities. Sometimes people complain about sensationalist examples of gutter journalism. If you disapprove of swearing, you can call it the language of the gutter.

2 Talking about things in the news

Complete the short conversations with the words in the box.

apparently	crisis	dreadful	heard	saying
charity	damage	harm	ridiculous	

1. A: I was reading a report in the paper about that earthquake.
   B: Oh yeah. It's awful, isn't it?
   A: Yeah, ... , but what it was .... was that the .... has been that much worse because there's been so much illegal building and the government's just been turning a blind eye to it.
2. A: I was reading an article in *The Times* about this awful .... in northern Uganda.
   B: Oh yeah? I haven't .... anything about it.
   A: No, I know. It was saying it's been really under-reported, but .... they've had this conflict for 18 years.
3. A: Did you see that guy on the news who wants to do the London Marathon naked?
   B: Oh yeah. They want to stop him, don't they?
   A: Yeah, it's .... I mean, he's doing it for .... , isn't he? And he's not doing anyone any ....

With a partner, practise the conversations and continue them. Use some of the techniques for developing conversations you practised in Unit 5.

3 Reading

Student A: Look at the newspaper articles on page 171.
Student B: Look at the newspaper articles on page 172.
Student C: Look at the newspaper articles on page 174.

For each of the articles you read, complete one of these sentence starters:

- I was reading this article / editorial / letter this morning about ... .
- Did you see that article / editorial / letter in the paper about ... ?

Decide what you think and feel about each article. Do you think it's true, awful, amazing, or what? Have you heard any similar stories?

Close your books. With a partner, have conversations like those in Activity 2. Take turns to talk about the articles you read. You may find you have read the same articles. Then change partners and repeat the exercise.

4 Word building

Complete these extracts from the articles you read with the correct forms of the words given.

1. **survive, complete**
   A cancer .... from Britain has just .... the New York Marathon.
2. **expertise, donate, close**
   .... have revealed that some charities saw a drop in .... and came to the brink of .... because of the millions that were given to the Asian tsunami appeal.
3. **encouragement, protect, develop**
   The role of governments should be to simply .... free trade and break down .... tariffs in Europe and America that so damage economic .... in Africa.
4. **mismanage, corrupt, resign**
   A high-profile charity has been accused by *The Tribune* newspaper of financial .... and .... , which has left millions of pounds unaccounted for and led to the .... of its leader.
5. **collect, harassment, technical, charity**
   I have .... for charity approaching me in the street and on my doorstep nearly every day of the week. They frequently .... me and try to make me feel guilty for saying no. These kind of marketing .... have no place in .... organisations and they should be banned.
6. **embarrassing, perception, donate**
   The report is an .... to the US government, coming in the wake of criticism at its .... mean response to recent disasters. The States is in fact by far the biggest .... of aid in absolute terms, providing over $7bn more than any other country.

Listen to the extracts and check your answers.

Now discuss these questions with a partner.

- Do you agree that some countries don't give enough foreign aid to underdeveloped and developing countries?
- Do you think there are any downsides to what charities do?
- Have you ever felt harrassed or guilt-tripped into giving money?

5 Charities

Complete the collocations with the verbs in the box.

distribute	fund	lobby	raise
fight	help	provide	support

1. .... children in need / people to help themselves
2. .... poverty / injustice / racism
3. .... awareness / money for charity
4. .... money / education and training / help for homeless people
5. .... emergency food supplies to victims / books to schools in Africa
6. .... the work of the UN / development programmes in West Africa
7. .... the government for help / for a change in the law
8. .... research into cancer / research into Alzheimer's

Now discuss these questions with a partner.

- Do you ever give money to any charities? Which ones? What do they do?
- How do charities raise money?
- Have you ever raised money for charity? How?
- Have you seen any adverts or campaigns run by any charities recently?

Writing: Putting your point of view

1 Planning (1): seeing both sides

You are going to read a short essay with this title.

'Cities offer a better environment to live in than the countryside.' Discuss.

Work with a partner. One of you should spend five minutes noting down as many reasons as you can think of for agreeing with this statement. The other should think of reasons for disagreeing.

Compare your ideas and then share what you thought of with another pair. Did they have any ideas you hadn't thought of?

2 Planning (2): weighing up the arguments

Read through your ideas. As you read, think about these questions.

1. Which ideas do you agree with?
2. Which do you disagree with?
3. Do you feel the statement in the title is basically right or basically wrong? Why?

Discuss your feelings with a partner.

3 Before you read

All of the words in red are connected to the essay. Discuss with a partner what you think the words mean. Use a dictionary to help you if you need to – or ask your teacher.

1. There's a problem with urban drift from the country to the city.
2. Some rural villages have become badly depopulated.
3. The university offers a broad spectrum of courses.
4. Being a foreigner here, I sometimes feel socially isolated.
5. I'm jealous of him. He seems to have such an idyllic life
6. A lot of the areas outside the city are slowly being urbanised.
7. Looking after the kids seems to eat up all my time – and money!
8. They've passed a new law outlawing any further construction in the green belt around the city.

4 While you read

Now read the essay. As you read, think about these questions.

1. How many of the ideas you thought of does the writer mention?
2. Does the writer basically agree or disagree with the statement in the title? Why?

One of the dominant social trends of the last century has been the growth of the city. Urban drift has resulted in mega-cities appearing all over the world and a correspondingly high level of rural depopulation. As such, it is worth asking if this is a direct result of cities being better living environments than the countryside.

First and foremost, cities are places of economic activity. Most people drawn to the city come in search of work and it is undoubtedly true that cities offer more opportunities: there is money to be made and a wide variety of jobs to be done. Furthermore, cities offer you a broader range of leisure-time activities: cinemas, theatres, bars, clubs and galleries all thrive in an urban environment. Another plus is the fact that cities provide a whole spectrum of differing life-styles, allowing you to choose whatever suits you best.

However, the competitive nature of cities inevitably causes stress. Individuals can fall through the safety nets society provides and end up homeless. Alcoholism, drug abuse and domestic violence are all unfortunate side-effects of city life, whilst the high crime rate guarantees suspicion, social isolation and loneliness for many.

A rural life seemingly offers an idyllic existence. In theory, living in a close-knit community means you can bring up your children safely. However, things are not always what they seem. Narrow-minded attitudes are common in the countryside and not even the most remote area is free from drug abuse or violence. Urban drift has left rural areas devastated and high unemployment can lead to despair or even suicide. At the same time, urbanisation is rapidly eating up the green belt.

All in all, therefore, I feel that cities do offer the best of all possible worlds, provided you are up to the challenge of making the most of city life.

5 Structuring your ideas

The essay is an example of an argumentative essay. It has five paragraphs. Spend a few minutes thinking about the function of each paragraph. Then compare your ideas with a partner.

If you were writing a similar essay in your own language, would you structure it in the same way?

6 Writing your introductory paragraph

In an argumentative essay, the opening paragraph sets the scene for the whole work. It is important to show you know why the subject is being discussed and to then introduce the question suggested in the title.

Complete these opening sentences with the words in the box.

growing	interest	problematic
impact	issue	recent

1. Second-language learning in schools has become a burning .... in educational circles.
2. Many .... studies have focused on the alarming increase in underage drinking.
3. There has recently been .... concern about the general standard of living on many high-rise estates.
4. The increase in space travel has generated widespread .... in the possibility of life on other planets.
5. The computer revolution of the last thirty years has had a massive .... on our lives.
6. The continuing illegality of certain drugs is becoming increasingly ....

Underline the parts of the sentences above that can be reused in other essays.

Read the essay title below. Then work with a partner and write an introductory sentence for the essay, showing why the topic is important.

'The reintroduction of the death penalty is the only possible solution to the increasingly violent world we live in.' Discuss.

7 Showing your attitude

In these sentences, both forms are possible. Circle the form that shows greater certainty. The first one has been done for you.

1. Research has suggested / has shown that this policy is misguided.
2. Professor Hoey has proved / has suggested that there are fundamental flaws with this position.
3. Much recent research has claimed / has found that there are strong links between power stations and incidents of disease.
4. It is perhaps / undoubtedly true that cities offer more opportunities.
5. It is supposedly / obviously easier to teach single-sex groups of students.
6. Alternative solutions to the problem are theoretically / perfectly possible.
7. A rural life offers / seemingly offers an idyllic existence.
8. It is often suggested that / It is clear that the law needs to be tightened.
9. It is widely believed that higher taxation / Higher taxation inevitably leads to a more equal society.
10. It is clear / claimed that the young are becoming increasingly socially isolated as a result of the large amount of time spent on computers.

We often follow sentences containing expressions that show less certainty with *However* or *but* and then argue against these 'weaker' positions.

8 Planning an essay

Work with a partner. Spend five minutes brainstorming why people might agree or disagree with the essay title in Activity 6. Then change partners and discuss whether you think the statement in the title is basically right or wrong.

For homework, write your own essay. Before you start, plan your paragraphs and decide which language from these pages you want to use.

Review: Units 1–6

1 Adjectives

Put the adjectives in the box into four groups of four.

challenging	high-powered	remote
conscientious	laid-back	rewarding
demeaning	light and fluffy	run-down
deprived	mouth-watering	smarmy
dizzy	ramshackle	stodgy
filling		

job	person
....	....
....	....
....	....
....	....

place	food
....	....
....	....
....	....
....	....

Add two more adjectives you learnt in the last 6 units to each list.

Work in pairs.
Student A: Explain five of the words above.
Student B: Close your book and guess the words. Then swap roles.

2 Vocabulary quiz

Discuss these questions in groups of three.

1. Why might someone be bullied?
2. Can you think of three things people often whinge about?
3. What happens if there's a drought?
4. Would you describe your boss as domineering or dominating?
5. Who would someone lobby and why?
6. What's the difference between an egomaniac and a know-all?
7. How would you describe someone who's always talking behind your back or saying nasty things?
8. What's the difference between harassment and discrimination?
9. Why would you sue someone?
10. What might you try to regenerate? How?
11. Can you think of anything that is an eyesore in your town?
12. What's the opposite of a compact city?
13. Can you think of four kinds of political movement?
14. Why would you kick up a fuss?
15. Who might be involved in a custody battle?
16. Why would you say 'Spare me the details'?
17. What might your stomach do if you're feeling peckish?
18. What's the opposite of giving someone praise?
19. How do you feel if you're knackered?
20. Can you think of three things that might happen if you have an allergic reaction?

3 Verbs

Complete the collocations with the verbs in the box.

bend	demolish	fund	oversee	ruin
boost	foster	live up to	reverse	slam

1. .... a child / good relations
2. .... down / the rules
3. .... research / the health service through taxation
4. .... a decision / the car into the space
5. .... the phone down / the door
6. .... your confidence a lot / the economy
7. .... the holiday / my new suit
8. .... the hype / my expectations
9. .... the old building / a huge plate of pasta
10. .... all new projects / the whole industry

Spend one minute memorising the collocations above. Then cover the activity. Your partner will read out the ten verbs. How many collocations can you remember?

4 What can you remember?

With a partner, write down as much as you can about the listening in Unit 1 and the text in Unit 3.

Unit 1: The conversation after the French class

Unit 3: Twin trouble

Which did you enjoy more? Why?

5 Grammar

Complete the second sentence using the word given, so that it has a similar meaning to the first sentence.

1. They think that anything up to 1000 people might have died.
   believed
   Up to 1000 people .... dead.
2. The transport system back home is miles better than it is here.
   comparison
   There's .... and the one here.
3. There's nothing like as varied a mix of people as in London.
   cosmopolitan
   It's nowhere .... London.
4. She's constantly pushing people around.
   boss
   All .... about.
5. He treats me like an idiot.
   seems
   He .... I'm an idiot.
6. Beijing University is similar to Oxford or Cambridge University.
   Chinese
   Beijing University is .... of Oxford or Cambridge.
7. I can't believe you stayed so calm.
   temper
   I .... if I'd been in your shoes.
8. It's really against the rules to do this, so don't tell anyone.
   we
   Strictly speaking, ... this.

6 Prepositions

Complete the sentences by adding the correct preposition.

1. The company's having a crackdown .... the use of the Internet in office hours.
2. She filed .... divorce because she felt she was constantly being taken .... granted.
3. Women are still subjected .... a lot of sexist comments.
4. The town is steeped .... history.
5. It is claimed that people who are obese in childhood are more prone .... heart disease later in life.
6. There's an increasing trend .... litigation.
7. Often the police simply let off offenders .... a caution.
8. You should never take the law .... your own hands.
9. They didn't give me any training. They just threw me .... the deep end.
10. He spent three years in prison after being wrongly convicted .... murder.
11. Losing my job put a big strain .... our marriage.
12. She was awarded £10,000 .... damages.

7 Look back and check

Work in pairs. Choose one of these activities.

a. **Do the role play in Activity 4 on page 15 again. This time, use the sympathising expressions in Activity 5 on page 25.**

b. **Look back at Activity 5 on page 25 and repeat the final exercise.**

c. **Look back at the vocabulary in Activity 1 on page 30. Ask your partner about any words you've forgotten. Then think of a dish you know how to cook. Explain to your partner how to cook it.**

8 Idioms

Complete each idiom with a noun. The first letters are given.

1. He didn't stop. Honestly, I couldn't get a word in e.................................... .
2. He's just weird. Honestly, he gives me the c.................................... .
3. He's supporting me now, but I'm not sure he will when it comes to the c.................................... .
4. I can't cope with any more work. I've got enough on my p.................................... already.
5. He just can't cope. He doesn't have the skills or experience. He's just totally out of his d.................................... .
6. To be honest, we didn't really venture off the beaten t.................................... . We just stuck to the usual touristy areas.
7. The teachers know what's going on, but they turn a blind e.................................... to it.
8. Only offering me £100 compensation just added insult to i.................................... .
9. My boss is constantly breathing down my n.................................... .
10. I'll eat most things, but I draw the l.................................... at insects!
11. He's such a lazy slob. He never lifts a f.................................... to help.
12. She's supposed to be showing me the r.................................... , but she hasn't helped me much.

Now discuss these questions with a partner.

a. Have you ever met anyone who gives you the creeps?
b. Have you ever felt out of your depth? When?
c. Have you ever been involved in a crunch match or had a crunch moment? What happened?

9 Adjective-noun collocations

Match the adjectives to the nouns they collocate with.

1. acquired ☐ a. deadline
2. mounting ☐ b. job
3. tight ☐ c. taste
4. irate ☐ d. pressure
5. demeaning ☐ e. customer

Now match these adjectives to the nouns they collocate with.

6. unrealistic ☐ f. mismanagement
7. valuable ☐ g. bang
8. controversial ☐ h. insights
9. almighty ☐ i. expectations
10. financial ☐ j. decision

Which verb(s) could you use with each of these adjective-noun collocations? Write an example sentence for each. Compare your sentences with a partner. Whose are more useful?

10 Passives

Complete the sentences with the correct form of the passive verbs in the box.

be affected	be dogged	be stranded
be buried	be evacuated	be submerged
be criticised	be stamped out	

1. A: .... you .... by that tornado last year?
   B: Yes, absolutely. We had to .... from our block of flats, because they thought it might collapse afterwards – and it did! I guess we were lucky not to .... alive, really!
2. This mate of mine was caught in these flash floods while he was on holiday. Apparently, the hotel he was staying in .... in about 20 feet of water. They .... on the second floor for two days waiting for the waters to recede. It was dreadful.
3. The government's second term in office .... by problems. Corruption still .... not .... , security hasn't improved and the government .... widely .... for its handling of the economy.

Now complete these sentences with the correct form of the passive verbs in the box.

be awarded	be started	be treated
be rescued	be thrashed	be upheld

4. Last month, a man from London .... £80,000 in compensation when his case for unfair dismissal .... by an employment tribunal.
5. Several people .... for minor burns after they .... from a fire in a pub in Oxford last night. Police believe the fire may have .... deliberately and are appealing for witnesses.
6. We .... 5-1 on Saturday. It was a dreadful game.

Writing

1 Collocations

Complete the collocations with the nouns in the box.

concern	increase	issue	solution
impact	interest	problem	studies

1. intractable / long-standing / serious / enormous
   ....
2. widespread / keen / close / lifelong / media
   ....
3. unworkable / drastic / partial / cost-effective
   ....
4. alarming / rapid / 10 per cent / small / marked
   ....
5. growing / national / public / grave / mounting
   ....
6. massive / profound / visual / disastrous / full
   ....
7. burning / contentious / global / live / real
   ....
8. recent / further / preliminary / laboratory / field
   ....

Choose five collocations that are new for you and write example sentences. Use your dictionary to help you if you need to. Now read your sentences to a partner, but instead of saying the adjectives, say *blank*. Can your partner guess the missing adjectives? For example:

A: Whilst this solution may seem attractive in theory, it is almost certainly utterly *blank* in practice.

B: Unworkable.

2 Weak and strong positions

Work with a partner. Complete these sentences so that they make sense. The second sentence should offer a counter-claim to the first.

1. It is supposedly easier to teach single-sex groups of students. However, ...
2. A rural life seemingly offers an idyllic existence. However, ...
3. It is often claimed that the young are becoming increasingly socially isolated as a result of the large amount of time spent on computers. However, ...
4. It is widely believed that higher taxation leads to a more equal society. However, ...
5. It is often suggested that traffic laws need to be tightened. However, ...

3 A job application letter

The letter below was written by a student. Her teacher has underlined eighteen mistakes. Try to correct them with a partner. The first one is done for you.

Dear Sir / Madam,

in response to

I am writing to respond to your recent advertisement for an office assistant. Please find my current CV here.

I feel I would be suitable for the post for a number of reasons. Firstly, I am fluent in Polish and German as well as I speak excellent English, passing the Level 8 Trinity exam last month. Secondly, I feel I possess the relevant experience, as I have previously worked for a summer school at the university where I have helped out in the office to do photocopying and other basic duties for the teacher staff. Working in a team, I gained a valued experience and developed good interpersonal skills. Over the past year I have also done some voluntary work for a charity shop which it supports disabled people. The shop is partly managed by disabled people and I did some of the admin work as well as working a shop assistant.

I am a dedicated worker, who am able to act both independently and as part of a team. I'm very much enjoying new challenges and would look forward to taking up a post in an English-speaking situation. I feel the post would also allow me extension my range of abilities. I hope you will agree that my track record so far shows this.

I am available for interview at any time and would be happy to provide references, if you are requiring them.

Should you need another information, please do not wait to contact me.

I am looking forward to hearing from you soon,

Yours faithfully,

Natalia Sokolova

Now write a letter applying for the following job.

Sammy's

Sammy's offers great retail jobs for great people making great food. We pay our staff as much as we can – instead of as little as we can get away with! We invest in, train and develop our workers (75% of our managers were promoted from Team Leaders). Our average hourly rate is £6.60. Many get over £7 an hour – it depends.

Sammy's is a growing concern, so if you're hard working, enjoy food and have a sense of humour, you'll probably fit right in. Send us a covering letter and your CV to apply.

I want to get rid of these bags under my eyes. • He's just got this permanently vacant look on his face. • Wipe your feet! • It's nice to be pampered now and again. • I just poked myself in the eye! • He totally botched it up. • You're meant to rinse it out after 15 minutes. • It's hereditary, apparently. • Plastic surgery completely ruined my life. • I'm blissfully happy now. • I'm thinking of getting a wig. • That must've cost him. • There's a steam room there. • I wish I was a couple of sizes smaller. • They perpetuate these stereotypes. • He's prepared to undergo surgery. • I'm having it bleached. • It'd be a bit more manageable shorter. • They can't be real! They must be fake. • Bitchy, bitchy! • I just feel a bit self-conscious. • I've got cellulite.

7 Hair and beauty

Conversation

1 Body collocations (1)

Complete the collocations with the words in the box.

chin	eyes	feet	hands	nails
eyebrows	face	hair	legs	nose

1. sharp / polished / incredibly long / chewed ....
2. bags under my / mad staring / bloodshot / big soulful ....
3. skinny / hairy / long / great / fat stumpy ....
4. bushy / thick / thin / plucked ....
5. filthy / rough / soft / delicate ....
6. size-13 / smelly / bare / flat / tiny ....
7. double / stubbly / cleft ....
8. huge / runny / pointy / flat / pierced ....
9. wrinkled / angelic / boyish / vacant look on his ....
10. bushy / spiky / greying / ginger / permed / wavy / tangled ....

Do you find any of these things really attractive or really off-putting?

How would you describe the different parts of your own body? Does your partner agree?

2 Body collocations (2)

Complete the questions with the correct form of the verbs in the box.

be	pick	poke	tread	wax
file	pluck	raise	water	wipe

1. Do you .... your eyebrows?
2. Do you know anyone who .... their nose?
3. Do you .... your nails?
4. Have you ever had your legs .... ?
5. What do you say if someone .... on your foot?
6. When do you need to .... your feet?
7. Have you ever .... yourself in the eye?
8. What things could make your eyes .... ?
9. In what jobs .... you on your feet all day?
10. What kinds of things might .... a few eyebrows ?

With a partner, act out the verb collocations in the questions above. Then discuss the questions.

Can you think of any other verbs that collocate with the parts of the body in Activity 1?

3 Listening

You are going to listen to five conversations connected with hair and beauty. Match one statement with each conversation.

1. ☐ 2. ☐ 3. ☐ 4. ☐ 5. ☐

a. Someone regrets doing something.
b. Someone is ill at the moment.
c. Someone is going somewhere to be pampered.
d. Someone is self-conscious about their appearance.
e. Someone has changed their looks because of work.
f. Someone has been lucky.
g. Someone has recently had their hair dyed.
h. Someone has changed a lot since they were younger.

Compare your answers with a partner and explain your choices. Listen again if you need to. Which person do you sympathise with most? Why?

4 Speaking

Discuss these questions with a partner.

1. Do you know anyone who has had a big change of image? Why did they change?
2. Do you think 13 is too young to be dyeing your hair? Did your parents ever stop you from having a particular image?
3. Have you been in a situation where you felt quite self-conscious?
4. Have you ever had any of the following?
   a facial a manicure
   a massage a pedicure
   a sauna

5 Using grammar: auxiliaries

Complete the sentences from the conversations with the correct auxiliary or modal verb.

1. A: Oh my God! What .... you done to your hair?
   B: It .... only supposed to lighten it a little.
2. A: An hour! No wonder it's come out the way it .... You're meant to rinse it out after 15 minutes.
   B: .... you?
   A: Yeah, it says here. .... you bother to read the instructions?
   B: No, but I wish I ....
3. B: People like to put you in a box, ... they?
   A: Well, that's their problem. You should just ignore them.
   B: It .... their problem, but at the same time it .... affect me and what I get to do.
4. A: A wig? I don't see that as much of an opportunity. I think I'd feel a bit self-conscious wearing one.
   B: Oh, I .... , and I .... always fancied having thick blonde hair. I think I could pass for a bit of a Marilyn Monroe.
5. A: Really? That ....'ve cost him.
   B: Yeah, but he .... owe me something special after my last birthday.
   A: Oh yeah, he completely forgot, ... he? So what .... you going to do while you're there?
   B: Well, all sorts. There's a steam room, which I love.
   A: Mmm, so .... I.

Listen and check your answers. Notice which of the auxiliaries are stressed. With a partner, practise reading out the conversations above.

For more information on using auxiliaries, see G6.

6 Using grammar: *have something done*

Look at how you can use this structure in different tenses.

- So why did you have it done?
- I was ready to have it chopped off.
- I'm going to have a crown fitted next week.
- It's time I had my roots done again.

Complete the conversations using the correct form of the *have something done* structure.

1. A: Are you going to be in this afternoon?
   B: No, I .... (hair / cut). I'll be back around seven.
   A: Are you .... (much / take off)? I quite like it long.
   B: Do you? I was thinking of .... (it / do) in a bob. It'd just be a bit more manageable.
   A: That's a shame. I'd just leave it. It looks really nice as it is. I .... (just / it / trimmed) if I were you – just tidied up a bit.
2. A: Have you seen Hazel's hair?
   B: No, what's she done to it?
   A: She .... (it / bleach). Honestly, it looks ridiculous.
   B: I can imagine. Mind you, I've had my fair share of disasters like that. I once .... (hair / perm). It was all the rage at the time, but as soon as I .... (it / do), I regretted it. I just looked like a complete idiot. I left it for a couple of days, but then I went back and .... (it / straighten). I'd had so many negative comments, I couldn't stand it.
3. A: All right. How are you?
   B: Dreadful, if you must know. I've got this really painful abscess behind a tooth. It's horrible – all filled with pus.
   A: OK, spare me the details! .... (it / look at)?
   B: Yeah, I went to the dentist's yesterday. He gave me some antibiotics to see if it'll clear up, but he said I .... (probably / tooth / take out) and a bridge put in.
   A: Ooh! Rather you than me! I .... (some bridging work / do) last year. It was a nightmare.

What things have you had done at the hairdresser's or the dentist's? Have you ever had to have something looked at? What? Why?

Complete the sentences with your own ideas using a *have something done* structure. Tell some other students.

- I was thinking of ... .
- I once ... .
- I really should ... .
- Last year ... .

For more information on using *have something done*, see G7.

Reading

1 Speaking

Discuss these questions with a partner.

1. Do you know anyone – or have you heard of anyone – who has:
   - had a facelift?
   - had liposuction?
   - had their nose done?
   - had their eyes done?
   - had their breasts done?
   - had their ears pinned back?
   - had their teeth straightened?
   - had a tattoo removed?
   - had a part of their body pierced?
2. Have you ever heard of anyone having any other kinds of plastic surgery?
3. Do you know anyone who you think should have one of these operations?

Real English: She's had her nose done.

If someone has their nose done, they have plastic surgery to make their nose look nicer. Maybe they have it made longer or maybe it's made smaller. People often say She's had a nose job. If you have your breasts done, you have implants and have them enlarged. This is often called having a boob job.

2 Before you read

You are going to read an article about plastic surgery. Before you read, discuss these questions with a partner.

1. How many reasons for having plastic surgery can you think of?
2. How many reasons for NOT having it can you think of?

Compare your ideas with another pair.

3 While you read

Now read the article and find out if any of your ideas are mentioned. Underline any other reasons for or against plastic surgery that are mentioned in the text.

Compare what you've underlined with a partner and discuss which reasons you agree or disagree with.

4 Speaking

Discuss these questions with a partner.

1. Which of the four people interviewed do you most/least like the sound of? Why?
2. Why do you think the kind of plastic surgery people have differs so much around the world?
3. Do you think surgeons should be held legally responsible if their operations go wrong?
4. Do you ever wish you were different? In what way? Are you going to do anything about it?

5 Using grammar: adverbs that modify adjectives

In the article, you read that plastic surgery has become far more socially acceptable than it used to be. We often use adverbs before adjectives to add shades of meaning.

Match the adverbs from the article with the adjectives they collocate with.

1. internationally	☐	a.	British
2. blissfully	☐	b.	disgraceful
3. clinically	☐	c.	qualified
4. badly	☐	d.	famous
5. absolutely	☐	e.	happy
6. uniquely	☐	f.	depressed

Can you remember what each collocation was used to describe?

Now match these adverbs with the adjectives they collocate with.

7. outrageously	☐	g.	produced
8. strictly	☐	h.	disappointed
9. locally	☐	i.	enforced
10. bitterly	☐	j.	normal
11. wrongly	☐	k.	convicted
12. perfectly	☐	l.	expensive

6 Speaking

Discuss these questions with a partner.

1. What kind of things do you think are becoming increasingly socially acceptable in your country?
2. Is there anything that's still not really socially acceptable?
3. Do you know any couples who seem blissfully happy together?
4. Are any people from your country internationally famous? Why?

For more information on using adverbial modifiers, see G8.

I feel like a whole new person!

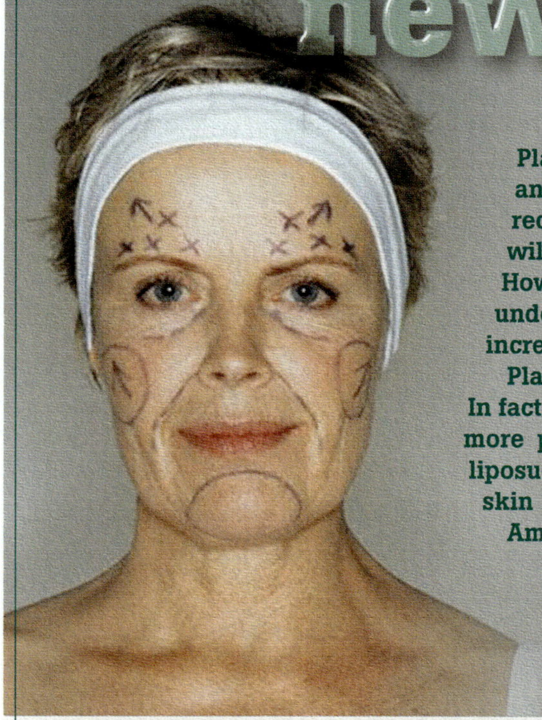

Plastic surgery has become affordable for many in recent years and has also become far more socially acceptable. Indeed, in a recent survey, 67 per cent of British women said they would be willing to undergo surgery to achieve their perfect look. However, it's not just women who are happy to put themselves under the surgeon's knife in the pursuit of beauty. Men are also increasingly choosing to surgically alter their appearance.

Plastic surgery is far from being a uniquely British phenomenon. In fact, it is a global boom industry, though different procedures are more popular in different countries. Whilst Brits tend to opt for liposuction or a 'tummy tuck' (an operation which removes excess skin and fat from the stomach area), all across Latin and North America women are going in the opposite direction and getting buttock implants. At the same time, eye-widening surgery is big in many Asian countries. We decided to ask a few different people how they felt about these trends. Here's what they told us.

Kevin

I can see people might need plastic surgery for reconstructive or for health reasons, but apart from that, I'm dead against it. There is no need to correct something that is natural, and plastic surgery just shows a weak-willed desire to conform to some kind of unobtainable ideal. I'm Chinese-American and what really gets my back up is how many women go for the eye-widening operations. I don't get it! I think it just demonstrates a lack of cultural pride and it's absolutely disgraceful that Asians feel the need to change their eyes in pursuit of this Caucasian ideal. I feel the same when I see African-Americans bleaching their skin. And the media doesn't help. They perpetuate these stereotypes of white equalling beautiful, but we do have minds of our own and we can choose to reject these images.

Charlotte

I don't really have any strong feelings on the matter, to be honest. Each to their own is what I say. It's easy to sneer at people who have plastic surgery, but you never know what you'd do if you were in their shoes, do you? And your perspective on things changes as you get older too. I mean, when I was 21, I was blissfully happy with my body – most 21-year-olds are, aren't they? But once I turned 40, I started feeling differently. Men stopped looking at me in the street and I lost a bit of self-confidence and I do have to admit, there are days when I look in the mirror and think to myself 'I wish my bum wasn't quite so big' or 'I wish I was a couple of sizes smaller'. So, if surgery makes people feel better about themselves, good luck to them!

Nicky

I know some people might think I'm shallow, but I couldn't care less about their opinions because plastic surgery changed my life. I had a nose job a few years ago and it was like a huge weight being lifted off my shoulders! I'd been literally clinically depressed about my nose for ages before that. I just REALLY hated my nose. It had this strange bit on the end of it that people always used to comment on. My sister's got the same thing. It's hereditary. In the end, I became obsessed with it and eventually it got to the point where I felt like it was taking over my life. The final straw was when some guy in the pub asked if it'd been bitten by a dog! I decided there and then to splash out and get it done – and life's been sweet ever since!

Katty

Plastic surgery completely ruined my life. I used to be a top model and an actress, and even though people were always telling me how gorgeous I was, I could never see it. I always thought I should be even thinner or have even bigger breasts. I was borderline anorexic for ages. I was convinced I had cellulite in my legs, so I had liposuction. There are lots of badly-qualified practitioners around operating semi-illegally, but I went to an internationally famous surgeon. He totally botched it up. It left my legs scarred for life and he refused to accept responsibility. It destroyed my career. Now I'm studying to be a lawyer and want to represent women who've had similar experiences.

I'm not very politically aware. • What we need is a bit more honesty and openness. • No-one won an overall majority. • The party's suffered from a lot of in-fighting. • It's a fine line between smooth and smarmy. • I just keep out of it all. • You're so apathetic! • What bugs me is the amount of money they've wasted. • I'm your typical floating voter. • He comes across as being very down-to-earth. • She never seems to get flustered. • They're so patronising. • He's just power-mad. • I don't like their stance on pensions. • The election was rigged. • Well, in my humble opinion, it's just blatantly unfair. • They need to encourage greater participation. • They treat voters like idiots. • You're such a cynic.

8 Politics and elections

Conversation

1 Reading and vocabulary: politics and elections in Britain

Read the text and underline the verbs that go with the nouns in red. Translate the whole verb + noun collocations into your language. Then discuss which things in the text are:

a. exactly the same in your country.
b. similar in your country.
c. quite different.

Many people feel the British electoral system is in need of reform. The government can decide to hold a general election any time within five years of coming to power. For the election, the country is divided into 646 areas or constituencies. In each constituency, the people who live in that area vote to elect one MP to represent them. The party with the majority of MPs forms the government. Where no party wins an overall majority, there is a hung parliament and the biggest parties form a coalition. In the UK, coalitions are rare. This is partly because of the 'first-past-the-post system'. In each constituency, the candidate who wins the most votes becomes the MP and all the other votes that have been cast for other candidates do not count towards the national result. This is why the Labour government in 2001 could win a landslide victory with a 166-seat majority, despite having only received 41% of the vote.

One suggested benefit of this system is that people have a more direct relationship with their MP. If you have a problem, you can write to your MP and they are obliged to answer you. They also hold weekly or monthly surgeries when you can go and visit them in person. However, some people believe we should adopt a system of proportional representation – where the number of MPs each party gets is in direct relation to the total number of votes cast nationally. So, if the Labour party were to poll 51% of the total vote, they would then have 51% of the members in Parliament.

In the UK, there are three main parties: Labour, which was traditionally left wing, but which moved to the centre to get elected, the Conservatives (or Tories) and the Liberal Democrats (Lib-Dems). The Tories were most popular in the eighties when Margaret Thatcher was their leader, but after 1997, they were in opposition. The party suffered from a lot of infighting. The Lib-Dems are the third party. They were traditionally in the centre, but have adopted more left-wing policies. There are also a number of Nationalist parties – in Scotland, Wales and Northern Ireland – which want either more autonomy or complete separation from England.

2 Listening

You're going to hear four people talking – Harry, Abigail, Miriam and Toby. Listen to the conversation and find out:

a. if they are going to vote and if not, why not.
b. who they're going to vote for and why.

Discuss who says the following and what they are talking about.

1. I caught the end of it.
2. It's a fine line between smooth and smarmy.
3. It's quite off-putting.
4. I've had enough of them.
5. They're only involved in a tiny proportion of schools.
6. I just don't see it helping integration.
7. I find him a bit shifty myself.
8. They're a bit lightweight, aren't they?
9. He tells it like it is.
10. They're never going to get in.
11. I keep out of all of it.
12. You're such a cynic.

Listen again and check your answers.

3 Speaking

Discuss these questions with a partner.

1. A new phenomenon in UK elections is negative campaigning. What do you think of the poster below? Do you find this kind of thing in your country?
2. How do you feel about religious schools?
3. Do you agree that all politicians are as bad as each other?
4. Would you describe yourself as a floating voter?

4 Using grammar: sentences starting with *What*

We often start sentences with What followed by verbs to express feelings and opinions. We use it to mean *The thing that*. For example:

- What annoys me is the way they treat us as if we couldn't think for ourselves!

Find examples of this structure in the tapescript for Activity 2 at the back of the book.

Complete the sentences with the pairs of words in the box.

annoys + way	concerns + that
drives + how	angers + amount
disturbs + fact	frustrates + lack
bothers + level	disappoints + not
upsets + seeing	

1. What .... me most is .... it's not an isolated incident. It's happened time and time again. It's really worrying.
2. What .... me most about him is the .... he talks to people. He's really patronising.
3. What .... me most is the .... of money they've wasted on useless projects.
4. What .... me crazy is .... arrogant they all are. They never believe they're in the wrong.
5. What .... me is the .... that you can now be basically detained without trial. They're constantly eroding civil liberties.
6. What .... me is .... all these people starving in Africa and knowing our government is doing nothing to help.
7. What .... me is .... so much what they've done, but the way it's been presented.
8. What .... me is the .... of crime in our cities. There's just so much!
9. What .... me is the .... of investment in education. We can't improve our schools as quickly as we'd like without more money.

Write six sentences of your own about the government, your prime minister, the opposition parties, the local council, your city, your country – or anything else you feel strongly about.

Tell a partner and find out if you agree or disagree.

Can you complete these sentence starters about similar things?

a. What I really like about what they've done is ... .
b. What's great about things here is ... .
c. What's really pleasing to see is ... .

5 Talking about politicians

Match the descriptions with the follow-up comments.

1. He seems very down-to-earth. ☐
2. I get the impression he's very passionate. ☐
3. He just comes across as being really arrogant. ☐
4. He's very smooth in front of the cameras. ☐
5. He's obviously very competent, but he's a bit dull. ☐
6. He's a complete fascist. ☐

a. He never listens to other people's points of view because he think he knows best.
b. He presents a very slick image. You never see him flustered or caught out.
c. He's just really right-wing! He wants to curb women's rights and get rid of all the immigrants – that kind of thing.
d. He hasn't got the spark or charisma to be Prime Minister.
e. You could imagine having a drink with him. He's got no pretensions.
f. He genuinely believes in what he's doing and wants to change things.

Now match these descriptions with the follow-up comments.

7. I get the feeling he's very ambitious. ☐
8. He's very charismatic. ☐
9. He just seems very honest. ☐
10. He comes across as being quite shifty in interviews. ☐
11. He just comes across as incredibly patronising. ☐
12. He's just a complete hypocrite. ☐

g. He never gives a straight answer. I just wouldn't trust him.
h. He's very straight with people. If he thinks something is bad, he says so.
i. He's just power-mad. He's only interested in getting to the top.
j. He complains about private schools, but he sends his son to one!
k. He talks down to people like they're children.
l. He gives some very powerful speeches. He's got this aura of confidence which people find attractive.

Work with a partner. Spend two minutes trying to memorise the descriptions.

Student A: Say one of the follow-up comments.
Student B: Close your book and respond with one of the descriptions.

Now discuss these questions. Try to use some of the language from this activity.

- Are there any politicians or public figures you like or respect? Why?
- Which politicians don't you like? Why?

Reading

1 Listening: voter apathy

Voter apathy is a big problem in many democracies. Do you know what it is?

Listen and complete this introduction to a radio news feature about voter apathy.

Voter apathy has reached (1) .... Turnout for the forthcoming election is expected to be the lowest in history with voters staying away from (2) .... in their millions. Politicians have come to be seen as remote from the people, self-serving and (3) .... As one commentator dryly noted, 'The issue now is not whether politicians lie or not. It's which liar you (4) .... !' On top of all that, there's also a (5) .... that it's not really politicians that run the show. They are often seen as puppets with no real power, whilst behind the scenes, big business (6) ....

2 Speaking

Discuss these questions with a partner.

1. Is voter apathy a problem in your country? Why?
2. Do you always vote in both local and national elections?
3. What are the consequences of voter apathy – both for society and for individuals who don't vote?
4. Which groups in society do you think are most / least likely to vote?

3 Before you read

You are going to read about some different ways people have tried to combat voter apathy. Before you read, write down three things you think would encourage more people to vote.

Compare your ideas with a partner. Who has the best idea?

4 While you read

Now read the article. As you read, think about these questions.

1. Do any of the ideas mentioned already happen in your country?
2. Would you like to see any of these ideas introduced? Why?
3. What downsides to each idea might there be?

Now discuss your answers with a partner.

5 Vocabulary focus

Match the nouns from the article with each group of collocations.

answer	goal	meeting	policy
election	joke	opinion	vote

1. crack a ... / a dirty ... / a sick ... / the ... fell flat / an old ...
2. cast a ... / get 22 per cent of the ... / the yes ... / a ... of confidence
3. demand an ... / a rambling ... / he never gives a straight ...
4. a cabinet ... / a stormy ... / disrupt a ... / hold a ... / a top-level ...
5. in the run-up to the ... / rig the ... / hold a mock ... / a local ...
6. put forward a ... / adopt a controversial ... / a ... aimed at the young
7. divide public ... / an ... poll / a difference of ... / in my humble ...
8. a long-term ... / an immediate ... / an unrealistic ... / set a personal ...

Now read the article again and find as many verbs / adjectives as you can that collocate with the nouns in the box below.

ways	the party line	system
participation	debates	

How many of the collocations are new for you and your partner? Look up any collocations neither of you know. Then think of when you might use each one.

6 Speaking

Make sure you understand the words in the box. Then discuss the questions below in small groups.

abortion	infrastructure and technology
civil rights	law and order
education	pensions
Europe	privatisation
foreign policy	the economy
government reform	the environment
health care	war and peace
immigration	welfare and poverty

1. What were the big issues in the last election in your country? Which of these issues were most important for you personally?
2. What kind of stance do the various parties in your country have on these issues?

The politics of persuasion

There's an old joke about voter apathy. A local council in Britain once held a meeting to find ways of combating the problem – and only one person bothered to turn up! To those living under dictatorships, the widespread disillusionment with politicians in many democracies must seem incredible and perhaps even offensive. However, for many – particularly the young – elections hold very little appeal. As a result, a vicious circle develops. If young people don't vote, candidates stop trying to appeal to them. If the candidates then don't appeal to them, they're even more reluctant to vote! Re-engaging with voters and encouraging wider participation in the whole democratic process has become one of the main goals for political parties of all persuasions. Here we explore six key ways in which a higher turnout could be encouraged.

1 Stop the spin!

Many voters claim they stay away from the polls more in anger than in apathy. The modern obsession with image and presentation means most politicians never give a straight answer, always stick to the party line and generally sound like they're endlessly repeating a well-rehearsed script. A bit more honesty, openness and information would go a long way. Most voters want to know about the mistakes as well as the success stories, the problems as well as the plans. They also want politicians to make big, brave decisions rather than always tailoring policies to fit public opinion.

2 Lower the voting age

Politicians often complain that the young seem uninterested in politics – and yet many feel the voting system treats the young like idiots! In Britain, you can smoke, have sex and start paying income tax at 16; you can join the army and die for your country at 17; and yet you can't cast your vote for a party in favour of or opposed to war, abortion, tax cuts, and so on until you turn 18. The young have many responsibilities. Perhaps it's time to start treating them like adults and give them more rights!

3 Pay more attention to civic responsibilities in schools

Some schools hold their own mock elections and encourage debates among pupils. Politicians and lobby groups are also occasionally invited in to address pupils. This can all surely only be for the good. Students could also learn to value their right to vote through studying, for example, the history of the struggles women faced to get the vote.

4 Encourage greater participation in grassroots democracy

Many western democracies actually limit participation in the democratic process to a solitary vote once every four of five years. Referendums on issues of national importance – such as those often held in Switzerland – would be one way of increasing interest. The South American cities of Porto Alegre, Belém and Santo André in Brazil and Villa El Salvador in Peru have gone even further and set up participatory budgets, where anyone and everyone can attend public meetings and vote on how public finances should be spent.

5 Make it easier to vote

Many people don't get round to voting simply because they're too busy. E-voting, SMS-voting and polling stations set up in shops, cafés or even pubs would take this into account and thus encourage greater participation.

6 Scrap the first-past-the-post system in favour of proportional representation

At the moment, a British government that has 38 per cent of the vote in a country where perhaps only 50 per cent of the people voted still has the power to rule! The first-past-the-post system, where the party that wins the most seats wins the election, is blatantly unfair. A system of proportional representation, where parties would be allocated seats according to the percentage of the overall national vote each received, would be far fairer and would ensure every vote cast actually counted!

Writing: Introductions to essays

1 Describing changes

Rewrite the sentences using the words in brackets so that the pairs of sentences mean the same. For example:

There has been an alarming increase in the spread of AIDS in recent years. (enormously)

The spread of AIDS has increased enormously in recent years.

1. There has been a massive decrease in the number of people using public phones. (plummeted)
2. There are more people committing suicide now than there used to be. (a rise)
3. Over the past decade, the number of cars on the road has escalated. (ever increasing)
4. The number of teenage pregnancies has continued to rise steadily over the last decade. (steady)
5. The hole in the ozone layer has doubled in size over the last five years. (twice / ago)
6. Since the 80s, there has been a continuous decline in the birth rate to just 1.3 children today. (slumped)
7. The number of people buying music on CD is falling. (Fewer and fewer)
8. Car crime has fallen over recent years, but violent crime is on the increase. (a drop / going up)

2 Speaking

Discuss these questions with a partner.

1. Do you think the statements in Activity 1 are true for your country? If not, what changes have occurred?
2. What has caused these changes?
3. What do you think the implications and results of these changes are?

'That's the gist of what I wanted to say, now find me some statistics to base it on'

3 Using grammar: cause or result?

Decide which pattern the verbs in the list fit into:

CAUSE → RESULT
a. Migration from the countryside ... chronic overcrowding in cities

RESULT ← CAUSE
b. Chronic overcrowding in cities ... Migration from the countryside

1. bring about
2. be brought about by
3. cause
4. be caused by
5. give rise to
6. result in
7. be the result of
8. lead to
9. stem from
10. be due to
11. play a part in
12. mean

Now complete these sentences with ONE word in each space.

1. The massive increase in state funding of hospitals has .... a part in the rise in life expectancy.
2. The massive rise in the price of oil is largely the .... of natural disasters, wars and ethnic conflicts in oil-producing countries.
3. The spread of AIDS has been .... by poor sex education.
4. The hole in the ozone layer has .... in increased incidences of skin cancer.
5. Some say the increase in teenage pregnancies is .... to the break-up of the traditional family.
6. Improving public transport should .... to a reduction in private car use.
7. The problems that beset the rail network largely .... from a lack of investment by successive governments.
8. Most of the effects of so-called natural disasters such as droughts and flooding are actually .... about by corruption and bad government.
9. The internet has given .... to a number of legal problems particularly around the area of copyright.
10. The rise in house prices in the UK has .... many young people cannot afford to get on the property ladder.

With a new partner, discuss the questions in Activity 2. Use some of the words above to show causes and results.

4 Vocabulary check

Complete the compound nouns from Activity 3.

a. state ....
b. life ....
c. ethnic ....
d. oil-producing ....
e. sex ....
f. the ozone ....
g. skin ....
h. teenage ....
i private car ....
j. the rail ....
k. natural ....
l. the property ....

5 Introductions

When we write introductions to articles and essays, we often follow this pattern.

1. Describe a trend.
2. Give further evidence / the cause / the result of this trend.
3. Pose one or more questions we aim to answer.

Put these sentences in order to make a good introduction to an essay.

Introduction 1

a. How has this situation come about?
b. A recent report has even suggested that the life expectancy of today's teenagers has actually decreased.
c. And just what can we do to reverse the trend?
d. Over the past decade, young people have become increasingly unhealthy.

1. ☐ 2. ☐ 3. ☐ 4. ☐

Introduction 2

a. Indeed, average speeds in the city are lower than they were a hundred years ago.
b. Is banning city centre traffic the only answer or is there a less drastic solution?
c. It has become increasingly difficult to move round our cities because of traffic congestion.
d. But what is to be done about it?
e. Over the past few years, the number of people using cars has escalated.

1. ☐ 2. ☐ 3. ☐ 4. ☐ 5. ☐

Introduction 3

a. Could the internet be creating new problems which will damage our society rather than improve it?
b. Increasingly, more and more people are using the internet.
c. There are obvious benefits, such as e-mail, the ease of buying and selling things, and the free availability of information.
d. Most people have access through their work and many are connected at home.
e. Nevertheless, it is worth asking if the internet is wholly a good thing.

1. ☐ 2. ☐ 3. ☐ 4. ☐ 5. ☐

6 Practice

Choose three of the exam questions below. Note down which trend is being discussed in each one. Think about the evidence / the cause / the result connected to each trend. Then decide which questions you will need to answer in the essay.

Now write an introduction for each question you chose. Try not to repeat exactly what is said in the questions.

1. Write a short essay explaining why there is still so much poverty in the Third World and how it could be eradicated.
2. You have recently seen a report suggesting people are unhappier than they used to be. Write an article for a college magazine explaining why this might be and how you could overcome it.
3. 'The main reason for the increase in teenage pregnancy is the loss of family values.' Write an essay saying if you agree and what solutions could be found for the problem.
4. Explain why English has become such an important language to learn and say if you think this is a good thing or not.
5. 'The only way to curb air traffic is to increase prices dramatically.' Write an article discussing the reasons for the increase in air travel, if it should be reduced and, if so, how.
6. 'If we don't do something about global warming now, our children will suffer.' Write an essay saying if you agree with this statement and what, if anything, we should do about it.

Show what you have written to a partner. Which introduction does your partner like best? Why?

7 Planning an essay

Choose one essay to write for homework. Work with your partner and spend five minutes brainstorming ideas for this essay. Think of as many reasons and solutions (or arguments for and against) as you can. Remember that at this stage you don't have to say if you agree with all the ideas.

Change partners. Does your new partner agree or disagree with all the ideas you thought of. Why?

For homework, write your own essay. Before you start, plan your paragraphs.

It's going to chuck it down any minute. • It's gone a bit chilly. • It's blowing a gale out there. • Glorious weather! • My skin actually blistered it was so burnt! • Bit muggy, isn't it? • We were snowed in. • It was rained off. • It was completely waterlogged. • There was a huge tailback on the motorway. • I avoid him like the plague. • They're going to erect a wind turbine in front of my house. • We're going to have to do something fairly drastic. • They claim global warming doesn't exist. • Well, they would say that, wouldn't they? • He's a leading advocate of nuclear power. • They're just nimbies opposing it.

9 The weather and the environment

Conversation

1 Talking about the weather

Match the questions with the answers.

1. Did you get caught in that shower earlier? ☐
2. Was that rain? ☐
3. Is it still raining outside? ☐
4. Hot today, isn't it? ☐
5. Is it still snowing out there? ☐
6. Is it OK if I close the window? ☐
7. Do you think I'll need a coat? ☐
8. Do you think I'll be OK in a T-shirt? ☐

a. Yeah, go ahead. It is a bit chilly, isn't it?
b. Yeah, scorching!
c. Yeah, it's pouring down.
d. Yeah, it's an absolute blizzard!
e. Yeah, it's quite mild out there.
f. Yeah, it's bitter out there!
g. Yeah, it's just started spitting. It's going to chuck it down any minute.
h. Yeah, I got absolutely soaked!

Spend two minutes trying to memorise answers a–h above. Then cover them. Now read out questions 1–8 while your partner answers. When you have finished, swap roles.

Now match the nouns in the box with each group of collocations.

breeze	fog	rain	sky	weather	winds

1. clear blue / overcast / there wasn't a cloud in the ....
2. thick / freezing / patchy ....
3. howling / gale-force / biting ....
4. torrential / tropical / fine ....
5. miserable / unpredictable / glorious ....
6. light / stiff / sea ....

Discuss these questions with a partner.

- Do you ever get any of the weather described in Activity 1 in your country? When? Where?
- What's your favourite kind of weather?
- What kind of weather do you find hardest to deal with? Why?

2 Listening

You are going to listen to six short conversations. As you listen to each one, try to answer these questions.

a. What kind of weather are the people talking about?
b. What kind of problems do they mention?

3 Vocabulary focus

Listen to the conversations again and complete each sentence with TWO words.

1a. The pitch was .... , so it was too muddy to play on.
1b. I could .... warming up a bit.
2a. I thought they said it .... to be nice and sunny today.
2b. I .... them having the reception in the garden if it stays like this.
3a. She just really .... the heat.
3b. .... that, though, it was amazing!
4a. They've just put out an announcement saying it's ....
4b. Anyway, listen, I'm almost .... money, so I'd better go.
5a. I was .... a minor car crash.
5b. We went skidding off the road and through all these bushes and we .... in this field.
6a. No, it's .... at this time of year.
6b. You've made your point, Jurgen. There's .... to rub it in!

4 Speaking

Discuss these questions with a partner.

1. Have you ever been to a wedding reception? When? What was it like?
2. Is drink driving much of a problem in your country? How strictly do the police enforce the laws? What's the punishment?
3. Have you ever had a close shave – when you were lucky no-one was really hurt?
4. Is there anything you think could only happen in your country?

5 Weather problems

Complete the sentences with the words in the box.

blisters	dropped	power cut	sunburnt
bucketing down	froze over	snowed in	

1. It was .... and all the parents drove their kids to school rather than letting them walk, so the traffic was horrendous!
2. There was a blizzard and we got totally .... We had to literally dig ourselves out.
3. There was a huge storm and then there was a .... We didn't have any electricity for about three days!
4. It .... to about minus twenty and all the rivers ....
5. I'm not really used to hot weather and it was absolutely scorching, so I got really badly .... It was horrible. I came out in .... everywhere.

Now complete these sentences with the words in the box.

chaos	foggy	skidded	tailback
downpour	icy	soaked	visibility

6. There was so much black ice on the roads we actually .... right off at one point. We were lucky no-one was hurt.
7. It rained for about ten hours non-stop and then it all froze during the night, so it was total .... on the roads in the morning.
8. It was the middle of winter and the roads were really .... and there'd been an accident, so there was a huge .... on the motorway.
9. The drive back up from the coast was a nightmare! It was really .... and it was night-time, so we had almost zero ....
10. I got .... cycling in to work yesterday! It was nice and sunny when I left my house, but then suddenly the skies opened and I got caught in this ....

6 Speaking

Discuss these questions with a partner.

1. Have you ever had any similar problems to those mentioned above? When? What happened?
2. Have you ever had any other problems because of the weather?
3. Have you ever had any other problems while you were driving or while you were a passenger in a car?

7 Similes

A simile is when we say something is like something else. For example, in Conversation 3 you heard that the heat when you get off the plane in Malaysia 'is like walking into a wall'.

Complete the sentences with the words in the box.

like a mudbath	like a log	like a sieve
like dirt	like a glove	like a pig
like cat and dog	like the plague	

1. It'd been raining so hard the pitch was ....
2. The heat was just unbearable. I was sweating ....
3. I can't believe those two are still together. They fight .... !
4. I don't know how she puts up with it. I'd leave him if I was her. He treats her .... !
5. A: Did you sleep well?
   B: Yeah, ...
6. I can't stand the guy! I avoid him ....
7. A: Do you like the cut of those jeans? Do they fit OK?
   B: Yeah, ... They're really comfy.
8. I've studied some of these things before, but I can't remember any of them! I've got a memory .... !

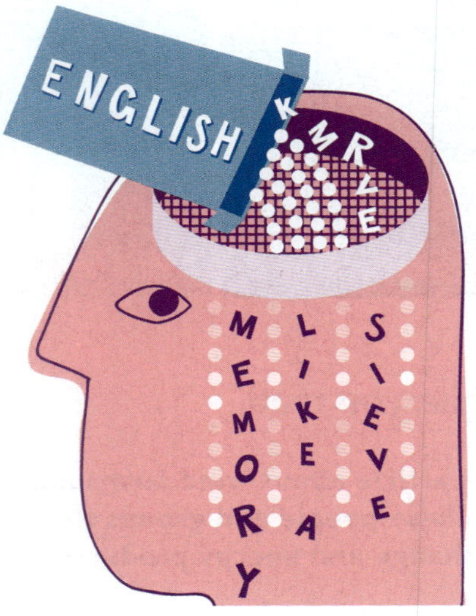

The similes above are fixed expressions. However, we also often make up our own creative ones. Write your own endings for the similes below.

a. It was total chaos in the office. Everyone was running around like … .
b. Have you seen the way he runs? He runs like … .
c. I can't stand him. He acts like … .
d. When we opened the box up, the smell was disgusting. It was like … .
e. You should've seen the place. It was like … .

Compare your ideas with a partner. Who has the best ones?

Reading

1 Before you read

Discuss these questions with a partner:

1. Have you noticed any changes in the weather in your country over the years? Do you know why this has happened? Do you worry about climate change?
2. Look at the photos. Do you have power stations like these near where you live? Have there been any protests about them? Why?
3. Can you think of any other ways of producing energy?

Hydroelectric plant

Coal-fired power station

Nuclear power station

Wind farm

2 While you read

Read this article about wind farms and make notes on what these people and groups think about climate change and energy production.

Professor Bellamy	The Countryside Alliance
Professor James Lovelock	Left-wing groups
The people of Saddleworth	Oil companies
Environmentalists	The writer

3 After you read

Compare your notes with a partner. Which of the arguments mentioned have you heard before? In what context? Were there any you hadn't heard before?

Storms of Protest

SADDLEWORTH MOOR in the north of England is a desolate place. Though lying just a few miles from the sprawling city of Manchester, it feels remote. There is generally a howling gale blowing across the moor and when the sky above is not simply overcast, then it's bucketing down! Someone told me that the sun did actually come out once and it was beautiful, but my experience of the place in the past has only been grim and miserable. It seemed almost bizarre to me, then, that anyone should be against the erection of seven wind turbines to generate clean, renewable energy. Surely this was the perfect place to situate them – basically dull, unattractive to tourists and – above all – windy. Yet Saddleworth is becoming another battleground in an increasingly confusing debate over wind farming and the future of the planet, a debate which is splitting the environmental movement and creating a number of unusual coalitions.

Typical of this confusion is hearing Professor David Bellamy leading the fight against wind farms. I had always thought of Professor Bellamy as an environmentalist and had made the false assumption that he would be a natural supporter of wind power. However, on reflection, Bellamy would be better described as a conservationist, whose main aim is to preserve natural habitats of plants and animals from destruction, rather than a campaigner on climate change. He has fought against other renewable energies, such as hydroelectric projects that threatened wildlife and wilderness, and has described the wind turbines as 'weapons of mass destruction' chopping up birds and bats.

Bellamy, along with other opponents, has argued that the wind farms are in fact uneconomic, and are only commercially viable because they are so heavily subsidised. This argument has been put forward by several newspaper commentators recently, who have then gone on to extol the virtues of nuclear power. This is in the face of years of protests from Greens who claim that nuclear power is both expensive and dangerous. And yet nuclear energy has recently been advocated by a leading green scientist, Professor James Lovelock, who was one of the first to draw attention to the problems of climate change. He argues that renewable energy such as wind simply cannot provide sufficient electricity for our energy needs.

But of course, it is difficult to imagine that the good people of Saddleworth would prefer to see a nuclear power station on their doorstep rather than seven 350ft wind turbines. On average it takes six years to get planning permission for nuclear plants because of the inevitable protest, and Professor Bellamy would be one of the first among those protesting, being anti-nuclear. So what's the answer?

Bellamy suggests reducing consumption of fossil fuels if people want to control greenhouse gases. Certainly, he has much support for this from environmentalists. However, just a few years ago, the government was forced to end increases in taxes on petrol because of a huge public outcry and demonstrations which saw the country almost brought to a halt. And at the heart of those protests was a right-wing group – the Countryside Alliance – representing people in the country, who said they relied on their cars and were being unfairly punished by high fuel taxes. These same people reject wind farms because they see the turbines as eyesores which spoil the countryside.

In turn, there are left-wing groups who see the attack on consumption as a way of continuing the oppression of developing countries. They see the West as trying to restrict these countries' industrial and economic progress under the guise of being environmentally conscious. And of course, these left-wing arguments get support from oil companies and the like, who claim that global warming doesn't even exist, albeit for rather more self-interested reasons.

And so it goes on. There are so many conflicting claims, each apparently fronted by some eminent scientist and backed up by a barrage of statistics. So who's actually right? What's the right solution? What worries me is that we will take so long in deciding that it will be too late. The damage will have been done. Yet what I also recognise is how convenient these conflicting arguments are. We can avoid making any changes to our personal lifestyles by passing the buck. Global warming isn't down to me jetting off to Barcelona for the weekend or having a dishwasher or driving everywhere; no, it's because those people in Saddleworth won't let us build our wind farms!

Real English: nimbies

Someone who agrees with the basic idea of developments such as power stations, prisons, rubbish dumps, immigration centres, etc., but who doesn't want them near where they live is often called a nimby. It comes from Not In My Back Yard. This kind of hypocritical opposition is often negatively described as nimbyism. Nimby is an example of an acronym – a new word made up of the first letters of a phrase. Another example is Dinkies (dual income no kids).

Can you think of any examples of nimbyism where you live?

4 Word building and collocations

Do you remember the words in the article which are based on these words?

environment (paras 1, 2)	commerce (para 3)
assume (para 2)	subsidy (para 3)
destroy (para 2)	permit (para 4)
oppose (para 3)	consume (paras 5, 6)
economy (para 3, 6)	conflict (para 7)

Look at the article again and check. Underline the words they are used with.

Which of the people / groups in the article do you agree with? Who do you disagree with? Why?

5 Using grammar: conditional sentences

Complete the conditional sentences with the verbs in the box.

be	find	grind	happen
stand for	deteriorate	get away	kick up
regret	turn		

1. Imagine what would happen. There'd .... a riot.
2. People would just .... ways of getting round it.
3. The police would just .... a blind eye to it.
4. People would .... such a fuss.
5. The government would never .... with it.
6. People just wouldn't .... it.
7. The country would just .... to a halt.
8. If they don't do something fairly drastic, the situation's just going to ....
9. If we don't face up to it, we're going to .... it.
10. If you ask me, it's bound to .... sooner or later.

Why do the last three examples use first conditional sentences instead of *would*?

Listen to the short conversation. Which of the expressions above do the speakers use?

6 Practice

Complete these sentence starters with your ideas for dealing with climate change and the issues raised in the article – or any other issues that worry you.

- I don't know why they don't just ... .
- They should just ... .
- If it was up to me, I'd ... .

Tell a partner and find out if you agree or disagree. Try and use some of the expressions from Activity 5.

10 Shopping

It's a pirate copy. • Maybe that's why the picture's so fuzzy. • It must've fallen off the back of a lorry at that price. • This is just the tip of the iceberg. The problem's much worse. • She was done for benefit fraud. • They're just worried it'll dent their profits. • We've been scratching our heads as to how best to tackle the problem. • The country's been crippled by rampant inflation. • The whole plan is fatally flawed. • The handle came off in my hand. • That's just perfect, that is! • Oh, my heart bleeds, it really does! • You don't think it makes my bum look big? • Hey, if you've got it, flaunt it! • It's a bit flimsy. • I don't suppose you could possibly do me a huge favour, could you? • I haven't the foggiest. Sorry. • Me? Sarcastic? You must be joking! • It cast a bit of a shadow over things.

Reading

1 Speaking

Make sure you understand the words in red. Then discuss with a partner which of these you think it's OK to do? Explain your ideas.

1. buy tickets for concerts or football matches from a tout
2. buy counterfeit DVDs or CDs
3. buy pirate copies of computer software
4. fiddle your tax return
5. do cash-in-hand jobs
6. get whole coursebooks copied for school
7. illegally download music from file-sharing sites on the internet
8. burn CDs for friends
9. buy cigarettes that've been smuggled into the country
10. make fraudulent benefit claims
11. buy counterfeit replica football shirts or designer clothes or fake brand-name perfume
12. buy goods that've been nicked

Can you think of any other examples of 'informal' economic activity? How do you feel about them?

Real English: nicked

Nicked is an informal word meaning 'stolen'. People also often say stolen things fell off the back of a lorry.

2 While you read

You are going to read an article about the black-market economy. As you read, try to answer these questions.

1. What new measures are the UK and US governments introducing? Why?
2. What has brought the issues of the black-market economy to the public's attention?
3. Why have the two governments' proposals been criticised?
4. What alternative approaches have been put forward?

3 Word check

Complete the sentences with the correct form of the words in the box.

cast	drain	rampant	dent
uncover	undercut	radical	resort
incorporate	draconian		

1. The police probe into the murder has .... a world of corruption and deceit.
2. The economy has been crippled by .... inflation. It's currently running at 250 per cent!
3. The endless litigation is .... the company's financial resources.
4. Unions are angry about what they see as the .... new laws.
5. We've tried to ensure that the new policy .... as many of your earlier suggestions as possible.
6. We're being priced out of the market. We're being totally .... by all the imports flooding in.
7. The whole plan is fatally flawed. It needs a .... rethink.
8. I think that last defeat .... their confidence quite badly.
9. I think we should be able to sort this problem out without having to .... to legal action.
10. The latest round of killings have .... a bit of a shadow over the city.

Out of the black, into the red!

THE TRAGIC DEATH of at least 21 Chinese migrant workers, drowned whilst illicitly gathering shellfish on the treacherous north-west coast of England, has cast a stark light onto the shadowy world of Britain's black-market economy. The 21, all illegal immigrants, had been picking cockles for slave-labour wages when the rapidly incoming tide cut them off. The police investigation that followed uncovered a world of ruthless gangs and people smugglers – and possible links to big businesses looking to find the cheapest labour possible.

The informal economy in Britain has recently been valued at around £100bn a year, though it has been claimed that even this figure is just the tip of the iceberg. The sector is vast and incorporates everything from those working secretly in cash-in-hand jobs whilst claiming unemployment benefit to organised criminals pirating the latest CDs and DVDs.

The government has promised action, this week introducing stiffer penalties for those convicted of benefit fraud and launching a clampdown on piracy. To support these changes, ministers have pointed to the fact that the billions lost in undeclared revenue substantially drains government resources, whilst untaxed labour undercuts wages in other jobs.

The US government has gone one step further, claiming that the underground economy provides the sea in which terrorist organisations – and their funds – can move, and introducing what some see as draconian new legislation, which makes, for instance, illicit downloading and file-sharing federal crimes, akin to domestic terrorism and punishable by up to ten years in prison.

Similar battle lines are being drawn around the world. The Mayor of Moscow has long been engaged in a fight against the country's rampant media piracy, whilst the issue of bootlegging came to the fore in Turkey following upwards of 20 deaths resulting from drinking counterfeit raki – the country's national drink.

However, a number of academics have suggested that these measures are rather missing the point and that the black economy may not be an entirely bad thing. The report points out, for instance, that the heaviest illegal downloaders of music are actually also among the biggest legal buyers of tracks. Similarly, despite fears that internet piracy would dent its profits, Hollywood has remained buoyant, with profits rising year on year. Furthermore, the academics claim that many parts of the UK's black economy should in fact be

encouraged because of the boost they give to deprived areas. They also note that 'off the books' employment is a cornerstone of how many people cope and even keeps the economy from collapsing in certain areas. Also highlighted by academics is the hypocrisy of raising VAT whilst wondering why people resort to buying fake goods and of tightening immigration laws and then scratching one's head when migrants feel compelled to use people smugglers. Finally, they note that many of those globally buying counterfeit products are actually in no position, financially speaking, to purchase the genuine articles, priced as they are at several times their 'street price'.

Radical new policy ideas are then suggested. Basic income tax should have a higher starting threshold; brothels should be licensed; tax on cigarettes and alcohol should be cut to discourage trafficking and it should be made easier for black-economy workers to make the switch to the mainstream economy. All very sensible ideas, you might find yourself thinking – but, of course, not likely to make their way into any of the major parties' next election manifestos!

4 Speaking

Discuss these questions with a partner

1. Have you heard any other stories similar to the tragedy of the Chinese migrant workers in the UK?
2. Do you agree that the US proposals seem draconian?
3. Are there any major investigations going on in your country at the moment? What into?
4. How many of the proposals suggested in the report do you think are sensible? Could you see any of them ever happening in your country?

5 Problems with things you buy

Discuss with a partner what kind of thing you think each of these sentences is most likely talking about.

1. I got it cheap in the market, but when I played it, the picture was just really fuzzy.
2. After the first two tracks, it kept jumping.
3. It shrank in the wash.
4. When I got it back home, I realised it was chipped.
5. The handle came off in my hand.
6. It wasn't compatible with my system.
7. It had a little rip in it.
8. The colours ran the first time I put them in the wash.
9. It was one of those flat-pack things – impossible to put together.
10. It just didn't really go with the rest of the outfit.
11. It's already coming apart at the sole.
12. I only noticed later there was a dent in the boot so it was difficult to open.
13. It was past its sell-by-date, so I just had to chuck it away.

Conversation

1 Speaking

Look back at Activity 5 on page 59. Then discuss these questions with a partner.

1. Have you ever had any of the problems mentioned?
2. Have you ever had any other problems with things you bought? Did you get a refund?

2 Listening

You are going to listen to Joanna talking to a shop assistant. She is trying to return something. As you listen, try to answer these questions.

1. What does she want to return? Why?
2. Is she happy at the end of the conversation? Why / why not?

Now listen again and complete the conversation.

A: Yes, love.
J: Hi. (1) .... you could help me. I bought these shoes from you the other week and they're already coming apart at the sole here, you see?
A: When exactly did you buy them? They look (2) ....
J: Well, I have been wearing them to work. I think I got them four weeks ago now.
A: Right. Well, I'm not sure we can do anything about it really. Have you got a receipt?
J: Well, no. I (3) .... bringing them back. I must've just thrown it away.
A: Well, (4) .... , we really can't give you any kind of refund. We could send them to be repaired, though, if you want.
J: I don't want to have them repaired. What I want is to get my money back.
A: I'm sorry, but that's just (5) .... It's against company policy to give refunds without a receipt and we certainly don't give them when items have been worn for some time.
J: Listen, if I spend (6) .... on a pair of shoes, I expect them to last longer than four weeks.
A: I understand what you're saying, but (7) .... that THAT'S the company policy. If you don't like it, you'll have to take it up with the manager.
J: Fine. Can I speak to him now?
A: SHE'S not here at the moment.
J: Well, when will SHE be back?
A: Next week. She's away on holiday.
J: Next week! Well, that's (8) .... ! Thanks a lot for your help!

With a partner, practise reading the conversation.

3 Being sarcastic

In the conversation in Activity 2, Joanna said, 'Well, that's just great, that is! Thanks a lot for your help!' She was being sarcastic. When people are being sarcastic, they exaggerate the way they say things.

Listen and repeat these sarcastic comments.

1. That's just fantastic, that is!
2. It couldn't have happened to a nicer person. It really couldn't!
3. Fascinating!
4. Charming!
5. Mmm! Lovely!
6. Lovely weather for it!
7. That's just perfect, that is! Just marvellous!
8. Thanks a lot! I hope I can do the same for you one day!
9. I bet that's just what you'd always wanted!
10. Oh, that's a great idea! That's really going to work, that is!
11. Oh dear. What a shame!
12. Oh, my heart bleeds, it really does!

Work with a partner. Take turns to read out the sentences below and to respond with one of the sarcastic comments above.

a. I asked him politely to turn the music down and he told me to get lost.
b. He spent an hour telling me about his pension plan.
c. My gran bought me a framed photo of the Queen for my birthday.
d. My knee swelled up to the size of a melon and all this horrible yellow stuff started coming out of it.
e. All the trains have been cancelled, I'm afraid.
f. There's absolutely nothing I can do about that.
g. That idiot Andrew lost £5000 at the casino.

4 Role play

With a partner, choose one of the problems in Activity 5 on page 59.

Student A: You are the buyer.
Student B: You are the seller.

Spend three minutes deciding what you are going to say. Look at the conversation in Activity 2 again and the sarcastic comments above, and choose any expressions you want to use. Then role-play the conversation.

5 Listening

Listen to three conversations. In which conversations is someone sarcastic? Why?

6 Using grammar: negative sentences

We often use negative sentences with a questioning intonation when we're not sure about things and want to check people's opinions.

Match the questions with the answers.

1. You don't think it's a bit extravagant?
2. You don't think it's a bit too revealing?
3. You don't think it's a bit frumpy?
4. You don't think it's a bit tacky?
5. You don't think it makes my legs look a bit fat and stumpy?
6. You don't think it's a bit flimsy?
7. You don't think it's a bit loud?
8. You don't think it'll look a bit out of place in our front room?

a. Yeah, it won't last very long, but you only really need it while we're here on holiday.

b. No. Anyway, you deserve it. Splash out for a change.

c. Hey, if you've got it, flaunt it! That's what I say!

d. Well, I did see my gran wearing something similar recently!

e. Well, it IS pretty bright, but that's never bothered you in the past!

f. Maybe it IS a bit too modern. You're right. It might clash a bit.

g. That's the point of souvenirs, isn't it? They're supposed to look cheap and nasty!

h. I wouldn't go that far, but maybe something longer or darker would be a better bet.

Spend one minute trying to memorise answers a–h above. Then cover them. Now read out questions 1–8 while your partner answers. When you have finished, swap roles.

Real English: a bit loud

If you describe someone's clothes as being a bit loud, you don't like them and think that they're too bright and/or that the patterns are too strong. You can also describe a person as being a bit loud if you think they like to be the centre of attention and talk too loudly.

Now look at these pictures. Have conversations starting like this:

A: What do you think of this?

B: It's OK.

A: You don't think ... ?

Writing: Letters of complaint

1 Speaking

Decide what you would do about each of these problems. Discuss your ideas with a partner.

a. An article in a newspaper has misrepresented the company you work for.

b. You have been asked to pay £500 excess baggage on a return flight, after the airline company introduced a new rule overnight. You paid nothing on the outward journey.

c. You turned up at the station with your family to catch your train home and found that all the trains had been cancelled for that day.

d. You contracted food poisoning from a local restaurant.

e. The hotel you stayed at on holiday, which was supposed to be four star, was next to a building site and its restaurant was closed for refurbishment.

f. Your washing machine broke down three times in the first year and the company refused to change it for a new one.

g. You ordered a present over the Internet especially for your partner's birthday, but it hasn't arrived and you have nothing else to give them.

h. When you moved out of your flat, the landlord refused to return the deposit of one month's rent, which you paid when you moved in. You didn't break or steal anything.

2 Listening

Listen to two people – Donna and Elspeth – talking. What was the problem? What would you have done in Donna's situation?

3 Reading

Read the letter of complaint Donna wrote to the rail company. As you read, try to answer these questions.

a. What has happened since Donna and Elspeth's conversation?

b. Were there any other complaints which Donna didn't mention to her friend?

354 Fairfax Road
London N19 0NG

11 May 2005

Patsy Newman
Customer Relations Manager
Station Buildings
Station Street
Banbury BA1 2PT

Ref: 5158

Dear Ms Newman,

I am writing regarding a complaint I made about the Goldlink train service on the Wednesday and Saturday of Easter this year, for which I have just received a totally inadequate response.

In your letter you apologised for the problems I suffered and thanked me for drawing attention to them. However, you also made it quite clear that as far as you were concerned, the customer is responsible for checking any changes in times of services due to engineering works. This point was reiterated when I phoned your customer care line. The call centre assistant told me that there were a number of announcements at the train station about disruption to services, but anyway 'there are always engineering works at the weekend, so what did I expect'.

Not only did I ring National Rail enquiries before my journey to check the times of trains, but I also specifically stated to the ticket seller that I wished to return on Saturday. At no time did anyone tell me there were engineering works, let alone that all trains were to be cancelled. The fact that you are trying to blame me for not planning my journey properly is only adding insult to injury.

On top of all this, you also completely failed to address my other complaints. You did not mention that our outward journey had also been cancelled, that the train we finally caught was overcrowded, and that my bag was stained by some unknown substance because your staff had neglected to clean the floor.

According to your customer charter, Goldlink 'aims to make the traveller's life easier', but you have made this traveller's life a nightmare. I would now like you to provide full compensation for the upset and inconvenience I have suffered. If not, I will be forced to take the matter further with the railways watchdog.

I look forward to a prompt and more satisfactory reply.

Yours sincerely,

Donna Ecclestone

Donna Ecclestone

Now spend two minutes trying to memorise the underlined expressions.

4 Useful expressions

Cover the letter. In pairs, try to re-write the whole expressions containing the words which were underlined in the letter. For example:

regarding — I am writing regarding a complaint I made

1. response
2. problems
3. clear
4. reiterated
5. stated
6. injury
7. failed
8. neglected
9. charter
10. compensation
11. matter
12. reply

Look back and check your ideas.

5 Using grammar: *Not only … / At no time …*

Look at these patterns.

- Not only did I ring National Rail enquiries before my journey to check the times of trains, but I also specified to the ticket seller that I wished to return on Saturday.
- Not only was the train late, but it was very overcrowded.
- At no time did anyone tell me there were engineering works.

Notice that we invert the subject and the auxiliary when we start a sentence or clause with Not only or At no time. We do this to add emphasis.

Rewrite these sentences using a similar structure. Begin with the expression in brackets.

1. The room overlooked a building site and it was filthy. (Not only)
2. Nobody informed us what was happening or why the plane had been delayed. (At no time)
3. There were over 18 students in the class and the room was dark and cramped. (Not only)
4. Our teacher was frequently late for class and she had extended breaks. (Not only)
5. We were not provided with any refreshments the whole time we were there. (At no time)
6. You have wasted my time and money. (Not only)
7. I was required to pay for the transfer to the airport and then I had to pay a service charge for my room. (Not only)
8. I asked several times, but nobody said children were not allowed at the event. (At no time)

For more information on using *Not only* and *At no time*, see G9.

6 *According to …*

We often refer to a company's promise using According to and then contrast it with the reality. We use a variety of words and expressions to introduce the contrast.

Complete these sentences using your own ideas.

1. According to your leaflet, all your staff are highly qualified. However, … .
2. According to your advertisement, the hotel was supposed to be close to the beach, but I was disappointed to find … .
3. According to your book, the track 'Funky Dollar Bill' is on Funkadelic's first album. In fact, … .
4. According to your article, our school is close to bankruptcy. On the contrary, … .
5. According to your brochure, prices are all-inclusive. Imagine my surprise when … .
6. According to your website, you deliver within four working days, but … .

7 Planning a letter of complaint

Have you ever had to complain about something or had a bad experience like those mentioned in this unit? Tell a partner.

You are going to write a letter of complaint about this experience. With your partner, look back at the letter in Activity 3 again. Could you use any of the expressions or structures in your own letter? Would you use the same number of paragraphs? Why / why not?

Write your letter for homework.

There's no need to bite my head off! • They used to be the best of buddies. • We just drifted apart, really. • She can't have seen us. • I'm glad we cleared the air. • She can be very stroppy sometimes. • I think we must've got our wires crossed. • He might just be on holiday. • Don't be such a drama queen! • What's that supposed to mean? • How do you get on with your flatmate? • I wish you wouldn't barge in like that. • What are you getting so worked up for? • It's not the first time. • I was sitting there like a lemon all evening. • We're very much on the same wavelength. • He's not exactly the tidiest person in the world. • He's no oil painting, I can tell you. • Are you taking the mickey? • I've had it up to here with them. • I wanted the ground to open up.

11 Relationships

Conversation

1 Before you listen

Match the verbs with the words they go with.

1. impress ☐ a. bright red
2. want ☐ b. close
3. go ☐ c. the subject
4. drop ☐ d. these lads
5. have ☐ e. the ground to open up
6. be ☐ f. some kind of falling out

Now match these verbs with the words they go with.

7. bite ☐ g. an argument
8. have got ☐ h. her a ring
9. get over ☐ i. my head off
10. feel ☐ j. a bit left out
11. give ☐ k. the whole evening
12. ruin ☐ l. a temper

You are going to listen to four women – Laura, Danielle, Caitlin and Amy – talking. They use all of the collocations above. What do you think their conversation will be about?

2 While you listen

Now listen to the conversation and find out what actually happened.

With a partner, retell what happened using the words in Activity 1 to help you.

3 Comprehension

Read the tapescript at the back of the book. Then discuss these questions with a partner.

1. What do you think had happened to Laura – the first speaker – before the conversation you heard started?
2. What do you think Michelle ordered in the restaurant?
3. What do you think happened between Amy and Michelle? Why doesn't Amy want to talk about it?
4. What do you think will happen when Amy comes back from the bar?

4 Using grammar: *must / might / can't*

Remember that we use must, might and can't to speculate about events in the past and present. For example:

- It must've been something fairly major for them not to be speaking.
- She might be annoyed about something completely different.
- She can't be coming. Otherwise, she would've arrived by now.

Complete these sentences by adding must, might or can't and the correct form of the verbs in brackets.

1. A: She .... (split up) with her boyfriend. Why else wouldn't he be here?
   B: Well, lots of reasons. He .... (just be) ill. You never know.
2. A: She .... (be) pregnant. She was off sick again this morning and she is ... you know, getting a bit big.
   B: She .... (be). I mean, have you ever seen her with a man?
   A: Well, it's either that or she's been eating too many doughnuts!
3. A: It's unusual for him not to be on time. Do you think we should go to the cinema? He .... (wait) there. We .... (just got) our wires crossed about where to meet.
   B: No, I spoke to him earlier and he definitely knew we were meeting here. He .... (be caught) in traffic.
   A: Well, it's either that or he's had some kind of accident. He would've phoned otherwise.
   B: Don't be such a drama queen. He .... (just forget) to recharge his phone or something. There could be any number of reasons. He'll be here in a minute. You'll see.
4. A: Why did Lauren leave so early?
   B: Well, it .... (have) something to do with the way everyone ignored her all night.
   A: We didn't exactly ignore her.
   B: No, but you didn't exactly welcome her either, did you? She .... (feel) quite left out with you lot going on about the old days all night.
   A: I suppose so. It .... (be) much fun for her.

For more information on using *must*, *might* and *can't* to speculate, see G10.

Real English: It might've had something to do with ...

This is a sarcastic way of saying we're 100 per cent sure of the reason for something.

A: *I can't believe we got burgled!*

B: *Yeah, well, it might've had something to do with the fact that YOU left the keys in the front door!*

5 Practice

Read these three short texts about missing people. Then speculate with a partner about what you think happened in each case. Try to use *must*, *might* and *can't*.

1. Linda Peyton has been missing for three weeks. It is known that she was staying in a hostel near Exeter until quite recently and it is thought that she has a boyfriend in Bristol, over 50 miles away. Linda is only 16 years old and should have been attending school. Her family are worried about her and would like her to get in touch and let them know she's OK. Linda had been living with her grandparents. According to her grandfather, Linda enjoys shopping, is very creative and had hoped to become a beautician.

2. Richard Withers, 43, went missing from his home in Eastbourne last October, leaving behind his glasses, credit cards and various personal documents. Richard was due to report to work at a local factory, but never turned up. His mother claims that he left the house that day 'in a distressed condition' because he had recently been beaten up in a street fight and had also been having some serious personal problems. Richard is a keen football supporter who often went to watch Brighton & Hove Albion play. His mother described him as 'a lovely, helpful man who wouldn't hurt a fly'.

3. Skip Hudson disappeared on Christmas Eve last year. That day, he was due to fly to Almeria in Spain with his fiancée and had gone to the bank in Cleethorpes to withdraw some money. He never came back and has not been seen since. Skip had apparently been looking forward to the holiday, despite his fear of flying. He had never flown before. There was a reported sighting of him on Boxing Day in a nearby town. Skip used to work as a mechanic in a local garage and was also a keen fisherman.

6 Reporting conversations

In the conversation, Caitlin said, 'Amy has bitten my head off in the past for fairly petty things.' This expression reports a conversation in a short way. There are a number of expressions like this.

Complete the sentences with the words in the box.

brick wall	confirmed	get	head	taking
chest	exactly	had	mood	took

1. He was .... the mickey out of my haircut.
2. He nearly bit my .... off when I asked him if he'd finished the work.
3. She didn't get her way, so she got into a right .... and stormed off.
4. Honestly, I tried to warn him, but it was like talking to a ....
5. I did explain why I hadn't done the work, but she wasn't .... sympathetic.
6. We .... a bit of a heart to heart about things, just to clear the air.
7. She was just going on and on about her husband. Honestly, I couldn't .... a word in edgeways.
8. I think things had been building up for a while and I just needed to get it off my ....
9. I only asked if he'd put on a bit of weight and he .... it completely the wrong way.
10. I had a horrible feeling things were going wrong between us – and when I confronted her about it, she .... my worst suspicions.

Underline the whole expression in each sentence. The first one has been done for you. Then discuss with a partner what you think was actually said in each of the conversations that is being reported.

Act out one of the conversations to another pair. Can they guess which conversation it is?

Reading

1 Listening

You are going to listen to two people having a row. As you listen, try to answer these questions.

1. What's the relationship between these people?
2. What're they rowing about?
3. What sparked the row?

2 Language focus: having an argument

Complete the sentences you heard with ONE word in each space.

1. I've had it up to .... with him!
2. He never .... a finger round the house!
3. .... who's talking!
4. What's THAT .... to mean?
5. Well, talk about the .... calling the .... black!
6. You're not .... the tidiest person in the world yourself.
7. He's a complete and utter ....
8. He's .... leaving stuff lying around all over the place.
9. I just wish he .... think about us a bit more.
10. I wish YOU .... get so worked up about petty little things all the time!

Listen to the conversation again or look at the tapescript at the back of the book to check your answers.

Can you think of any other situations where you could use the expressions in sentences 1 and 5?

Which of the expressions above do you think you're most likely to use? Why?

3 Speaking

Discuss these questions with a partner.

1. Who do you sympathise with most in the conversation – the mum, the dad or the son? Why?
2. Do you ever row with the people you live with? With your colleagues or boss? What usually sparks the rows?
3. Have you ever fallen out with anybody because of a row?

4 Using grammar: *She's not exactly ...*

We often make our criticisms of people and things softer by using not exactly. Look at the patterns that follow not exactly.

- He's not exactly the most tolerant person I've ever met.
- He's not exactly the best-looking guy in the world.
- She's not exactly an oil painting, is she?
- He didn't exactly cover himself in glory.
- It's not exactly rocket science, is it?

What do you think the last three examples mean?

Respond to these sentences using the ideas in the box and not exactly.

best	Bill Gates	help
generous	positive	sharp

1. A: She's so tight-fisted.
   B: Well, she's ....
2. A: It's a rubbish film.
   B: I think that's a bit strong, but it's ....
3. A: She's such a whinger.
   B: I know. She's ....
4. A: He sat around most of the time while we did all the work.
   B: I know. He .... , did he?
5. A: His business is still tiny.
   B: No, I know. He's .... yet, is he?
6. A: She's just thick.
   B: Well, I wouldn't go that far, but she's ....

Write some of your own not exactly sentences about people, restaurants, films, books or places you know. Tell a partner your ideas.

5 Using grammar: *I wish you wouldn't do that!*

In Activity 2, you saw these two sentences:

- I wish you wouldn't get so worked up about petty little things all the time!
- I just wish he'd (= he would) think about us a bit more.

We use these structures to complain about annoying things other people do a lot – or things they don't do, but that we'd like them to start doing.

Complete the sentences using *'d* or *wouldn't* and the verbs in the box.

assume	keep	talk down	tell

1. I wish you .... interrupting me when I'm talking!
2. I wish you .... me when you're going to be late back! I've been worried sick about you!
3. I wish my dad .... to me all the time. He doesn't seem to realise I'm not a little kid anymore!
4. I wish you .... I'm unhappy all the time just because I don't walk around grinning like an idiot!

Now complete these sentences using *'d* or *wouldn't* and the verbs in the box.

barge into	call	get	stop

5. I wish you .... my room like that! You didn't even knock!
6. I wish you .... putting words in my mouth! You keep twisting what I'm trying to say.
7. A: Hi Andy.
   B: I wish you .... me that! My name's Andrew!
8. I wish you .... so worked up about stupid little things all the time. You're going to give yourself a heart attack if you're not careful!

Make three sentences like these about people you know.

Tell a partner your complaints.

For more information on using *wish* like this, see G11.

6 Reading

The class should divide into two groups. You are going to read about two different students, both of whom share a house with three other people.

Group A: Read the article below.
Group B: Read the article on page 174.

Imagine you are the person you read about. Think about these questions.

1. How do you get on with the people you share with?
2. What kind of problems are you having?
3. What do you think the root of the problems is?

When you have finished reading, compare your ideas with someone else who read the same article as you.

They're just good-for-nothing layabouts!

Martin Green, 21, is doing a degree in Middle-Eastern History and Politics at the School of Oriental and African Studies. He lives in a student house share with three other people.

I guess that if I'm honest, I'd have to say that student life isn't all it's cracked up to be. I'm sure lots of people think we're busy having an amazing time and are quite envious of what they imagine our lives to be like. Well, they shouldn't be is all I can say! I've worked hard to get where I am today and I don't intend to waste this opportunity just so I can go out clubbing every night! This course is my ticket out of the life I've had so far. I come from a working-class background and am the first person in my family ever to get into uni, so I feel quite a heavy burden of responsibility. I don't want to end up like my dad and my brothers, working down the mine or in a factory. That's why I take my studies seriously. It's probably also why I just can't get on with the losers and layabouts I have to share a house with! I think they must all have been spoiled when they were kids. They seem to have led sheltered, pampered lives and have never had to work for anything – everything's just been provided for them and so now they don't know how to look after themselves. They can be really thoughtless and selfish too. They eat my food from the cupboards and take stuff from my room without asking. It's out of order, it really is. Another thing I wish they wouldn't do is take the mickey out of my accent. They all seem to think it's hilarious that I'm from the north! Don't they realise they sound comical to me?

Toby is the worst of all. He seems to be the ringleader and is a real party animal – with the emphasis on 'animal'! He comes home in the small hours, totally drunk and turns all the lights on, turns his music up really loud and wakes the whole house up – without any regard for anyone else's feelings! He's a total slob as well. He's always leaving half-eaten pizzas lying around in the front room and he never washes up! It drives me mad! The sooner I graduate and start working and can afford to get a place of my own, the better, because I've had it up to here with this lot!

7 Role play

Work with a partner who read a different article to you in Activity 6. If you read about Martin Green, read the role-play card on page 172. If you read about Toby Jenkins-Jones, read the role-play card on page 176. Plan what to say and then role-play the row!

I was laid off last year. • Jobwise, things are really improving. • We're still lagging behind the rest of the world in terms of health. • It was a bit of a let-down. • I do worry about the increasing wealth gap. • The boom is completely unsustainable. • I've got grave reservations about it myself. • It's got completely out of hand. • Credit cards are too much of a temptation. • We ran into cash-flow problems. • I'm saddled with a £10,000 debt. • Nothing ventured, nothing gained. • The population is dwindling. • They emigrated to escape the famine. • We've got a pension crisis on our hands. • We're struggling. • There's a real buzz about the place. • I did, but I wish I hadn't. • It's the new tiger economy.

12 Economics and finance

Conversation

1 Speaking

***The Economist* magazine recently carried out a survey into the relative quality of life in 111 different countries. They ranked countries according to these categories:**

- average income
- health and life expectancy
- job security and unemployment
- sexual equality
- climate
- political stability and security
- political freedom
- family life: divorce rate, teenage pregnancies, etc.
- community life: church attendance, trade union membership, etc.

On a scale of 1 (= poor) to 10 (= excellent), how would you grade your own country for each category? How would you compare your country to its neighbours?

Tell a partner about your choices. Use some of these structures:

- In terms of ... , I'd give my country an 8 because ... .
- I think we'd deserve a 9 or 10 for ... because ... .
- I think we'd only score a 4 or 5 for ... because ... .
- When it comes to ... , I'd only go for a 3 because ... .

2 Talking about the quality of life

Complete the sentences with the words in the box.

breakdown	downturn	lag	rocketed
booming	laid off	repressive	springing up

1. We've been really badly hit by the .... in the economy. Tens of thousands of workers have been .... this year.
2. There's been a real .... in family life over the last 20 years. The divorce rate has .... , and more and more kids are being brought up by single parents.
3. The economy is .... at the moment. New businesses are .... all over the place.
4. There's more political freedom than there used to be. The government is a lot less .... these days.
5. Don't talk to me about sexual equality! It's common knowledge that women's wages still .... a long way behind men's!

Now complete these sentences with the words in the box.

breakdown	defaulted	mess	safe
bust	dwindled	recession	thing

6. There's no such .... as a job for life anymore. No-one's job is .... these days.
7. Since we .... on our loan from the World Bank, the economy has been in a real ....
8. The economy has been in .... for ages now. Loads of businesses have gone ....
9. There's been a real .... of community life. People these days just tend to do their own thing.
10. Trade union membership has .... to almost nothing!

Make a list of any new collocations or expressions in the sentences above. Can you use any of them to talk about the categories in Activity 1? Tell a new partner your ideas.

Real English: go bust

An everyday way of saying a company has gone bankrupt is it's gone bust. People often also say the company went under, went down the pan or went to the wall.

3 Before you listen

You are going to listen to a radio programme about the country that topped *The Economist's* survey. Before you listen, tell a partner which country you'd expect it to be and why.

4 While you listen (1)

Listen to the introduction and take notes on the following:

1. what led to the mass emigration from the country
2. the factors that contributed to the economic turnaround
3. the results of the economic miracle of the 1990s

Compare what you heard with a partner.

5 Speaking

Discuss these questions with a partner.

1. Were you surprised that this country came in at number 1?
2. How much do you know about the country?
3. Was there anything that surprised you in the introduction?
4. Do many people emigrate from your country? Where to? Why?
5. Have you heard any other stories regarding national economies and the World Bank / IMF (International Monetary Fund)?

6 While you listen (2)

Now listen to the three Irish people who moved back home after living abroad – Ian, Jackie and Mary. As you listen, decide which person:

a. has found moving back a bit of a let-down. ....
b. is concerned about the growing wealth gap. ....
c. feels their privacy is sometimes invaded. ....
d. thinks the new Ireland is over-rated. ....
e. left Ireland because of limited employment opportunities. ....
f. got fed up with some of the Irish people they met abroad. ....
g. found it really easy to find work on their return. ....
h. enjoys the irony of the new employment situation in Ireland. ....
i. expresses serious reservations about the changes. ....

Now read the tapescript at the back of the book and underline the expressions that make these points. Are there any other expressions you'd like to ask your teacher about?

7 Voicing your opinion

Complete the sentences with the words in the box.

doubts	favour	minds	slight	support
fan	opposed	practice	stand	theory

a. It's a nice idea in ...., but I just don't think it works in ....
b. I have to say, I've got grave .... about it myself.
c. I'm basically in .... of it, but I do have a few .... reservations.
d. I'm a big .... of the idea. I fully .... it.
e. I'm fundamentally .... to the whole idea.
f. I don't really know where I .... on it. I'm still in two .... about it.

Check your answers and practise saying the expressions.

Put the sentences in order of strength – from 1 (totally disagree) to 6 (completely agree).

8 Practice

How do you personally feel about the following? Decide which of the expressions from Activity 7 you could use to voice your opinions about each. You might also want to use this expression to explain how you feel – *I couldn't care less about it!*

- a cut in welfare spending
- unregulated business activity
- the European Union
- a maximum 40-hour working week
- free dental care for all
- globalisation
- a 5-per-cent cap on wage increases for the next five years

Now compare your ideas in groups of three.

Reading

1 Before you read

Have you done any of these things?

1. got a mortgage
2. used a credit card
3. borrowed money from a friend or family
4. taken out a student loan
5. taken out a loan from a bank to start a small business
6. never borrowed any money

What problems are sometimes associated with these things?

2 While you read

Read the article and find out if any of the problems you thought of are mentioned.

3 Speaking

Complete each sentence with the name of one of the people in the article. If you don't think any of the names fit a sentence, then leave it blank.

1. ....'s just a whinger. I don't know why s/he's complaining.
2. I really feel sorry for ....
3. There's a lot of truth in what ....'s saying.
4. ....'s obviously brought the situation upon her/himself.
5. ....'s not thinking about the long term enough.
6. ....'s talking rubbish.
7. .... hit the nail on the head when s/he said that.
8. ....'s quite blasé about things.
9. I would hate to be in the situation ....'s in.
10. ....'s obviously a bit of a crackpot.

Discuss what you have written with a partner. Explain why you agree or disagree with your partner's choices.

Lenders and borrowers – all are we!

As the UK personal debt breaks the one trillion pound mark, six people talked to Channel 9 News Online about debt.

Jake

It may seem strange to say I wish I'd never gone to university, but sometimes I really regret I ever did. Studying media communications for three years has left me saddled with a £15,000 student loan to pay off and the employment situation is pretty dismal at the moment, which doesn't make the future look too bright. I would've been better off just getting straight into the job market when I was 18.

Brian

I see the government says it wants to encourage small businesses. What a joke! The whole financial system is skewed in favour of the big boys and they always just lobby to protect their interests. My garden-ornament business had cash-flow problems last year, which meant I needed a temporary loan to pay my staff. My bank just refused point blank to extend my credit. I even occupied the bank manager's office one day! My business ended up going to the wall. Now I open the paper today and I see some cable company is negotiating with the banks to restructure £12 billion of debt. There's no justice.

Lizzie

My parents had problems with debt, which meant I couldn't get a credit card before I left home and I swore blind I wouldn't get one when I did leave home. But then you get out into the big bad world and you're just surrounded by temptation. We're bombarded with adverts for this and that and then you're offered easy credit. A few years ago, I was persuaded to celebrate New Year in Egypt. I took out a loan to pay for the holiday and cover my expenses and then I got a credit card 'just for emergencies'. The next thing I knew I'd spent £3,000 on the card. I tried to juggle the debt by transferring the money onto another credit card, but by then I'd got into the habit of spending and I ran up a debt on that card too. Over the next two or three years, things just got completely out of hand, and now I'm £38,000 in debt and at the point of declaring myself bankrupt.

Joseph

This whole sorry debt-ridden country is going to come crashing down and it's going to be a hard, hard landing. You mark my words, this whole economy is built on borrowing and credit, and it's just unsustainable. I have a small place with a bit of land, which I bought when I was made redundant. I rear chickens and goats, and grow a lot of my own food. I reckon I'm almost self-sufficient now, so I know that on that day when the shit finally hits the fan, I'll be prepared.

Malcolm

All that 'never a borrower nor a lender be' stuff is all just rubbish, if you ask me. There isn't a successful businessman in the world who hasn't had to borrow money to either get started or to expand. If you worry about what you owe, if you let it play on your mind, you'll never take the risks you need to take in order to be successful.

Angela

We borrowed a few thousand pounds off my parents-in-law to buy our house and now I just wish we hadn't. It's just something they constantly hold over us and it's caused a lot of friction – like last year when we said we weren't going to stay at Christmas. My mother-in-law got all upset and then my father-in-law started saying 'You're so ungrateful. All the things we've done for you and you just throw it back in our faces.'

4 Using grammar: auxiliaries and modals

Look at these examples from the article and answer the questions.

- It may seem strange to say I wish I'd never gone to university, but sometimes I really regret I ever did.
- We borrowed a few thousand pounds off my parents-in-law to buy our house and now I just wish we hadn't.

1. What verbs do the auxiliaries in red refer to?
2. What tenses do they represent? Why are they different tenses?

For more information on using *wish*, see G12.

Complete these sentences with auxiliaries or modal verbs.

1. A: I wish I'd never taken out that loan.
   B: Yeah, well you .... , so you'd better start paying it back.
2. A: Didn't you read the small print?
   B: No, but I wish I .... now.
3. A: I wish we had a bit more money. We could buy it.
   B: Yeah, well we .... So just forget about it.
4. A: How's business?
   B: I wish I could tell you we were doing well, but we .... We're really struggling.
5. A: I don't suppose you could lend me a tenner, could you?
   B: I wish I .... , but I'm skint at the moment.
6. A: I wish the kids would help out more round the house.
   B: Well, they .... until you start making them.
7. A: Did you go to the meeting yesterday?
   B: Yeah, but I wish I .... It was a complete and utter waste of time.
8. A: I wish you could come with us.
   B: I know, but there's no way I .... I'm just broke.

Spend two minutes memorising B's responses. In pairs, student A – read out your sentences. Student B – give your responses with your books closed. When you have finished, swap roles.

Real English: skint / broke

These are informal ways of talking about having no money at the moment.

I'm totally skint. I don't suppose you could lend me a fiver?

He's broke – and he's lost his job. I don't know what he's going to do.

5 *How's business?*

Complete the replies to the question *How's business?* with the correct forms of the verbs in the box.

be hit	boom	cut	lose
struggle	be inundated	break	get rid of
make	take on		

1. OK. We're managing to .... even at the moment.
2. Terrible. We .... already .... two of our biggest customers so far this year.
3. Terrible. We .... really ....
4. Great. Business ....
5. Terrible. It looks like we .... a big loss this year.
6. Great. We .... with orders. We're thinking of expanding.
7. OK. We .... too badly by the recession so far.
8. Great. We .... ten new people since last year.
9. Terrible. We've had to .... twenty people so far this year.
10. Terrible. We're going to have to .... costs drastically over the next year.

Do you know any businesses which are struggling or booming at the moment? Why?

6 Role play

You are attending a business convention. Spend a few minutes deciding what kind of business you have. Decide how you are doing and why. Try to use some of the language from Activity 5. Now have conversations with some other students. Find out about their businesses.

Writing: Anecdotes and stories

1 Speaking

Discuss these questions with a partner

1. Do you ever write stories in e-mails or letters?
2. Is there an anecdote that you have told a lot of people recently?
3. How do you usually bring these stories up in conversation or writing?

2 Starting and ending anecdotes

We usually introduce an anecdote by saying what it is about – an accident, something surprising, etc. We then finish the anecdote with another general comment about how we felt or what we learnt from the experience. These general comments are often fixed expressions.

Complete the sentences with the words in the box.

books	had	killed	mistake	shock
died	hilarious	laughing	mouth	tell
ground	hurry	learn	shave	

1. I had a really close .... the other day.
2. I could've been .... I was lucky, really.
3. When it happened, we all just fell about ....
4. Did you hear about the accident I .... the other week?
5. Honestly, I could've .... , I really could.
6. I saw this absolutely .... thing the other day.
7. I just wanted the .... to open up. It was terrible.
8. Actually, I'm in Glen's bad .... after last week.
9. Oh well, you live and .... , I suppose.
10. I won't make that .... again.
11. I had the biggest .... of my life the other day.
12. I certainly won't be doing that again in a ....
13. That's the last time I'm going there, I can .... you.
14. Honestly, me and my big ....

Decide which of the sentences are introducing an anecdote. Which sentences do you think could appear in the same anecdote?

3 Reading

You are going to read an e-mail from Megan to her friend Janice. What happened to her? Has anything like this ever happened to you or anyone you know?

4 Using grammar: tenses in anecdotes and stories

Complete the e-mail by putting the verbs in the correct form. Compare your answers with a partner and discuss these questions.

1. Which tense is used to show completed actions which follow another completed action?
2. Which tense is used to emphasise that an action happened *before* another action?
3. Which tense shows that an action was incomplete when another action happened?
4. Why does she use present tenses in the middle of the story?
5. Why does she say the kid *must've* sneaked up?

5 Further practice

Complete the sentences using appropriate past forms.

1. I'd just left the house when ....
2. I'd just sat down when ....
3. It'd been raining heavily, so ....
4. I'd been travelling all day, so ....
5. No sooner had I done it than ....

Now complete these sentences with past perfect forms.

6. .... , so I was absolutely exhausted.
7. .... , so there was a huge tailback on the motorway.
8. By the time we got to the party, ...
9. By the time we left, ...

Re: Total nightmare!

Hi Janice,

How's it going? Finally got round to writing – sorry it wasn't sooner, but I've been completely snowed under since I got back from holiday. Actually, it's a good job you wrote to me because I had both my mobile and laptop stolen a month or so ago, so I (1) .... (lose) a whole load of e-mail addresses and phone numbers. It's been a bit of a disaster, really.

The way I had the mobile and laptop stolen was such a scam. I (2) .... (sit) outside a café in town with Gareth, this guy I work with. We'd just been to a meeting and we (3) .... (stop off) for a coffee on the way back to the office. So we were sitting there, having a coffee and there were these kids hanging about nearby – Gareth even made some comment about them looking a bit dodgy – when I got a phone call from my mum. I guess we were talking for about five minutes and I (4) .... (just hang up) when this guy (5) .... (come) up to us with a map and started asking us for directions. He looked perfectly respectable – quite well-dressed – and while we (6) .... (talk) to him one of these kids nearby must've sneaked up and just (7) .... (snatch) the phone.

The guy with the map suddenly shouts, 'Hey, that kid's just run off with your phone,' and, 'Someone get him'. Both me and Gareth just instinctively leap up and start to run after the kid, but neither of us are that quick on our feet and the lad just sprints off into the distance. Of course, we then turn round and find the guy with the map (8) .... (go) – along with my laptop, which I (9) .... (leave) on the table. Apparently, he'd just strolled off without anyone even noticing – everyone was just so focused on this kid.

Honestly, I couldn't believe it. I (10) .... (feel) such an idiot. I mean, I (11) .... (actually hear) of something similar happening to someone else I knew, but it was all so slickly done. I guess you live and learn. I certainly (12) .... (fall for) that trick again.

On a lighter note – check out the photo in the attachment. He was a busker I saw in Barcelona. Ignore the grass skirt for a moment, but isn't he the spitting image of your mate, Barry? He could be his twin! I did actually ask him, but he turned out to be Czech, so I guess they can't be related, unless they were separated at birth. Freaky!

Anyway, good to be back in touch. Drop us a line soon. By the way, send me your telephone number as well. I did try to ring you, but I must've remembered it wrongly. The number was in my mobile!

See you soon.
Love,
Megan

6 Ways of doing things

Which verbs were used to replace these ideas in the e-mail?

> Both me and Gareth just instinctively *get up very quickly* and start to run after the kid, but the lad just *runs off very fast* into the distance.

Rewrite the sentences with the correct forms of the verbs in the box.

crawl	shoot	snatch	sprint
glare	slam	sneak	stroll

1. The car came out of the side road very quickly.
2. I went down the stairs very quietly.
3. I got into bed, exhausted.
4. I took his bag very quickly.
5. I ran very quickly down the road.
6. I walked leisurely through the park.
7. I looked at him angrily.
8. I put the phone down angrily.

What are these verbs ways of doing?

gaze	mumble	smash	strut
giggle	peek	sprint	trudge
leer	screech	stare	whisper

Work in pairs. Take it in turns to act these verbs out. Can you guess the verbs your partner is acting?

Real English: me and ...

Although me and Gareth leap up is not grammatically correct (Megan should have written Gareth and I leap up), it is commonly used by English speakers today, especially in informal situations.

7 Planning an e-mail

Choose one of the anecdotes you discussed in Activity 1 or any other story you discussed in this unit.

You are going to write an e-mail about this experience. Decide which language you could use to introduce and end the story. Think about the different verbs and tenses you could use to make your story sound more interesting.

Write your e-mail for homework.

Review: Units 7–12

1 Grammar

Complete the sentences. Write ONE word in each space. Negatives such as *don't* or *aren't* count as one word.

1. A: What do you think of this top?
   B: It looks nice. It's fine.
   A: You .... think it's a bit .... revealing?
   B: No, not at all. It suits you.
2. A: I wish I'd never started talking to you about it!
   B: Yeah, well, you .... !
3. A: Didn't you say anything to her about it?
   B: No, but I wish I .... now.
4. A: Did you manage to book an appointment?
   B: Yeah, I'm .... that tooth taken out tomorrow.
5. A: The flight was delayed and we had to sleep in the airport.
   B: Really? That .... have been much fun.
6. A: I ended up having to stay in hospital for a week.
   B: You poor thing. That .... have been horrible.
7. Let's put it this way. He's not .... the most interesting guy I've .... met in my life!
8. I wish you .... keep interrupting me all the time!
9. Imagine what .... happen if they did that! There .... be a riot! People would kick up .... a fuss!
10. .... I really hate about him is .... arrogant he is!

Compare your answers with a partner.

2 Grammar: *I wish*

Complete these sentences with *I wish* + *subject* + *verb*. The first one is done for you.

1. *I wish my boss wasn't so* boring and dull. I mean, I do have to work with her.
2. .... leave his stuff lying around all over the place.
3. .... such a high opinion of herself. She's so big-headed!
4. .... such a bully. He made my life hell for ages!
5. .... as my teacher. I remember every class with him as absolute misery!

3 Grammar: *must / might / can't*

Work in pairs. Look back at Activity 5 in Unit 11 on page 65. Read the three short texts again and discuss what you think happened in each case.

Now complete these sentences by adding must, might or can't and the correct form of the verbs in brackets.

1. A: I think Linda Peyton .... with her boyfriend in Bristol somewhere. (live)
   B: Yeah, so do I. I suppose she .... some kind of argument with her grandparents or something like that. Perhaps that's why she left. (have)
2. A: Richard Withers .... suicide. There's no other explanation. (commit)
   B: I don't know. He .... some kind of trouble or fight with the people who beat him up. That's a possibility. (get into)
   A: Yeah, but why would he have left all his things at home in that case?
   B: Who knows? He .... a forgetful kind of guy. (just / be)
3. A: I haven't the foggiest about Skip Hudson. Anything could've happened to him. He .... at the cash point, or he .... because he was so scared of flying. Who knows! (be mugged, just / disappear)
   B: No, he .... ! Why would he have done that? He had a job, a girlfriend, everything. (just / disappear)
   A: Don't know. Him and his girlfriend .... problems for a while or something like that. (have)

Did you make any similar guesses?

4 Common mistakes

Work with a partner. Decide how best to correct these mistakes.

1. The dentist said I'll probably have to take a tooth out.
2. I wish I wouldn't be so fat!
3. It would cause a riot if they would do that here.
4. He's quite shifty. He's never giving a straight answer.
5. His car mustn't have been that expensive, because he doesn't exactly earn a fortune, does he?
6. I was disappointed bitterly with the result.

5 Verb collocations

Match the ten verbs with the words they collocate with.

1. perpetuate		a.	a very sheltered life
2. skid		b.	a big row
3. wipe		c.	stereotypes
4. dent		d.	an election
5. lead		e.	responsibility for your actions
6. hold		f.	right off the road
7. spark		g.	your feet
8. confirm		h.	my suspicions
9. accept		i.	civil liberties
10. erode		j.	your confidence

Spend one minute memorising the collocations above. Then cover the activity. Your partner will read out the ten verbs. How many collocations can you remember?

With a partner, try to think of one more common collocation for each of the ten verbs.

6 Adjectives

All the adjectives in the box have been used in the last six units. Which nouns can they collocate with? Use a dictionary to help you if you need to.

bloodshot	shallow	subsidised
draconian	sick	torrential
gale-force	strictly enforced	unrealistic
hereditary	stubbly	waterlogged

Compare your ideas with a partner.
Now discuss these questions.

1. Have any governments passed any new laws recently that you think are draconian?
2. What kind of things do you think are sick?
3. Do you know anyone who's ever had unrealistic plans for the future?
4. What kinds of things are hereditary in your family?

7 Look back and check

Work in pairs. Choose one of these activities.

a. **Look back at Activity 5 in Unit 10 on page 59. Check you remember all the vocabulary. Then choose a problem each and role-play two different conversations. In one, you are an angry customer, in the other you are an apologetic shop assistant. To help you prepare, read Activities 2 and 3 on page 60 again.**

b. **Look back at Activities 6 and 7 in Unit 11 on page 67. Decide who is going to take which role. Read the relevant text and then do the role play again. Make sure you use some of the grammar from Activity 5.**

8 What can you remember?

With a partner, write down as much as you can about the texts you read in Unit 7 and Unit 10.

Unit 7: I feel like a whole new person!

Kevin

Charlotte

Nicky

Katty

Unit 10: Out of the black, into the red!

Now work with another pair of students and compare what you can remember. Who remembered more?

Which text did you enjoy more? Why?

9 Idioms

Make complete idioms by matching the beginnings to the endings.

1. The whole thing's just a storm ☐
2. It's out ☐
3. It was the final ☐
4. We must've got our wires ☐
5. That was a close ☐
6. It raised ☐
7. It's just the tip ☐
8. It completely blew ☐

a. me away.
b. of the iceberg.
c. a few eyebrows.
d. in a teacup.
e. straw
f. shave.
g. crossed.
h. of the question.

Work with a partner. Discuss what context you could use each of these idioms in.

Now choose three of these idioms to talk about experiences from your life. Tell a different partner.

10 Vocabulary quiz

Discuss these questions in groups of three.

1. Can you think of three reasons why some people are apathetic about politics?
2. Can you think of two other ways of saying 'I don't know'?
3. How could you pamper someone?
4. What kind of things might you have a heart to heart with someone about?
5. What happens if a joke falls flat?
6. What happens when there's an absolute blizzard?
7. When might a party form a coalition?
8. What could cast a shadow over a city? Over a wedding?
9. Can you think of three things that are all the rage at the moment?
10. When could you say 'Talk about the pot calling the kettle black'?
11. What's the difference between wavy, curly, permed and tangled hair?
12. What's the problem if clothes are a bit frumpy? A bit flimsy?
13. When would you say to someone 'Don't rub it in'?
14. What's the opposite of taking new workers on?
15. When are the small hours?
16. Can you think of three things you could botch up?
17. What happens when an election is rigged?
18. What kind of things are shallow people interested in?
19. Can you think of three things that really get your back up?
20. Where do you usually find the small print? Why is it important to read it?

11 Real English

Match the eight sentences to the responses.

1. So what're you up to these days? Are you still working for that company? ☐
2. Did you see that shirt he was wearing yesterday? ☐
3. Did you see how cheap those jeans in the market were? ☐
4. I can't believe how much opposition there's been to that plan to build a youth club for teenagers in the centre of town. ☐
5. Have you seen Michael recently? ☐
6. Why aren't you cycling? What's happened to your bike? ☐
7. Is there any way you could lend me a fiver? Just till Monday. ☐
8. I don't understand why I'm so skint. I only got paid last week. ☐

a. I know! It was a bit loud, wasn't it?
b. I know. They must be off the back of a lorry!
c. No, they went bust a few months ago.
d. Well, it might have something to do with the fact you bought five pairs of shoes at the weekend!
e. I know! I hate that kind of Nimby attitude!
f. No, but I heard he's had a nose job. Have you seen it yet?
g. It got nicked!
h. Sorry. I would, but I'm totally broke.

Spend two minutes memorising the responses above. Then cover the activity. Your partner will read out the eight sentences. How many responses can you remember?

12 Word building

Complete the sentences with the correct forms of the words in the brackets.

1. Our whole .... system is fatally flawed. (elect)
2. He's a very .... politician. (charisma)
3. Overall .... of imported fruits has rocketed. (consume)
4. I'm just sick of all your .... and hypocrisy. (deceive)
5. She's had her eyes .... altered! (surgery)
6. Downloading music illegally is now .... by up to ten years in jail! (punish)
7. People don't trust the government, but there's widespread .... with the opposition parties too. (illusion)
8. If you are going to have your nose done, be careful who you go to. There are lots of badly-qualified .... out there. (practise)

Writing

1 Opposites

Write possible opposites of the words in red.

1. The number of mixed-race marriages has doubled / .... over the last decade.
2. The cost of purchasing property in the capital has plummeted / .... over recent years.
3. There has been a slight / .... increase in sales of bottled water over the last few years.
4. There has been a significant rise / .... in the number of people studying Chinese.
5. Incidences of allergies and eczema have increased / .... dramatically in recent years.
6. More and more / .... people are making use of alternative or complementary medicine.
7. The incidence of obesity has fallen slightly / .... over recent years.
8. The past few years have seen a major reduction / .... in asthma among those who are most prone to it.

Do you think any of the statements above are true for your country?

2 Ways of doing things

Put the verbs in the box into four groups of four.

gaze	mumble	snatch	strut
glare	peek	sprint	trudge
go on	slam	stain	whisper
leer	smash	stroll	yell

Ways of talking and shouting

....
....
....
....

Ways of looking at things

....
....
....
....

Ways of walking and running

....
....
....
....

Ways of taking things – or damaging them

....
....
....
....

When might you do each of these things?

3 A letter of complaint

In each line of this letter, there is one spelling or punctuation mistake. Correct the mistakes.

Dear Sir / Madam,

1 *It is with regret that I find myself having to write to you, to complain*
2 *about my recent expereinces with your company.*
3 *Last Tuesday that is the 24th of September, I was booked onto Flight*
4 *AJA426 from Tokyo to London, departure time 16:45. Naturally I*
5 *tried to check in, only to be told that my ticket was invallid and that*
6 *the flight was already fully booked. It was, only after making*
7 *repeated enquiries, that I was finally informed that, in fact, a mistake*
8 *had been made and that I could baord the flight after all. What upset*
9 *me most was the fact that nether an explanation nor an apology was*
10 *ever offered. This however, was not all.*

11 *Once seated on the plane, I found that I had been placed in the econimy*
12 *section, despite the fact I posessed a first-class ticket. I explained the*
13 *situation to your staff, but at no time was any atempt made to*
14 *relocate me. As a result I spent the next ten hours in a state of*
15 *severe discomfort but again no apology or compensation was offered.*

16 *Were I not a regular busines flyer with your airline, I might not*
17 *have bothered to write. However, as I am shore you treat such*
18 *complaints as mine with the serioussness they deserve, I trust you*
19 *will investigate this mater fully and take any necessary action.*
20 *Furthermore I trust you will also see fit to provide full compensation*
21 *for all the upset and inconvenience I have suffered. If not I will be*
22 *forced to take the issue further, with the airlines watchdog.*

I look forward to hearing from you soon,

Yours faithfully,

Beth Gibbons

Compare your corrections with a partner. Do you agree on the errors?

The whole plot's a bit convoluted. • It was such a harrowing film. • I was in floods of tears by the end. • It's a bit of a feel-good film. • The ending's quite uplifting. • I was just squirming in my seat watching it. • I nearly wet myself it was that funny! • I've vaguely arranged something. • I don't suppose anyone fancies going for a pint? • I would've if I hadn't got something else on. • It's an open-mic stand-up evening. • Full-on free-form jazz isn't really my kind of thing. • How about a bit of gender-bending experimental theatre, then? • It's a bit of a thorny issue. • The place has been re-vamped. • Come on! Let's see you on the dancefloor, shaking your stuff! • It's a bit of a young crowd.

13 Books, films and music

Conversation

1 Describing films

Would you go and see a film which was described in any of the following ways? Why / why not? Explain your decisions to a partner.

amusing	explicit	hyped-up	predictable
art-house	gory	moving	soppy
convoluted	gripping	off-the-wall	tense
disturbing	harrowing	over-the-top	uplifting

Choose four of the adjectives to describe films or TV programmes you've seen. Tell a different partner about them.

2 Listening

You are going to listen to four short conversations in which people talk about films. Listen and match two of these sentences with each conversation. Two sentences aren't true for any conversation.

1. The film had a happy ending.
2. A speaker apologises for something.
3. The film wasn't in English.
4. A speaker is persuaded to do something.
5. One of the speakers cried during the film.
6. One speaker accuses another speaker of something.
7. The film was violent.
8. A speaker got into an argument with someone in the cinema.
9. The speakers agree the film was incredible.
10. One of the speakers is thinking of going to see a blockbuster.

Explain your choices to a partner. Listen again if you need to.

3 Listen again

Listen to the first conversation again. Complete the conversation.

K: What a depressing film!

B: Oh, I know, I'm sorry. I wouldn't have suggested it (1) .... more about it.

K: No, it's not your fault. I thought it'd be good too – it had (2) .... I mean, it said in the paper it had light touches and a really uplifting ending.

C: I guess that scene with the priest was kind of funny.

K: Yeah, but (3) .... And I don't see how topping yourself really constitutes a happy ending.

C: I think you were supposed to (4) .... a release for him.

K: Mmm. I can't say it felt like that to me. Just depressing.

B: Yeah, absolutely. So what are we doing now? Are you just going home or what?

C: I don't know. What have you got in mind?

B: (5) .... about going to get something to eat.

C: Oh, right. I'm not actually that hungry, but I don't mind coming along for a drink. Kathy, what about you?

K: I am (6) .... , but I should really get back and do some work.

B: Oh, come on, one night off (7) .... Go on.

C: Yeah, you're not going to get much work done by the time you get home, are you?

K: Oh, all right. You've (8) .... Where were you thinking of going?

Real English: topped himself

In the first conversation, the speakers talk about a film in which a man tops himself. This is a very informal, jokey way of saying kills himself or commits suicide. It's best not to use it in more formal situations or with people you hardly know.

4 Speaking

Discuss these questions with a partner.

1. Do you read film reviews? Have you ever been let down by one?
2. Has anyone in an audience at the cinema ever spoiled a film for you? What happened? Did you say anything to them?
3. Do you know any film / music / art snobs?
4. What do you think of the Harry Potter films?

5 Describing scenes of films

Complete the conversations with the words in the box.

floods	gross	mile	twist
gory	hilarious	moving	wet
gripped	lost	squirming	zoomed

1. A: I was in .... of tears by the end.
   B: I know. It was so ....
2. A: That scene where they're robbing the bank was just ....
   B: Yeah, it was OK, but I didn't think it was that funny.
   A: Come on! It was brilliant. Honestly, I nearly .... myself.
3. A: I thought the battle scenes were amazing.
   B: Yeah? They were a bit .... for my liking – the way the camera .... in on people's arms and heads being chopped off …
   A: Yeah, I can see that, but I don't mind all that blood and guts.
4. A: I thought it was a really good .... at the end.
   B: Oh, come on! You could see it coming a .... off.
   A: Do you think so? I wasn't expecting it at all.
5. A: I thought the opening fifteen minutes were brilliant.
   B: Yeah, I know. I was quite .... for the first half, but then it just .... its way – and the ending was just ridiculous.
   A: Yeah, it was totally unbelievable, really over the top.
6. A: What about that scene when he's in the toilet? It's so .... !
   B: I know. I was literally .... in my seat.

Work with a partner. Find two films you've both seen, but don't tell each other what you think of them yet. Then work on your own and spend two minutes deciding which words from this activity and Activity 1 you could use to describe different scenes in each film.

Now work with your partner again. Tell each other what you thought about the film and the scenes you liked or disliked. Agree and disagree with each other as in the conversations above.

6 Using grammar: unreal conditionals 1

Underline the conditional sentences below and discuss the questions with a partner.

A: Did you say anything?
B: If I'd been in Britain, I would've.

A: Do you have to go now?
B: I wouldn't if I hadn't told my boss I'd be at the meeting.

A: Can you give me a lift to the airport?
B: I would if our car wasn't being repaired.

1. What tenses are used in the conditional 'if' parts of each sentence? Why?
2. Why does the first sentence use *would've* whilst the third only uses *would*?

Write similar conditional sentences to respond to the following:

1. Did you go and see that film in the end?
2. You should've complained.
3. Can you lend me some money?
4. Did you finish the work I asked you to do?
5. Why don't you come with us?
6. Do you go out much?

7 Using grammar: unreal conditionals 2

Match the sentences and the follow-up comments.

1. You should've told me it was your birthday. ☐
2. I should've left the party earlier. ☐
3. He can't have seen us. ☐
4. They should start taxing the rich a bit more. ☐
5. He must be involved in some kind of criminal activity. ☐

a. I'm sure he would've said hello.
b. I would've got you something.
c. There's no way he could've afforded that car on his salary.
d. I wouldn't be feeling so tired this morning.
e. They could invest more money in schools then.

In a–e, why aren't full conditional sentences with 'if' used?

Add three follow-up comments to each of these sentences.

6. I sometimes wish I'd never moved here.
7. Why didn't you tell me about it earlier?
8. They should cut taxes.

For more information on using unreal conditionals, see G13.

Reading

1 Using grammar: keeping your options open

Match the five sentence starters to the endings.

1. I've vaguely arranged
2. I was vaguely thinking
3. I should really try to
4. I'm toying with the idea of
5. I'm supposed

a. of going to the cinema tonight.
b. maybe going ice-skating tomorrow.
c. to be going out with some people from work later.
d. to go out somewhere with Ben tonight.
e. go to the gym today, I suppose.

We often follow sentences like those above with an extra comment. Put the words in order to make five common follow-up comments.

6. suggestions / to / I'm / but / open
7. looking / it / out / I'm / for / to / but / get / excuse / of / an
8. do / I / suppose / with / anyone / don't / fancies / me, / they / coming?
9. confirmed / yet / haven't / we / but / anything / got / definite
10. the / if / the / wouldn't / be / world / didn't / it / but / end / of / I

2 Practice

Spend three minutes thinking of your plans for the rest of today / tomorrow / this weekend. Make sure you use at least two of the sentence starters from Activity 1 when you report your plans – even if you need to lie! Then have conversations with some other students like this:

A: So what're you up to tonight?

B: I'm not really sure. I should probably try to do a bit of studying, I suppose … but it wouldn't be the end of the world if I didn't, though! Why? What've you got on?

A: Well, I was vaguely thinking of maybe going bowling. I don't suppose you fancy coming with me, do you?

B: Oh, yeah. I'd love to. Where were you thinking of going?

Continue each conversation until you have sorted out where and when to meet.

3 Before you read

You are going to read an extract from a listings magazine. Check that you understand the words in the box, using a dictionary to help you if necessary. Then decide which section you'd expect to find each in: *Music*, *Film*, *Comedy*, *Theatre* or *Clubs*.

a devoted, dressed-up crowd	outstanding tenor
a middling blockbuster	trad stand-up acts
an open mic jam session	spin a wildly eclectic mix
long-awaited sequel	stark, minimal set design
show-stopping songs and choreography	
MC	

Compare your choices with a partner.

4 While you read

Imagine you are on holiday in London for a week. Read the extract from a listings magazine on the opposite page. It tells you some of the things that are on in town tonight. Mark the items you like the sound of with a tick (✓) and those you don't like the sound of with a cross (✗).

When you finish reading, compare the things you marked with your partner. Could you go on holiday with them?

5 Vocabulary focus: collocations

Match the adjectives in the box with their most likely group of collocates.

improvised retro thorny up-and-coming

1. .... issue / matter / question / problem
2. .... area / director / young actress / lawyer
3. .... scenes / speech / music / dialogue
4. .... clothes / music / style / bands

Now match these adjectives with their most likely group of collocates.

experimental promising supportive veteran

5. .... young player / start / new band / actor
6. .... jazz pianist / campaigner for human rights
7. .... music / operation / procedure / stage
8. .... environment / person / boss / group

Now go back and underline the collocates for these eight adjectives in the text you read. Are there any collocations you don't understand?

What's on?

MUSIC

Audioslave @ The Forum, Kentish Town
Hardcore rock from former Soundgarden and Rage Against The Machine members. Not for the faint-hearted!

Lee Urbaniak @ The Spitz
A night of full-on free-form jazz from the veteran saxophonist and his band.

The Eighteenth Day of May @ The 12-Bar Club
Bluesy folk music followed by an open mic jam session.

Cosi fan Tutte @ Somerset House
Outdoor concert performance of Mozart's comic opera featuring the outstanding tenor Gregory Turay.

FILM

That Obscure Object Of Desire @ The Curzon
Re-release of Luis Buñuel's surrealist masterpiece about a reclusive aristocrat's torturous infatuation with an evasive teenage girl.

Mulan @ Odeon Leicester Square
Disney classic loosely based on the Chinese legend of a girl who disguises herself as a man in order to take her sick father's place in the army.

Revenge @ Odeon Holloway Road
The latest action hero, Steve Mortensen, takes (surprise, surprise) revenge on the alien killers of his parents in this middling CGI blockbuster.

Ape King II @ The ABC
Long-awaited sequel to the epic sci-fi fantasy saga, starring Jennifer Johnson-Smith and Kyle Lagerfeld and set in a futuristic California in the wake of a nuclear war.

COMEDY

Big Night Out @ The Comedy Club
Up-and-coming comedienne Joanne Newsom tops a very promising bill, which also features the always amusing Cooper Jones and the very skilful Danny Dawkins as MC.

Old Rope @ The Deptford Creek
Improvised sketches jostle for attention alongside more trad stand-up acts at this weekly club, compèred by the glamorous Lady Edna.

THEATRE

The Lady and the Leopard @ The Apollo
Long-running musical that remains a perennial family favourite, despite never having met with critical acclaim. What it lacks in plot, it more than makes up for with show-stopping songs and choreography.

Carl and Carla @ Diorama Hall
Experimental gender-bending work tackling the thorny issues of identity, sexuality and desire. Clocks in at just over four hours long!

King Lear @ The National
Ambitious new production with some stellar performances from a seasoned cast. Jason Gordon-Davies is magnificent as Lear and the stark, minimal set design is a revelation.

CLUBS

Blow Up @ The Wag Club
London's premier retro club spins a wildly eclectic mix of soul, psychedelia, dancefloor jazz, soundtracks and more to a devoted, dressed-up crowd.

Larger @ Warp
Banging techno, happy hardcore and hard house at this recently revamped venue now able to hold a capacity of 2000 up-for-it mixed / gay clubbers.

Balance @ The Shaftesbury
Smooth R'n'B and hip-hop flavours for a well-dressed, well-heeled crowd of thirty-somethings still keen to shake their stuff on the dance floor.

OTHER

Jacobson & Worth
Opening night launch for this new gallery. Strong collection of contemporary abstract works and video installations.

South London Poets @ The Larrick
Rose Elizabeth reads from her new collection. Followed by friendly and supportive workshop for newcomers and poets from the floor.

Urban rites weekly skate
Weekly marshalled roller-skating trek around London covering approximately 12 miles and accompanied by a portable sound system. Meet at Hyde Park Corner.

6 Listening

You are going to hear two friends talking about their plans for tonight. As you listen, decide:

a. which of the things from the listings page they discuss.
b. what they end up deciding to do.
c. why they decide against the other things they mentioned.

Real English: a bit arty-farty

If something sounds a bit arty-farty, it sounds pretentious and as if it's trying to impress you with how creative and different it is.

7 Role play

You are going to have similar conversations with some different students about the events you marked in the listings page. First, look at the tapescript on page 154 and find three expressions you'd like to use in these conversations. Then talk to some other students. In each conversation, decide on things you'd both like to do this weekend.

There was a coup there in '67. • They're currently waging a guerilla war. • We should've intervened. • Hopefully, the ceasefire will hold. • He should be indicted for war crimes. • Apparently, they've reported some collateral damage. • The police were a bit heavy-handed. • It's just fuelling tensions. • The atrocity has provoked a backlash. • We need to stem the spiralling violence. • I'd take what they say with a pinch of salt. • I don't call that precision bombing! • We're beginning to bridge the divide. • We're beginning to acknowledge their grievances. • There are a lot of entrenched attitudes. • They just twist everything to their own ends. • These people are harbouring terrorists. • You've got to laugh – or else you'd cry! • There's light at the end of the tunnel at last.

14 War and peace

Conversation

1 Speaking

Check you understand the vocabulary in red in the questions below. Then discuss the questions with a partner.

Can you think of any countries:

a. that have compulsory military service?
b. that have been invaded?
c. that have been occupied?
d. that are widely seen as rogue states?
e. that have had conscription?
f. where there's been a civil war?
g. where there was a coup and which then had a military dictatorship?
h. where guerilla warfare is currently being waged?
i. where acts of genocide have been committed?
j. where there are regular border skirmishes?

How much do you know about what happened in each place?

Real English: conscription

Conscription occurs during wartime when the army is short of soldiers. If you're conscripted, you are made to join the armed forces. In American English, conscription is called the draft and you can get drafted. If you somehow manage to get out of doing this, you might get called a draft dodger.

2 Talking about war and terrorism

Complete the conversations with the correct form of the words in the box.

declare	get rid of	indict	pull out
descend	go off	pose	step up
foil	hail	prop up	stick

1. A: Have you heard? They've .... a ceasefire.
   B: Yes, but it's only a temporary one. It'll never last.
2. A: Have you heard? They're .... all the troops.
   B: Yeah, I know. The whole place will .... into civil war now, just you wait and see.
3. A: Have you heard? They've decided to invade.
   B: I know. They've got a nerve! They've been .... the regime for years and now they decide they want to .... it.
4. A: Have you heard the news? They've managed to .... a gas attack on the underground.
   B: Really? I just heard there'd been an incident somewhere.
5. A: Have you heard? A huge bomb's .... in the capital. Thirty-seven dead.
   B: Oh God! No! They're really .... their campaign, aren't they?
6. A: They're just using terrorism as an excuse to invade.
   B: How do you know? The country might .... a real threat.
7. A: We'd be .... as liberators if we went in there.
   B: You must be mad! They'd see us as invaders and occupiers.
8. A: I think it's great the Prime Minster has decided to .... to his guns and do what he thinks is right.
   B: Are you serious? He should be .... for war crimes.

With a partner, practise the conversations. Try to continue each conversation for as long as you can.

Have you heard any news about wars recently? How do you feel about it?

3 Listening

You're going to hear three people talking – Jackie, Don and Brian. As you listen, take notes about:

a. which film Jackie talks about and what it was like.
b. the scale of the genocide.
c. how Jackie feels about her country's role in that conflict.
d. how this differs from her previous comments about war.

4 Word check

Complete these sentences from the conversation with the correct form of the verbs in the box.

change	distract	have	see
come	hack	intervene	twist

1. It was really harrowing. It .... me in floods of tears.
2. You .... what I said. All I meant was that it's pointless trying to bomb countries into democracy.
3. We all just sat back and let it happen. I think we should .... , we really should.
4. You .... your tune!
5. They bring in all these so-called experts just to .... us from what's really going on.
6. All kinds of factors .... into play.
7. They basically just .... people to death with machetes.
8. They probably .... us as aggressors.

Work with a partner. Discuss who said these sentences and what they were talking about. Listen to the conversation again to check if you need to.

5 Speaking

Discuss these questions with a partner.

1. Had you heard about the Rwandan conflict before?
2. Why do you think no-one intervened in the conflict?
3. What's the most harrowing film you can remember seeing?
4. Which of the following do you think are acceptable reasons for going to war? Why?
   a. You think another country might attack you – so you attack them first.
   b. You want to prevent human rights abuses.
   c. One country has invaded another and this threatens to destabilise the whole region.
   d. You want to intervene in a genocidal inter-ethnic conflict.
   e. You want to defend your economic interests.
   f. You think another country is funding and arming terrorist groups.
   g. You want to bring about regime change in another country.

6 Using vocabulary: war reporting

In the conversation, Don and Jackie spoke about their distrust of the media. Can you remember why they feel like this?

Complete this text with the words in the box.

a war machine	fanatical	propaganda
biased	loyal	tyrant
censor	precision bombing	
collateral damage	pre-emptive strikes	

I've stopped watching the news when there's a war on. It's so one-sided and (1) .... They twist everything to make you get behind 'our boys'. If you believe everything you hear on the news, then the enemy always has (2) .... , whilst we just have an army; they fire wildly at anything that moves, we carry out (3) .... ; their leader is always a demented (4) .... , ours is always statesmanlike and dignified. When we kill innocent people, it's called (5) .... – when they do it, it's civilian casualties. When we attack first, it's (6) .... – when they do it's a sneak missile attack without provocation. They (7) .... all their newspapers; our journalists just operate under reporting guidelines. Our generals give press briefings; theirs just churn out (8) .... Our soldiers are professional, (9) .... and brave; theirs are brainwashed, blindly obedient and (10) .... Honestly, it makes me sick the way we're encouraged to view the enemy as less than human all the time. The press is all just part of the problem.

Now discuss these questions with a partner.

a. Do you watch / read much news? Where do you usually get your news from? Why?
b. Do you agree with the writer that the media influences the way people think about wars? Can you give any examples?
c. Are there any sources you don't trust? Why?
d. Do you think war reporting ever makes a positive difference? In what way?

Reading

1 Speaking

Look at the quotes below and discuss the questions with a partner.

1. Which do you like best?
2. Are there any you disagree with? Why?
3. Are there any you don't get? Can your partner explain them to you?

- To make peace with the enemy, one must work with that enemy, and that enemy becomes your partner. *(Nelson Mandela)*
- Honest disagreement is often a good sign of progress. *(Gandhi)*
- Melt their weapons, melt their hearts, melt their anger with love. *(Shirley MacLaine)*
- If the battle for civilisation comes down to the wimps versus the barbarians, the barbarians are going to win. *(Thomas Sowell)*
- Victory against terrorism will not take place in a single battle, but in a series of decisive actions against terrorist organisations and those who harbor and support them. *(George W Bush)*
- I don't worry about terrorism. I was married for two years. *(Sam Kinison)*
- One is left with the horrible feeling now that war settles nothing; that to win a war is as disastrous as to lose one. *(Agatha Christie)*
- Peace is not the absence of conflict but the presence of creative alternatives for responding to conflict – alternatives to passive or aggressive responses, alternatives to violence. *(Dorothy Thompson)*
- The man who throws a bomb is an artist because he prefers a great moment to everything. *(G K Chesterton)*

2 Reading

Read the first paragraph of the article on the next page and discuss these questions with a partner.

1. Which of the quotes above do you think the writer would most sympathise with? Do you think it's true?
2. Do you know much about the conflict in Northern Ireland?
3. Can you explain the diagram and what happens at each stage?

Now read the rest of the article and find out more.

Then re-explain the conflict with a partner, using the diagram to check you've both understood the article.

3 Speaking

Discuss these questions with a partner.

1. Do you know any other conflicts in the world which are at these different stages?
2. This model is sometimes applied to marriage and divorce. What do you think might happen at each stage?
3. Can you think of any other personal conflicts it could be applied to?

4 Word check: nouns

Look back at the article and find the adjectives / nouns which collocate with these nouns.

violence	struggle	ground	peace
riots	involvement	bombings	sacrifice

5 Word check: verbs

Match these verbs with the noun phrases they collocate with.

1. be denied ☐
2. contain ☐
3. open ☐
4. abandon ☐
5. provoke ☐

a. fire on thousands of protestors
b. the whole disastrous policy
c. a backlash against the government
d. all access to a lawyer
e. the rioters with water cannons

Now match these verbs with the noun phrases they collocate with.

6. bridge ☐
7. resolve ☐
8. reach ☐
9. acknowledge ☐
10. entrench ☐

f. the conflict through violence
g. a decision about what to do
h. the gap between both sides
i. its role in the whole sorry affair
j. attitudes on both sides

Can you remember how the verbs were actually used in the text?
Go back and underline them.

6 Speaking

Discuss these questions with a partner.

1. Has the government in your country abandoned any policies? Why?
2. What other gaps or divides could you bridge? How might you do it?

Us and them?

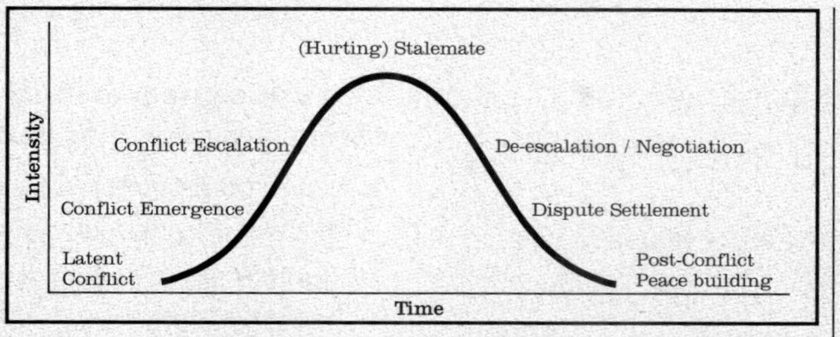

Another bomb goes off, more people are killed. A politician steps out in front of the cameras and talks of monsters attacking us. 'They are evil, inhuman terrorists. They must be destroyed, we must never give in to terrorists and never negotiate with them. Terrorists only understand the language of violence,' and so on. These statements may seem like natural reactions, but we often miss the fact that they may also contribute to escalating a conflict by de-humanising those involved and removing any cause or reason for their actions. This in turn allows those attacked to respond in heavy-handed ways, which in turn may fuel bitterness, remove options for dialogue and therefore encourage further violence. Recognising this, and understanding it as one of several stages conflicts can typically go through (see diagram above) may help us to reconsider our reactions to terrorist atrocities. Here we explore these stages of conflict as illustrated in Northern Ireland over the last forty years.

Latent conflict

Antagonisms between different sides are often present, but not publicly acknowledged. Up until the late sixties, the Catholic minority in Northern Ireland were frequently discriminated against by the Protestant majority – the Unionists – who ran the country and wanted to remain part of the UK. Catholics were denied access to jobs and good housing, and were unfairly represented in Parliament.

Emergence

Open conflict is usually triggered by one or more incidents. In this case, it emerged as a result of peaceful civil rights demonstrations by Catholics. The Unionist government claimed the civil rights movement was a front for the terrorist group, the IRA (Irish Republican Army), which wanted to create a united country with the Republic of Ireland in the south. The demonstrations were banned and when the protests continued, protestors were attacked by unionist groups and the police. The situation quickly developed into full-scale riots, which saw a number of deaths – mainly on the Catholic side. At this point, some Catholics actually accused the IRA of failing to protect their people. Subsequently, in 1969, the IRA split, with one group wishing to take up armed struggle to create a united Ireland. For many people north and south of the border, it was a decision they didn't agree with, and non-violent nationalist groups continued to reject violence throughout the following 30 years.

Escalation

In an attempt to contain the spiralling violence and crush the newly formed Provisional IRA, the British government introduced imprisonment without trial (or *internment*) of all those suspected of terrorist involvement. Those arrested were overwhelmingly Catholics. Prisoners were frequently beaten and denied basic human rights. In 1972, 13 civil rights protestors were killed when the British army opened fire on protestors. Far from crushing the IRA, internment proved to be a breeding ground for further hatred and support for terrorism. By the time the policy had been abandoned in 1974, over 1200 people had been killed on both sides of the divide.

Stalemate

The violence continued at a steady rate with an average of more than 80 killings a year throughout the 1980s. IRA attacks on the British mainland and the killing of 11 civilians in Enniskillen further entrenched views. The British army killed three IRA members in Gibraltar, sparking one of the bloodiest months of the Troubles. Both sides were locked in a conflict they couldn't win and were paying high costs in terms of lives and the economy, yet neither had an obvious way out.

De-escalation

In the early 1990s, the IRA's political wing made contact with the British government and began secret dialogues with a view to ending the armed struggle.
Typically, the push to enter negotiations is helped by events which confirm the need to move on. This happened in 1993 with a series of bombings on the British mainland including one in Warrington where two children, Tim Parry and Jonathon Ball, were killed. The then Prime Minster, John Major, was later to talk of it as a turning point. 'If we abandoned our attempt at peace … how many other innocents would have their lives cut short?' he asked. The attack also provoked a greater backlash amongst Republicans against the IRA. The following year, the IRA declared a ceasefire.

Dispute settlement

For agreement to be reached, both sides have to track back through the conflict and acknowledge hurt and grievances. Both sides have to offer change. In 1998, the Unionist and Republican parties signed the Good Friday agreement, recognising each other's rights and setting up power sharing.

Peace building

Signing an agreement does not necessarily lead to a lasting peace. Leaders have to convince their followers, and local resentments and stereotyping of the opposing parties have to be tackled. There is also a culture of criminality associated with paramilitary groups like the IRA, which has to be broken down. Northern Ireland, after ten years of 'peace', has far from resolved these issues with power-sharing institutions regularly suspended and low-level violence continuing. Yet peace remains and efforts of people to bridge community divides continue and none are working harder than the remarkable parents of the Warrington bomb victims who set up the Children's Peace Centre. The centre runs workshops to get children to acknowledge and understand diversity and try to resolve conflicts through dialogue. Reading the responses of participants in the Children for Peace programmes gives hope for the future. As one said: 'Although someone said that to die for one's country is the ultimate sacrifice, I now know that to live for one's country is better'.

Writing: Describing visual information

1 Speaking

Discuss these questions with a partner.

1. What factors do you think contribute most to a feeling of job satisfaction?
2. What kind of jobs would you expect people to be happiest / unhappiest in? Why?

Now look at the chart below. It shows the results of a survey into levels of job satisfaction.

3. What do you find most surprising about this information?
4. Why do you think those in certain blue-collar jobs seem to be much happier than those in white-collar jobs?
5. What would you imagine the pleasures and the downsides of each of these jobs would be?

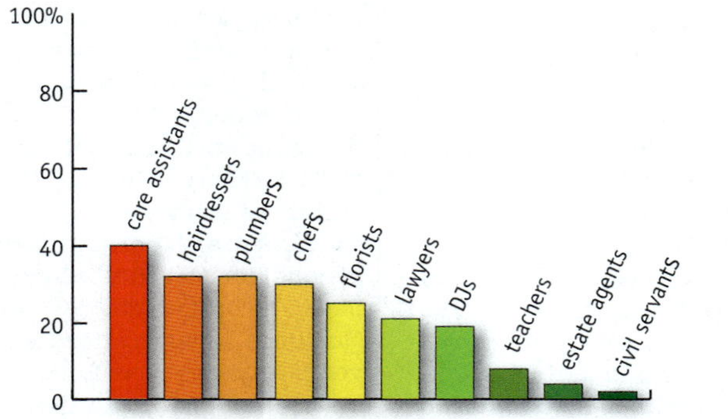

Percentage classifying themselves as very happy

2 Commenting on visual data

Complete the sentences with the words in the box.

case	inspection	revealed	significant
from	morale	seems	with

1. As can be seen .... this chart, a .... proportion of blue-collar workers seem content with their lives.
2. As .... by these figures, a financially-rewarding job is no guarantee of job satisfaction.
3. As can be seen from a closer .... of the figures, there almost .... to be an inverse relationship between income and job satisfaction.
4. As shown in this chart, the teaching profession is suffering from a serious loss of ....
5. As is often the .... with surveys, the limited number of respondents means the results should be treated .... caution.

3 Interpreting research data

In these sentences, both choices are possible. Circle the ones that make the *stronger* claims.

1. The results indicate / establish that there is a link between living near power lines and cancer.
2. Table 9 shows / suggests that many in the overseas research community still require help with their written English.
3. These experiments call into question / undermine much previous research.
4. Figure 8 clearly depicts / helps to clarify the relationship between the two elements.
5. Temperature changes had an influence on / distorted the results of the experiment.
6. The results depicted in Figure 3 validate / go some way towards supporting this theory.
7. Most commentators haven't fully taken / have failed to take these findings into consideration.
8. The findings demonstrate / suggest a need for further research into the matter.

4 Practice

Make three comments about the chart below using some of the sentence starters from Activity 2.

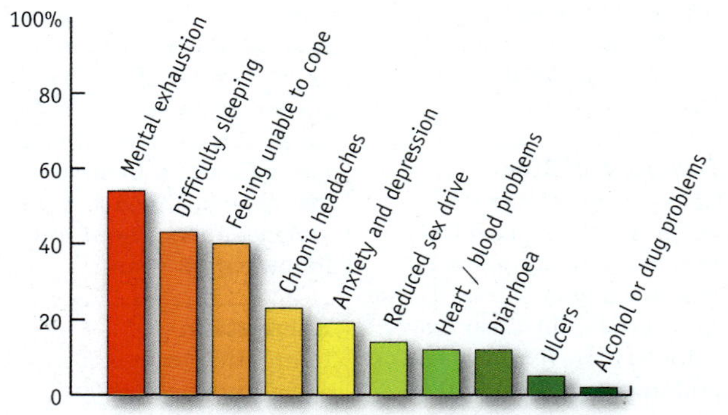

Health problems reported in the last year by people working 48 hours a week or more

Compare your comments with a partner. Now try to make some interpretations of the data, using some of the language from Activity 3.

5 Describing charts

Complete this short essay about the chart in Activity 1 with ONE word in each space.

This chart shows the results of a recent survey into levels of job satisfaction across a wide (1) .... of occupations.

Perhaps surprisingly, the overall (2) .... appears to be for those in more blue-collar jobs to classify themselves as very happy, (3) .... those in the usually more financially-rewarding white-collar sector claim disturbingly low levels of happiness.

(4) .... can be seen from the chart, the happiest workers are care assistants, of (5) .... 40 per cent described themselves as very happy. A slightly lower proportion of (6) .... hairdressers and plumbers (32 per cent) placed themselves in this category, with 30 per cent of chefs also opting for it. A (7) .... of all florists, just over a fifth of all lawyers and just (8) .... a fifth of all DJs seem content, whilst only an alarming 8 per cent of teachers feel similarly. At the bottom end of the survey, a (9) .... 4 per cent of estate agents are happy in their jobs whilst an (10) .... tinier proportion of civil servants feel the same.

6 Describing numbers

In this kind of academic writing, we need to vary the way we talk about the figures. Otherwise, the writing quickly becomes monotonous.

Replace the underlined statistics in these sentences with the expressions in the box.

an almost insignificant number	only slightly fewer
the overwhelming majority	just over half
just under a third	upwards of a third
only a tiny percentage	

1. 52 per cent of shoppers surveyed claimed to feel less confident about the state of the economy this year than last and 49 per cent said this was affecting their shopping patterns.
2. Only 2 per cent of the annual defence budget is currently spent on clothing and footwear.
3. 96 per cent of those polled said they would support a change in the law.
4. 35 per cent of all city dwellers have been affected by violent crime, though surprisingly 31 per cent of those living in the country have also been hit.
5. Only 0.2 per cent of those questioned claimed to support the proposals.

7 Using grammar: relative clauses

We often use relative clauses to link connected ideas together. Look at these examples:

- The bank currently has more than 2.4 million borrowers, the vast majority of whom are women.
- A prescribing error occurred in approximately 3 per cent of all medication orders written at the hospital, of which 18 per cent were potentially serious.

We generally use *of whom* to connect ideas about people and *of which* to connect ideas about things.

For more information on using relative clauses like this, see G14.

Connect the pairs of sentences with a relative clause using *of whom* or *of which*.

1. Only 800 escaped from the camps. 650 of the escapees were recaptured.
2. The government donates approximately 1.3 billion dollars in overseas aid per annum. The majority of this money goes to Eastern Europe.
3. Over a thousand people died in the conflict. Only a small percentage of those who died were actual combatants.
4. There has been a sharp increase in crime over the last twelve months. A considerable amount of this crime was juvenile crime.
5. Your body needs between 1.5 and 1.8 litres of fluid a day. The bulk of this fluid should be water.
6. During this time, just over 250 responses were received. Only a small percentage of these were negative.
7. Italian is a Romance language currently spoken by some 66,000,000 people. The vast majority of speakers live in peninsular Italy.
8. There were 1,113 motorcycle casualties in the country last year. 63 people involved in motorcycle accidents died.

8 Writing

Write a short essay (150–250 words) describing the chart shown in Activity 4. Use the essay in Activity 5 to help you. Try to use as much language from this unit as you can.

It's an ancient initiation ceremony. • It turned out well, all things considered. • It was a pretty lavish affair. • I burst into tears when they exchanged their vows. • His children contested the will. • Please pass on my condolences to the family. • I'd like my ashes scattered in my garden. • It wasn't at all solemn. • Consider it a perk of the job. • Whatever he told you, it was wrong! • Whoever did that should be shot! • Yeah, OK Dad. Whatever! • It's not as though I didn't ask politely. • It's just that the food was a bit dreary. • It's very multicultural.

15 Ceremonies, celebrations and culture

Conversation

1 Speaking: ceremonies

When might you have the following kinds of ceremonies?
What usually happens at each one?

1. a wedding ceremony
2. a funeral ceremony
3. a naming ceremony
4. a graduation ceremony
5. an initiation ceremony
6. an opening ceremony
7. a closing ceremony
8. an awards ceremony

Have you been to any of these kinds of ceremonies? Which of the adjectives in the box could you use to describe them?

ancient	civil	formal	moving	simple
brief	elaborate	lavish	religious	solemn

2 Listening

You're going to hear four conversations about ceremonies. Listen and answer these questions about each conversation.

1. What kind of ceremony do they talk about?
2. Which of the adjectives in Activity 1 could be used to describe the ceremony?
3. Did the person who took part in it enjoy it? Why / why not?

3 Listen again

Try to complete the gaps from the extracts of the conversations. Then listen to check your answers.

Conversation 1

B: ... We HAVE been together for almost ten years.

A: Well, exactly. I mean, why now? (1) .... you really needed a public statement of your commitment. I mean, you've got three kids!

B: Well, that's mainly it, actually. There were just all these (2) .... if we weren't.

B: ... when we actually exchanged our vows, I did get a bit emotional. It was weird. I thought I was going to (3) ....

A: I don't know. It's not that surprising. It's a big thing, (4) .... you've been together. I think it's a shame. You should've had some kind of party, made more of it.

Conversation 2

B: Still, my parents were happy and I only really did it for them. They (1) .... about it for ages. You know, like they had to get the photos of their clever son.

A: Ah yes, the photos, I'll look forward to seeing those.

B: (2) .... ! I might have to burn them before you get the chance!

Conversation 3

B: Oh, it was great in one way, but I did feel a bit uncomfortable.

A: Yeah? (1) .... ?

B: Well, God knows how much the whole thing cost.

A: Yeah, so what's wrong with that? It sounds great.

B: It was, it was. (2) .... I couldn't help thinking it was all at the taxpayers' expense (3) .... the whole thing was meant to be celebrating achievements in helping the needy, it just seemed a bit hypocritical.

- Do people living together have the same rights as married people in your country? Do you get any tax or other benefits for being married? Is this a good thing?
- Have you ever done something because your parents really wanted you to do it – even though you really didn't want to?
- Have you got any photos of yourself you don't like? Why don't you like them?
- Have you ever felt uncomfortable about having money or spending money? When?

4 Death, wills and funerals

Complete the sentences with the words in the box.

buried	cut	mourn	procession
condolences	grieving	shroud	went
cremated	left	split	wreath

1. The whole family was .... over the will, because their father .... everything to his youngest son.
2. I was really sad to hear about John. Can you pass on my .... to his family when you see them?
3. I'd like to send the family a .... just to pay my respects.
4. Her husband died about three years ago, but she's still .... for him. It was a huge loss for her.
5. I don't understand how people can .... someone they've never known or met. I mean, all those people who waited for hours to see the Princess's funeral .... and were wailing by the side of the road! I just don't get it.
6. He said he wanted to be .... after he died, and have his ashes scattered in the rose garden of our local park. He loved it there.
7. When I die, I'd like to be .... , but not in a coffin. I'd like to be just wrapped in a .... so I'll go back into the earth.
8. He .... very suddenly. It was totally unexpected.
9. He .... his son out of his will, so his son's not going to inherit any of his fortune. Apparently, though, he's going to contest it.

Now discuss these questions with a partner.

a. How would you like to go? Would you have any special requests for your funeral? What music would you like played?
b. How else can you pay your respects when someone dies?
c. Do you agree with the speaker in number 5?
d. Have you ever inherited anything? Have you heard any stories of families being split over a will? Why?

5 Using grammar: *-ever*

In Conversation 1, you heard that getting married is 'a big thing, however long you've been together'. We add -ever to question words to mean 'it doesn't matter how / what / who, etc.' Complete these sentences with *however*, *whoever*, *whatever*, *wherever* or *whenever*.

1. .... he told you, just ignore it!
2. .... hard I try, I just can't seem to get through to him.
3. I'll be in all day, so just come round .... you like.
4. Well, ... did it must've been sick in the head.
5. .... I phone, I just get a recorded message.
6. .... we went, we had people offering to sell us things.
7. I'm going to finish this, ... long it takes.
8. Within reason, I can wear .... I like to work.

For more information on how to use these words, see G15.

6 Using grammar: *It's not as though*

Complete each dialogue by adding one of the 'It's not as ...' sentences to the second line and one of the 'It's just ...' sentences to the third.

a. It's not as if you're always taking a sickie.
b. It's not as if he doesn't know you.
c. It's not as though he would've laughed at you or got annoyed.
d. It's not as though you were great friends before.
e. It's not as though it was that expensive.

f. It's just that everyone else seemed to understand him.
g. It's just that he hasn't actually invited me.
h. It's just that we don't need it. It's a real waste.
i. It's just that I was actually trying to be friendly to him.
j. Maybe that's why I feel so bad about it!

1. A: Why did you buy that?
   B: What's the problem?
   A: I know.
2. A: I just felt a bit stupid asking him to repeat what he said.
   B: Why?
   A: I know.
3. A: I feel funny about asking for a day off.
   B: Come on.
   A: Yeah, I know.
4. A: Do you think he'll mind me coming to the party?
   B: Of course not.
   A: Yeah, I know.
5. A: I can't believe he was so rude to me.
   B: What are you getting so upset about?
   A: Yeah, I know.

Read the conversations in pairs. Try to continue each conversation.

7 Practice

Write similar dialogues in pairs starting with these sentences.

1. I feel a bit guilty, not inviting him to the wedding.
2. I was surprised there weren't more people at the festival.
3. I really shouldn't have any more cake.
4. I really should get going.

Reading

1 Speaking

You are going to read an article about London life and multiculturalism. First, discuss these questions with a partner.

1. Does your country have any special public days? Are they usually celebrated in any particular way?
2. Do you personally celebrate any particular holy days? Which ones? How? Why?
3. Do you know what any of these days are? Do you know what usually happens on them?

   Chinese New Year
   Divali
   Easter
   Eid-ul-Adha
   Hannukah
   Ramadan

2 While you read

Now read the article. As you read, answer these questions.

1. What do you learn about the festivals and holy days in Activity 1?
2. How does the writer feel about them all being celebrated in London?
3. Why does she feel like this?

WE ARE ALL **DIFFERENT**, WE ARE ALL THE **SAME**!

London is one of the most multicultural places on earth. It is estimated that there are over 300 different languages spoken in the city – no mean feat, considering there are slightly under 200 different countries in the world! Obviously, such large numbers of such varied people all living and working alongside each other is a relatively new phenomenon and, in a sense, something of a social experiment. There are some who can only see the problems brought about by the situation: the ghettoisation of certain immigrant communities; the suspicion and prejudice with which people can come to view each other; the erosion of old certainties and ways of doing things. One of the main battle-lines of the multicultural experiment has been the separation-versus-integration argument and it is in London's schools that many of the attempts at conflict resolution take place. Whilst a minority of the capital's children go to single-faith religious schools, the vast majority attend mixed-sex, multi-faith schools – and that includes my daughter.

Rachel is ten now and is already an expert on the various celebrations and holy days of importance in our south London neighbourhood. She could quite easily inform you that the Hindu and Sikh festival of lights, Divali, which celebrates the victory of good over evil and knowledge over ignorance, is followed by the Jewish holiday of Hanukkah, eight days in which the Jews' struggle for religious freedom is celebrated. Then there's Eid-ul-Adha, the festival that marks the end of the holy month of Ramadan, a time of fasting and reflection for the Muslim community. She's learned about the importance of the colour red and of *jiaozi* dumplings for the Chinese during their New Year and, of course, she's studied the significance and history of Easter and Christmas. School assemblies and project work have allowed her to see the common links that unite us across all these divides – the importance of food and family and friendships to one and all. Rachel has friends who can claim to be Anglo-Turkish, Anglo-Somali, Anglo-Colombian, Anglo-Iraqi, Anglo-Irish and Anglo-Chinese and she takes it for granted that all of these are possible identities, bringing with them their own rich mix of traditions and culture.

The London she's inherited is a world away from the England I grew up in a small coastal town in the 1970s. There was one black kid at my school and two Asians – plus one Jehovah's witness, whose mother used to have him exempted from school assemblies, where we were all forced to sing lacklustre hymns (and where we egged one another on to sing dirtier and dirtier alternative versions!). My English 'culture' seemed to consist of football on a Saturday, my dad going down the pub on a Sunday whilst my mum slaved over a roast (before finally seeing the light and filing for divorce!), too much cheap chocolate at Easter, Harvest Festival in the autumn, when we were coerced into taking tins of baked beans to the old folk in our street, and cold turkey sandwiches for a week after Christmas. Racism was commonplace and taken as a given. I can even remember a Saturday night TV show that featured white guys all blacked up and pretending to be jazz dancers! The food was dreary and bland – meat and two boiled veg – and our holidays were spent with relatives in different parts of the country.

It amazes me that this is the England some white people of my generation pine after: a world I remember as only existing in black and white! The England Rachel inhabits – and has dragged me into as well – is Technicolor in comparison. She's already travelled more than I did until I was at least twice her age; she can use chopsticks and loves sushi; she wants to learn Arabic when she starts at secondary school, or maybe Spanish, and doesn't find it strange to meet Londoners called Saroj or Zhong Hua or Jamir. She has become what I suppose we all must become – a citizen of the world – for we all now live in an ever shrinking world and this requires us to exercise our imagination, our sensitivities and our empathy. Now more than ever before, it is vital that we understand that yes, of course, we all have our differences, but we are also all remarkably the same!

3 Speaking

Discuss these questions with a partner.

1. Does your town / city sound similar to the writer's description of London? In what way?
2. Has there been much immigration into your country? Where from? What're the biggest ethnic groups?
3. Do you know any people who've moved to your country? Where are they from originally? Why did they move?
4. Do you know anyone who's emigrated? Where did they move to? Why?
5. Do you agree with the writer that 'we are all different, we are all the same'?

4 Prefixes

The article talks about multi-faith schools and Anglo-Turkish students. What do these prefixes mean here?

Can you think of three more words which use the prefix 'multi'?

Do you know what these prefixes usually mean?

anti-	hyper-	post-	pro-	sub-
counter-	over-	pre-	semi-	under-

How many words beginning with each can you think of? Use a dictionary to help you if you need to.

5 Using grammar: *Considering*

Complete the sentences with the words in the box.

how badly	how little	how often
how few	how many	how quickly
how late	how much	how rarely

1. I got two As and a B, which is no mean feat, considering .... I studied!
2. I don't think losing 3-1 is a bad result when you consider .... we played.
3. I don't think the final results were really that impressive, considering .... money they'd spent on it.
4. I don't actually feel that bad today when you consider .... I went to bed!
5. She was just unbelievably patient with me, especially considering .... times I've let her down.
6. Considering .... I practise, I'm still not really very good.
7. I think we all coped pretty well with that, considering .... of us had ever done anything like that before.
8. Considering .... we managed to get it finished, I think we've done a pretty good job, actually.
9. You're amazingly good at this, considering .... you say you play.

Real English: all things considered

We often add all things considered at the end of a sentence to emphasise that something positive happened in spite of lots of problems.

The meeting went pretty well, all things considered.
It wasn't a bad day, all things considered.

What kind of problems might have happened in these situations?

For more information on how to use *considering*, see G16.

6 Practice

Complete these sentences with your own ideas.

1. I think the dinner went pretty well, considering ....
2. We don't get on all that badly, considering ....
3. It was a bit of a let-down, actually, especially when you consider ....
4. My English is pretty good, considering ....
5. I think ...., all things considered.

I suffer from chronic migraines. • It could be post-traumatic stress. • She came home infested with head lice. • It's just quack medicine. • All the car fumes and pollution really exacerbate it. • I get really wheezy and out of breath. • She's all skin and bones. • I feel really bloated. • She was diagnosed last year. • I was devastated. • She's really struggled ever since. • I'm a big fan of stem cell research. • It's a slippery slope. • It's a complete minefield. • It could pave the way for a cure. • There's an over-reliance on antibiotics. • It's a highly resistant bug. • I've got grave concerns about vivisection. • He's very prone to infections. • She stuck needles in my ears. • I had to go through IVF to conceive.

16 Health and medicine

Conversation

1 Medical problems

Look at the sentences. Check you understand the words in red. Then discuss these questions with a partner.

a. Do you know what causes any of these medical problems?
b. What kind of problems does each condition result in?

1. I get chronic migraines sometimes.
2. He had a minor stroke about a year ago.
3. She's going through the menopause at the moment.
4. I get terrible hay fever at this time of year.
5. She gets terrible arthritis in her hands and knees.
6. She's got pretty bad eczema.
7. He's clinically obese.
8. The specialists said they think he suffers from Attention Deficit Disorder.
9. I've got asthma.
10. I suffer from terrible insomnia sometimes.
11. I think he's suffering from post-traumatic stress.
12. My son came home from school the other day totally infested with head lice.

Which of these problems are described in more detail below?

a. It itches like mad and she scratches it like crazy. I think it's exacerbated by wheat and dairy products.
b. He's been really down since then and he's on anti-depressants. Still, it could've been worse. He could've been paralysed.
c. She's having problems sleeping. She gets hot flushes and she's prone to mood swings as well.
d. My nose runs like mad and I can't stop sneezing and my eyes water and everything. It's horrible!
e. I get really short of breath sometimes and have to carry an inhaler with me all the time.
f. He can't sit still for more than two minutes and he's got a really short attention span.

Do you know anyone who's ever had any of the problems in 1–12?

Real English: He suffers from Attention Deficit Disorder.

Attention Deficit Disorder affects certain young children. Its common medical acronym is ADD, which is pronounced A-D-D. Its main symptoms are hyperactivity, impulsive behaviour and inability to concentrate.

2 Acronyms

Discuss these questions with a partner.

a. How many of these other common acronyms do you know?
b. Which two are pronounced as whole words – not letter by letter?
c. Do you know what any of them stand for?

AIDS	CJD	IVF	MS	PMT	STD
BSE	HIV	ME	MRSA	SARS	TB

Now complete these sentences with the acronyms.

1. They seem to have the AIDS problem more or less under control, but there's been a worrying rise in other kinds of ....s.
2. She's in a really bad mood at the moment. I think it's .... She always gets like this before her period.
3. It was awful! During the height of the mad cow outbreak, she ate some beef infected with .... and then contracted ....
4. She had .... treatment a few years ago and ended up having twins.
5. Our offices in China had to close down during the .... outbreak of 2003.
6. For ages, the government buried its head in the sand and tried to pretend the .... problem didn't exist. Then suddenly, people started testing .... positive and they had to face up to it!
7. My aunt's got .... It's horrible. She's basically wasting away. She's almost paralysed now and needs constant care.
8. It was awful! He didn't bother to get vaccinated before he went to the Congo and then he contracted .... while he was there. He came back literally coughing blood!
9. To begin with, the doctors just thought he was so tired because of depression, but eventually they diagnosed him as having ....
10. My granddad's really reluctant to go into hospital. He's convinced he'll contract that killer superbug thing, ...

3 Speaking

Discuss these questions with a partner.

1. How much of a problem is AIDS in your country? Do you think they're doing enough to combat it? Are any other STDs a problem?
2. How worried do you feel about things like SARS and Avian Bird Flu? Would you go on holiday to a country that had had an outbreak of one these kinds of diseases?
3. Have there ever been any outbreaks of BSE in your country? Did mad cow disease make you think twice about eating meat?
4. Have you ever heard of MRSA before? Do you have similar problems in your hospitals?

4 Listening

You are going to listen to four short conversations in which people talk about health and medicine. Listen and match two of the sentences with each conversation.

1. .... and ....   3. .... and ....
2. .... and ....   4. .... and ....

a. Someone thinks they should've done something earlier.
b. Someone is overweight.
c. Someone thinks their friend got the wrong end of the stick.
d. Someone has been getting withdrawal symptoms.
e. Someone gets recommended quite a lot.
f. Someone is cautious about expressing too much optimism.
g. Someone practises complementary therapies.
h. Someone completely hit the roof.

Explain your choices to a partner.
Listen again if you need to – or read the tapescript on page 156.

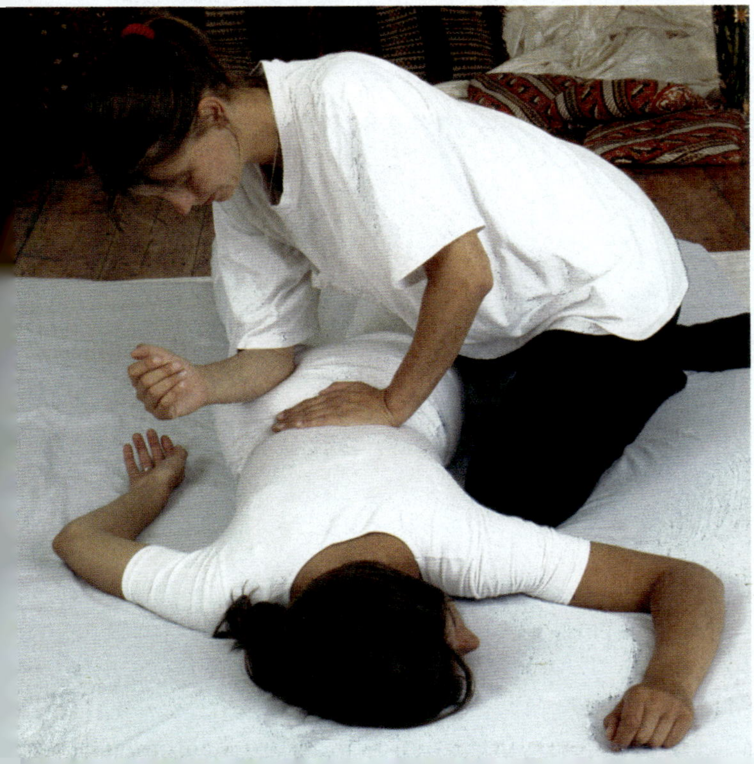

5 Speaking

Discuss these questions with a partner.

1. Have you ever tried any complementary therapies like shiatsu, aromatherapy or acupuncture? When? Why?
2 Do you think it's true that dieting can be unhealthy?
3. Have you ever taken sleeping pills? Do you ever take anything in these situations?
   - to calm you down
   - for headaches
   - to help you stay awake
   - when you have a cold
4. Do you take any other kinds supplements? Why?

6 Using grammar: perfect tenses

Complete the sentences from the conversations by putting the verbs in brackets in the correct perfect tense. Use contracted forms ('ve, 's, 'd, etc.) where appropriate.

1. I used to be a dental nurse and I .... to find it all a bit repetitive and predictable. (start)
2. She suggested that I quit and retrain – so I did. And I .... since. (not look back)
3. I set up on my own about two years ago now and the practice .... and .... (just / grow / grow)
4. Oh, the acupuncture course? Yeah, that's great. I'll .... by September. (finish)
5. I had this mole on my leg and it .... all red and itchy. (get)
6. It meant I avoided having to go through chemo and it .... all .... OK, really, because it went into remission a year or so ago and I .... much better since then. (turn out, feel)
7. I .... myself trying to get rid of this belly for weeks now! (kill)
8. No, you must .... it, mate. It can't be right. (mishear)
9. A: So how did it go the other day? The dinner with Dan's parents.
   B: Oh no! I .... to you since then, ... I? (not speak)
10. She .... only just .... to get off sleeping tablets. She .... hooked on them for years and she .... more and more and more and then about three months ago she decided to quit and she just stopped cold and .... to cope ever since. (manage, be, take, struggle)

Listen and check your answers. Practise reading out the sentences. Make sure you use the contracted forms of the auxiliary verbs.

For more information on how to use perfect tenses, see G17.

Reading

1 Medical issues

Discuss with a partner whether or not there is a difference in meaning between each of these pairs of words.

1. giving blood and donating blood
2. donating organs and removing organs
3. plastic surgery and cosmetic surgery
4. a chronic condition and a terminal condition
5. an abortion and a miscarriage
6. cloning and genetic modification
7. suicide and euthanasia
8. vivisection and testing on animals
9. being disabled and having learning difficulties
10. hereditary diseases and genetic diseases

Now discuss these questions.

- Have you ever given blood? Do you get paid for giving blood in your country? Should you?
- Do you know any famous people who are disabled or have a learning difficulty?

Now use these sentence frames to talk about the different procedures mentioned above?

a. I'm a big fan of .... I fully support it.
b. I think .... is fine in theory, but I just don't think it works in practice.
c. I've got grave reservations about ....
d. I think .... is OK, so long as it's only done as a last resort.
e. I'm fundamentally opposed to ....
f. I don't really know where I stand on .... I don't have a strong opinion either way.

Real English: disabled

Disabled is a more acceptable word to use than handicapped when talking about people with permanent physical injuries and illnesses. People who have severe permanent problems affecting the brain may be described as mentally disabled. However, people who suffer from problems such as dyslexia and autism are more commonly described as having learning difficulties.

2 Reading

Read the following stories and decide if you think the rulings are good or bad and why.

UK designer baby given the go-ahead

A couple have won their battle in the high court to allow them to select eggs for IVF treatment in order to create a baby who can provide matched tissue for their sick four-year-old son.

The boy suffers from a rare genetic blood disorder which will eventually become terminal without a bone marrow transplant. An extensive search for a donor has proved fruitless and the couple claimed that the only option now available to them was the radical stem cell treatment.

Doctors welcomed the ruling, which overturned a previous ban, although those involved in IVF also sounded a note of caution as the procedure has only a very small chance of success.

Approval given for cancer-free designer babies

FOUR COUPLES who have all been affected by the same form of hereditary cancer have been given approval to have their IVF embryos screened for the genes causing the disorder.

It is claimed that the ruling by the government's fertility watchdog will allow selection for a much wider range of genetic problems than was previously permitted.

Discuss your ideas with a partner.

3 Listening

Now listen to Charlotte and John talking about one of the stories in Activity 2 and answer the following questions:

1. Which story are they talking about?
2. What do they each think about the story?

4 Discussing medical ethics

Which of the following sentences did the people in the listening use?

a. It's progress.
b. It's got to be worth a try.
c. It's creating false hopes.
d. It'll probably come to nothing.
e. It's a slippery slope.
f. It'll drain money away from other areas.
g. We'd be better spending the money on other things.
h. It'd be worth a fortune if it all goes right for them.
i. They should just let nature take its course.
j. If you believe in the sanctity of life, we shouldn't do it.
k. I think they're really entering dangerous territory.
l. When it comes down to it, it's all about money.
m. The whole procedure's totally untested.
n. The whole thing's a bit of a minefield.
o. The whole thing's sick.
p. The whole thing's just asking for trouble.
q. It could revolutionise the way we treat disease.
r. It could pave the way for new treatments.
s. It could save thousands of lives.
t. It's like some kind of futuristic nightmare.

Listen again to check your ideas.

5 Practice

Student A: Look at the newspaper extracts on page 175.
Student B: Look at the newspaper extracts on page 171.
Student C: Look at the newspaper extracts on page 172.

For each of the extracts you read, complete this sentence.

- Did you see that story about … ?

Decide what you think and feel about each article. Which of the expressions from Activity 4 could you use?

Close your books. In pairs, have conversations similar to the one in the listening. Take turns to talk about the texts you read. You may find you have read some of the same texts. Now change partners and repeat the exercise.

6 Word building 1

Complete the sentences with the correct form of the words in the box.

age	estimate	mature	resist
continue	fertile	rely	short

1. We have an .... population and not enough young people to support and look after them.
2. Many bugs have become .... to antibiotics, which have been over-prescribed.
3. We should try and reduce people's .... on drugs for dealing with stress.
4. There are an .... three million sufferers of HIV/AIDS in Ethiopia out of a population of around 65 million.
5. People who suffer from the condition hear a .... ringing in their ears.
6. The health service is in crisis because of a .... of qualified nursing staff.
7. There has been a rise in .... in men over recent years, which has contributed to the fall in the birth rate.
8. He went .... grey at the age of 17.

7 Word building 2

One way to help you use the different forms of words is to create a table like the one below. Use a dictionary to complete the table.

Verb	Noun	Adjectives	Adverb
continue	continuance	continual continued continuous	....
....	commerce	commercial commercialised	....
estimate ....-estimate ....-estimate	estimate	estimated	
rely on	reliance on over-reliance on reliability	.... un................ .... on	....
revolutionise	revolution revolutionary counter-revolutionary	....	

Notice that some words have more than one adjective or noun form which have only a subtle difference in meaning. The difference is often more a question of collocation. A good dictionary will highlight these collocations. Does the one you use highlight them?

Writing: Book reviews

1 Speaking

Discuss these questions with a partner.

1. Do you read much? In English or in your own language?
2. What kind of things do you tend to read most?
3. What was the last book you read? Was it any good?
4. How do you decide which books to read? Do you ever read book reviews? Which ones?

2 Describing books (1)

Decide if the following comments are positive (P) or negative (N).

1. It's a witty satire of modern political life. ☐
2. It's puerile and offensive. ☐
3. It's a riveting read. ☐
4. It's an incisive commentary on the conflict in the Balkans. ☐
5. It's a very underrated book. ☐
6. I personally found it really heavy going. ☐
7. It's written in a clear, concise style. ☐
8. The plot was totally preposterous. ☐
9. After all the hype, I couldn't see what the fuss was all about. ☐
10. It's a tremendous page-turner. ☐
11. The style is wordy and verbose. ☐
12. The ending was perhaps a touch predictable. ☐

Compare your ideas with a partner.

3 Describing books (2)

You are going to tell some other students about a book you really like. Use some of the language above and the sentence starters below.

It's called … and it's by …

You might've heard of the author. He / She also wrote …

It's an absolutely hilarious / terrifying / riveting read.

It's really moving / gripping / fast-paced / evocative / disturbing.

The main character is … and it's set in …

First and foremost, it's a book about …

I think the main reason it had such an impact on me is because …

It's been made into a film starring …

It's the kind of book that would appeal to …

Now tell some other students about the book you chose.

4 A review

This review was written by a Brazilian student studying for an advanced exam. Complete the gaps with the words in the box.

appeal	cope	indifferent	moved
protagonists	childhood	heroine	internal
narration	unfold		

By the River Piedra I Sat Down and Wept
by Paulo Coelho

In this novel, which has become an international best-seller, Paulo Coelho recounts an intimate love story. The (1) …………………… , Pilar and the hero, a spiritual leader who remains nameless throughout the book, have known each other since (2) …………………… . Separated in their teens, they meet again eleven years later. She has a strong temper, but never lets her emotions overwhelm her, whilst he is a priest, searching for an answer to his (3) …………………… conflicts. Both of them are united by their desire to pursue their dreams.

This novel conveys deep, moving feelings, and the style is clear and incisive, but also quite poetic. Bit by bit, Paulo Coelho allows snippets of their lives to (4) …………………… before us. His book not only portrays the romantic journey taken by the two main characters, but is also a love-filled encounter between the writer and his readers. Paulo Coelho tells us about religion, love, life and death. He writes from the heart, and his two (5) …………………… reveal their souls to us as well.

They face difficulties and they have to (6) …………………… with their own feelings of guilt as well as the prejudices of society. They are searching for their own peculiar versions of truth; they want to be real, fulfilled human beings and both feel they deserve peace and happiness. Above all else, they long to be loved, and no reader could fail to be deeply (7) …………………… by their story.

This novel should certainly (8) …………………… to a wide range of readers. The relationship is memorable and eloquently described. With precision and remarkable depth of feeling, Coelho plunges us into a profoundly enchanting universe of emotional authenticity, and it is impossible to remain (9) …………………… to this account. From beginning to end, our emotions are transfixed and we are both touched and gripped by the (10) …………………… . This is a truly brilliant piece of work.

Have you ever read this book? If you have, what did you think of it? If you haven't, does the review make you want to? Why / why not?

5 Using grammar: adjectival clauses

Look at these two sentences. Why do you think the introductory clause in the first uses a past participle (*separated*) whilst the second uses an *-ing* form (*tackling*)?

Separated in their teens, they meet again eleven years later.

Tackling the thorny issues of love and fear of rejection, this is perhaps Coelho's masterpiece.

Compare your ideas with a partner.

For more information on how to use adjectival clauses, see G18.

Complete these sentences with either the past participle or the *-ing* form of the verbs in the box.

base	die	look	publish	start
bless	leave	narrate	revolve	use

1. .... by a young Chinese entrepreneur in post-1997 Hong Kong, the final chapters of the novel are the most impressive.
2. .... with supernatural powers, Taki decides to travel across Japan and rid the ordinary people of the evil demons that threaten them.
3. .... the idea of human relationships as a way of exploring man's relationship with God, the writer takes us on a spiritual journey to enlightenment.
4. Loosely .... on a real-life murder in Los Angeles in the 1950s, this novel is a dark psychological thriller that takes you into the depths of the human soul.
5. First .... in the 1930s, this book has continued to delight generation after generation of children.
6. .... around a love triangle in turn-of-the-century Paris, this novel explores the themes of love, lust and betrayal.
7. .... the childish part of his life behind him, the young protagonist sets out on the journey of a lifetime.
8. .... from the premise that the desire for world peace is almost universal, the book sets out to explode cross-cultural myths and explore the deep similarities we all share.
9. With her parents .... likely to divorce and her brother already .... , our heroine falls into the depths of depression that only that special someone can pull her out of.

What kind of book do you think each sentence describes? Which sound worth reading to you and which don't? Why?

6 Using grammar: adverbial modifiers

In each of these sentences, two adverbs are more probable. Cross out the least likely one.

1. The narration is really / very / absolutely appalling.
2. The protagonist is actually not very / quite / really all that likeable, though I personally found this an interesting twist.
3. Sinclair produced three follow-ups to this, his first, novel, though none were quite / almost / nearly as good.
4. The relationship between mother and son is slightly / downright / crucially unhealthy.
5. Whilst the main characters are very well-portrayed, the minor characters aren't handled very / really / that well.
6. The plot is very / absolutely / really intricate and it is not until the very last page that all the loose ends are tied up.
7. This revelation comes at a slightly / vitally / crucially important moment.
8. The so-called hero turns out to be utterly / fully / disturbingly amoral.
9. This novel proved highly / massively / extensively controversial on its release.
10. The ending comes as a complete shock and is emotionally / totally / bitterly devastating.

For more information on how to use adverbs like this, see G8.

7 Planning a book review

Write a review (250–300 words) of either a book you've read recently or the book you talked about in Activity 3. Use the review in Activity 4 to help you. Try to use as much language from these two pages as you can.

'Oh, we don't sort things into categories like fiction and nonfiction anymore, sir. Now it's either 'popular' or 'elitist'.'

She cackles like a witch. • He's very self-deprecating. • It had this dreadful canned laughter all the way through. • He said it really deadpan. • And she goes, 'Are you taking the mickey?' • He's so gullible. • I could see them sniggering at the back. • I just got the giggles. I couldn't stop myself. • It wasn't exactly a barrel of laughs. • Funny peculiar or funny ha ha? • Oh, that's hilarious, that is! • It's a spoof horror film. • It's a bit too slapstick for my liking. • That's so corny! • I don't get it. • I've forgotten the punchline now, but it was really funny. • That's not very PC. • It's fire-fighter, not fireman. • I didn't really see the funny side. • They're always playing jokes on me at work. • He's got a very irreverent sense of humour. • I was in absolute hysterics. • Go on then. Have a good laugh at my expense!

17 Humour

Conversation

1 Describing people's sense of humour

Match these sentences to the follow-up comments.

1. She's got a really infectious laugh.
2. She doesn't laugh – she cackles!
3. She's got a very dry sense of humour.
4. She's got a weird sense of humour.
5. She's got a bit of a sick sense of humour.
6. She's got a very irreverent sense of humour.
7. She's got quite a self-deprecating sense of humour.
8. She's got a really annoying laugh.

a. She just comes out with some really odd comments sometimes and then proceeds to laugh herself stupid about them.
b. She cracks a lot of tasteless jokes about death and people having accidents.
c. Whenever she starts laughing, it just sets everyone else off.
d. She sounds like a witch.
e. She sounds like some kind of braying donkey or something. I hate it!
f. She's quite sarcastic and deadpan.
g. She's not afraid to take the mickey out of the boss or the people above her.
h. She takes the mickey out of herself all the time.

Real English: take the mickey

If you take the mickey out of someone, you laugh at them and make fun of them, often in a friendly way. In informal, spoken English young people often say take the piss instead. Some people find this expression offensive.

Now discuss these questions with a partner.

- Do any of the sentences above describe people you know?
- What kind of sense of humour would you say you had?
- Do you think there's a national sense of humour in your country? How would you describe it?
- Do you know anyone who has no sense of humour whatsoever?

2 Listening

You're going to hear four conversations where a speaker is telling another person about something that happened to them.

Listen and answer these questions.

1. Did the speakers in the stories laugh? Why / why not?
2. Did anybody else laugh? Why / why not?
3. Would you have laughed in any of these situations?

Have you ever played a practical joke on someone? What did you do?

Have you ever had a practical joke played on you? What happened? Did you laugh?

3 Ways of laughing

Complete the sentences with the words in the box.

burst	cracks	giggling	stitches	tears
chuckling	giggles	sniggering	straight	

1. He told this hilarious story. I had .... rolling down my face by the end! Honestly, he had us all in ....!
2. It was awful! The two of us were just .... uncontrollably in class, and of course, because we were in the front row, we were desperately trying to keep a .... face, which just made things worse.
3. When the priest told me I could kiss the bride, I just got the .... I don't know why. I just did.
4. I .... out laughing when he asked me. I know I shouldn't have, but I just couldn't help it.
5. He's really funny, that guy. He just .... me up.
6. My son's got a stutter. I get really annoyed when I see other kids .... about it behind his back. It's just not nice.
7. A: What are you .... to yourself about?
   B: What? Oh, it's nothing. I was just remembering something I saw on the bus the other day.

Can you act out any of the sentences above?

Now discuss these questions with a partner.

- Have you ever got the giggles? Where? Why?
- When was the last time someone had you in stitches?
- Do you know anyone who completely cracks you up? How?

4 Idioms: *It was a joke!*

When we use words like *joke*, *laugh* and *funny*, it doesn't always mean that we found things funny.

Which of these statements show the speaker found the situation funny? What situations would you use the other statements in?

1. They had me in stitches.
2. It was an absolute joke!
3. I was the laughing stock of the class.
4. The whole thing was a complete farce.
5. Don't make me laugh!
6. They all had a laugh at my expense.
7. That's a great joke.
8. He had me in hysterics by the end.
9. The whole situation was a bit funny.
10. Oh that's hilarious, that is. Hah, hah, hah.
11. I couldn't keep a straight face.
12. You're joking.

Real English: a bit funny

If you describe someone as really funny, it probably means you think they're very amusing, a good laugh. However, if you say someone – or something – is a bit funny, you mean they're strange or peculiar. If you think something funny is going on, you suspect there might be something illegal happening.

A: He's a funny guy.
B: Funny peculiar or funny ha ha?

5 Intonation

We use *You're joking* to respond in both serious situations and to amusing anecdotes. The intonation changes depending on the context.

Listen to the two different ways of saying these responses. Repeat what you hear.

1. Yeah, yeah, yeah.
2. It was really funny.
3. Really?
4. Right.
5. You're joking.
6. Oh great.
7. It was OK.
8. Mmm.

Work with a partner. Write short conversations using these responses.

6 Talking about comedy

Can you think of a film, TV show or comedian that these sentences could be describing?

1. It's a sitcom.
2. It's a spoof horror film.
3. It's a political satire.
4. It's full of very slapstick humour.
5. The humour in it is quite dark.
6. It's all just puerile lavatorial humour.
7. There are some moments of real unintentional humour in it.
8. I love her stuff. It's quite quirky, off-the-wall humour.
9. His act is rubbish. It's full of all these really corny jokes.
10. It's not laugh-out-loud funny. Most of the humour is quite subtle.

Compare your ideas with a partner. Then discuss these questions.

a. What's the funniest film you've ever seen? What's the funniest book you've ever read? What's your favourite sitcom?
b. Do you like stand-up comedians? Who's your favourite?

Reading

1 Telling jokes

Discuss these questions with a partner.

1. Are you any good at telling jokes?
2. What kind of jokes do you prefer?
3. Are there any kinds of jokes you tend not to laugh at? Why?

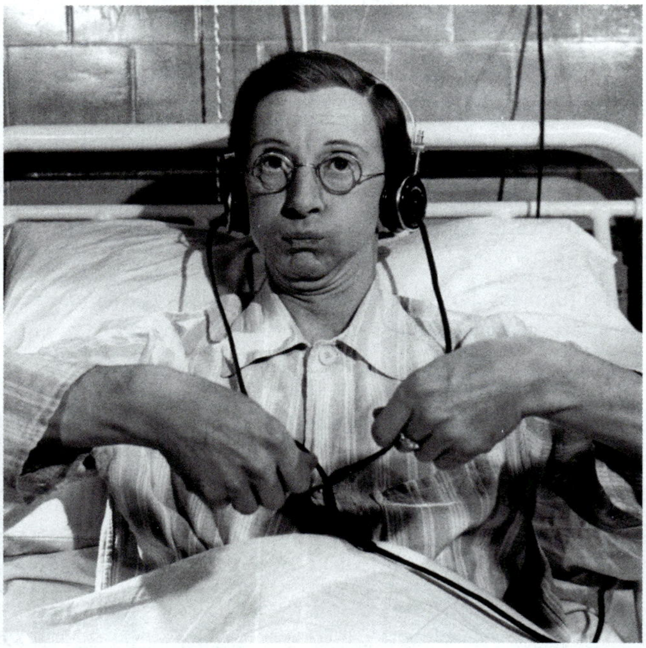

2 Listening

You're going to hear someone tell a joke. Before you listen, check you understand the words in the box.

a check-up	burden him with chores
a very severe stress disorder	nag him
a nutritious meal	regain his health

Based on the words in the box, have you got any idea what the joke might be about?

Now listen to the joke. Do you think it's funny?

Have you heard the same joke in your own language?

Real English: And she goes

In spoken English, we often report direct speech with the word go. It's especially common in jokes and humorous stories. A lot of younger people use the word like to report things they thought or felt.

And she goes, 'Oh … he said you're going to die!'
And I was like, 'That's the most outrageous thing I've ever seen!'
I was like, 'Why DO I bother? What IS the point?"

3 Using grammar: tenses and jokes

Look at the tapescript of the joke you just heard on page 157. Then discuss these questions with a partner.

1. What tenses are used most in the joke?
2. Can you find any examples of past or future tenses? When are they used?

Complete this joke by adding the verbs in the box in the correct tense. Some of the verbs will need to be in the negative.

be	call	do	rush	stick
blame	chop off	play	sew	suffocate

Ben and Lenny are at work in a timber yard when Lenny accidentally (1) .... his arm .... with a saw. Ben (2) .... the arm in a plastic bag and takes John to a surgeon. A few hours later, Ben sees Lenny in the pub. His arm (3) .... back on again and he (4) .... darts. 'Wow!' thinks Ben, 'that surgeon is great!' A couple of weeks later, Lenny accidentally cuts his leg off. Ben puts the leg in a plastic bag and (5) .... Lenny back to the surgeon. That evening, he (6) .... astounded to see Lenny playing football in the park. 'Wow!' thinks Ben, 'that surgeon is really something else!' A few months later, Lenny cuts his head off. Ben puts the head in a plastic bag and carries Lenny to the surgeon. The following day, the surgeon (7) .... Ben and says 'I'm sorry to have to tell you this, but Lenny is dead.' '(8) .... yourself,' says Sam. 'I'm sure you (9) .... all you could.' 'I'm not blaming myself,' says the surgeon, 'I'm blaming you. If you'dput some holes in that plastic bag, the poor guy (10) .... !'

4 Practice

Work in pairs. You are each going to read three different jokes.
Student A: Look at the jokes on page 173.
Student B: Look at the jokes on page 175.

Choose the joke you like best. The jokes are mostly in the past tense, but you're going to tell them mainly in the present. Spend four or five minutes trying to memorise the joke. Practise telling it to yourself in your head. You can add or change things if you like, if you think it will make your joke better. For example, you could exaggerate things.

Now tell your joke to your partner.

Read the rest of your partner's jokes. Do you agree that they chose the best one? Do you find any of the six jokes offensive in any way? Why?

5 Political correctness

If you tell certain kinds of jokes, you might well be accused of not being very PC – politically correct.

Tell a partner what you understand this to mean.

Now compare your ideas with this dictionary-type definition.

> **po'litically correct** [adj.] **1** describes a person who thinks that language or actions which could offend people – especially people likely to be discriminated against in society – should be avoided. **2** describes words that are used instead of other words to avoid being offensive.

Who might these kinds of jokes be most offensive to?

ageist jokes	homophobic jokes	racist jokes
anti-Semitic jokes	Islamophobic jokes	sexist jokes

'We're trying to come up with a less offensive term for political correctness'

6 Reading

Read this short article and then discuss these questions with a partner.

1. What reasons are put forward for adhering to political correctness? Do you agree with them?
2. Where does the opposition to political correctness come from? Do you think there might be any other reasons for opposing PC language and ideas?
3. Can you think of any more examples of PC language?
4. Do you have similar debates about the use of certain words and expressions in your language?

Does your dictionary contain notes about how to avoid causing offence for any of these words?

black	gay	girl	he	man	Ms	partner

Now look at the article again and find ten useful new collocations or expressions. For example:
heated debate

POLITICAL CORRECTNESS AND IDENTITY POLITICS

THE DEBATES SURROUNDING political correctness have become increasingly heated over the last few years as British and American universities attempt to take a firmer stand against all forms of overt discrimination. The rise of identity politics in the West – such as feminism, the civil rights movement, and gay and disability rights movements – has led to greater care being taken with the language used to describe different groups of people. In other words, more consideration is being given to the relationship between potentially offensive language and the continued existence of discrimination.

At its heart, political correctness is simply a form of linguistic etiquette or politeness. All it requires of us is not to use blatantly offensive or derogatory language. It asks us not to use negative words for women or gay people or the disabled, and it questions the function of jokes about such people.

However, at the same time, the phrase 'political correctness' has long been used to belittle and deride those concerned with the creation of a more just and equal society. Some social commentators are so appalled by attempts to critique the way we express ourselves that they have accused political correctness of being everything from humourless to an affront to free speech. It is claimed that "the PC brigade" wants to brainwash us into accepting their left-wing ideals, to straitjacket thought and to erode the very fabric of our society.

That notwithstanding, political correctness has had a major impact on the way we use many everyday words. Whilst many of us may still struggle with gender-neutral job titles such as 'fire-fighter' or 'flight attendant' (instead of 'fireman' and 'air hostess'), we find it easier to address letters to a Ms Leslie, to talk about people who have learning difficulties instead of people being backward or retarded, and to refer to our partners instead of our boyfriends and girlfriends. Similarly, perhaps the majority of people nowadays have no wish to return to the pre-political correctness era when racist abuse was common currency on the streets and jokes about women drivers were rife. Even dictionaries have been affected by the PC movement, with most now adding notes on how best to avoid potentially offensive language.

He's out on bail. • They've been detained in custody. • He got a suspended sentence. • There were mitigating circumstances. • He was released pending further investigations. • He was charged with gross misconduct. • He was done for reckless driving. • That's libellous! • I don't care if he's an eminent scholar – he's talking rubbish! • He was left destitute. • I was only five minutes over, but I still got clamped. • I could've murdered him! • He pulled a knife on me. • We were caught in the thick of it. • I was a bit shaken-up. • It was totally unprovoked. • The police just waded in. • His clothes were torn to shreds. • They've managed to track down the culprits. • They should lock them up and throw away the key! • My bike got nicked from right outside my house! • They've charged him with inciting racial hatred.

18 Crime

Reading

1 Crimes

Decide how serious you think each of these crimes is. Mark each one as either A (really serious), B (quite serious), C (less serious) or D (not very serious at all).

armed robbery	☐	handling stolen property	☐
causing GBH	☐	indecent assault	☐
disorderly conduct	☐	reckless driving	☐
extortion	☐	libel	☐
forgery	☐	manslaughter	☐
fraud	☐	obstructing the course of justice	☐
inciting racial or religious hatred	☐	hacking into a computer system	☐

Real English: GBH

GBH stands for grievous bodily harm. If you cause GBH, you assault someone and cause them very serious injuries. In Britain, it's punishable by up to five years in prison.

Compare your decisions with a partner and explain your choices. Can you think of five other crimes?

2 Verdicts and sentencing

Read the text. Which of the words in red can you translate into your language?

If you are suspected of having committed a crime, you can be arrested and detained in police custody for up to 36 hours before a decision is made about whether or not to charge you. If you're charged with a crime, you are then asked whether you are going to plead guilty or not guilty. If you plead guilty, you're not then normally needed in court – unless you've committed a serious crime. If you plead not guilty, you will usually be released on bail – allowed to go free, provided you leave a sum of money to guarantee you will appear in court. There may be conditions attached to your bail.

Most minor cases are heard in a Magistrates' Court, where the magistrate decides the verdict. However, serious cases are usually referred to a Crown Court, where trial is by jury. The jury consists of twelve people and they hear the case for the prosecution and the case for the defence before reaching their verdict. If you're found innocent, you're then released. However, if you are convicted of the crime you were charged with, the judge then passes sentence. The judge may decide that there are mitigating circumstances and thus give a more lenient sentence. The maximum sentence is life – which usually means between 15 and 20 years. There's no death penalty in the UK. It was abolished in 1965.

Recently, there has been much debate about sweeping changes planned for the English legal system. The government wanted to introduce trial without jury for complicated fraud cases and three-month detention without charges being brought in certain cases related to terrorism. These plans were highly controversial.

Discuss with a partner to what extent the things in the text are the same in your country.

3 While you read

You are going to read about six different legal cases. As you read, decide what sentence – if any – you think is appropriate in each case.

4 After you read

Work in groups of three. Discuss each case and what sentence you feel is appropriate. Explain your reasoning and reach unanimous decisions.

You be the judge

1 In the dock: *Chariot*

The parents of two troubled teenagers who took their own lives are seeking unspecified damages from their favourite band – heavy metal outfit, *Chariot*. It is alleged that the group glorify suicide and that their songs contain subliminal messages which prompted the death pact. One song, "Life is Death", features the lyrics "Do yourself in. Do it now". On the night of their deaths, the pair drank a 12-pack of beer and smoked marijuana whilst listening repeatedly to this track, before shooting themselves. In their defence, *Chariot* point to the teenagers' turbulent home lives and long-standing history of drug abuse.

2 In the dock: One man (and his dog)

A pensioner who recruited a friend to drive him home after a long night's drinking has landed him in court. Whilst James Murray was well over the legal limit, having "admittedly had eight or nine beers", driver Bear McLagan was stone cold sober. This was not the problem, legally speaking. What led to him being charged with reckless driving was the fact that Mr. McLagan is completely blind. Despite being accompanied by his guide dog, it was Mr. Murray who somehow managed to provide directions on the two-mile journey from The Green Moose bar home. Nobody was injured during the trip.

3 In the dock: The Internet service provider

An eminent nuclear physicist is suing the Internet provider, Smartline Internet, for allowing libellous material to be posted on their service. Professor Juan Baptista claims that three messages posted anonymously on a newsgroup site were potentially damaging to his professional reputation and that, as a result, the ISP should have removed them. Smartline claim they are not the publishers of the comments and thus not responsible in the same way as a newspaper would be for an article and that the case represents "an assault on freedom of speech".

4 In the dock: The jilted lover

A 34-year-old woman, left seething after her boyfriend left her for another woman, is in court today facing charges of breaking and entering, cruelty to animals and criminal damage. Melissa Martins drove to her former lover's house six days after their three-month relationship had ended, kicked in his back door and then proceeded to slash his wardrobe. Shirts and trousers were left in shreds and Ms. Martins also cut the ends off all the socks in the house. Finally, she kicked her ex's prized Persian cat, Nobby, so hard it later died of internal bleeding. In her defence, Ms. Martins claims she was not in her right mind at the time.

5 In the dock: The government

The Benet people, an indigenous minority group, took the Ugandan government to court over a land dispute, which they claimed represented a gross violation of their basic human rights. The Benets are native to the Mount Elgon area in the east of the country, but were forced off their land and left destitute when the region was designated a national park. The move was intended to help boost tourism. The Benet are dependent on agriculture and argue that their displacement challenges their very existence as a tribal people.

6 In the dock: The superhacker

A man dubbed "the worst hacker of all time" has been granted bail. Gary McKinnon, 39, is facing possible extradition to the United States following claims that he gained illegal access to numerous US military and NASA computers, and deleted crucial information. It is alleged that McKinnon's actions led to certain state computers being disabled on occasion and resulted in a tracing operation that cost over $1 million. McKinnon plans to contest the charges and believes they are the result of post-9/11 paranoia. He portrays himself more as a curious voyeur than a threat to national security and says he was stunned at how easy the systems were to break into.

5 Vocabulary focus: collocations

Match the adjectives in the box with the groups of collocates.

crucial   internal   gross   turbulent

1. .... misconduct / negligence / human rights violation
2. .... history / time / home life / market / flight / region
3. .... factor / role / decision / information / stage / step
4. .... organs / flight / affairs / bleeding / investigation

Now match these adjectives with the groups of collocates.

eminent   long-standing   numerous   subliminal

5. .... advertising / messages
6. .... occasions / reports / challenges / inaccuracies
7. .... historian / scientist / explorer / scholar
8. .... tradition / history / agreement / problem / interest

Which of the adjective + noun collocations are new for you? With a partner, try to agree on a good example for each one.

For example, gross misconduct could involve being drunk at work, selling pirate material or downloading offensive material at work. It often results in dismissal.

Conversation

1 Talking about crimes

Match the verbs with the words they go with.

1.	hijack	a.	him up at gunpoint
2.	spray	b.	the door in
3.	overtake	c.	the rampage
4.	hold	d.	graffiti all over the walls
5.	kick	e.	my flat
6.	break into	f.	on a blind corner
7.	go on	g.	a security van

Now match these verbs with the words they go with.

8.	smash up	h.	on a double-yellow line
9.	force	i.	a bar
10.	fail to declare	j.	his signature
11.	do	k.	her to have sex
12.	forge	l.	all his earnings
13.	nick	m.	something from a shop
14.	park	n.	70 in a 30-mile-an-hour zone

What crimes do each of these expressions describe?

Have you heard any stories about people committing these crimes recently? What happened?

2 Listening

You're going to hear five short conversations.

Listen and decide which of the people have been victims of crimes.

Discuss with a partner if you think the statements about each conversation are true or false.

1. a. The guy who robbed them got away on foot.
   b. They felt worse after the event.
2. a. There was hardly anyone on the road when he was caught.
   b. He's going to contest the fine.
3. a. Adrian was unlucky to be caught.
   b. They think the punishment was too harsh.
4. a. There was apparently no motive for the killing.
   b. Someone chased the killer.
5. a. They live in a dangerous part of town.
   b. They think Ricki is over-protective.

Listen again and check your answers.

Real English: He got done for drink-driving.

In informal spoken English, we often say someone got done for a crime instead of they were convicted of it. It is more commonly used to talk about less serious crimes. For example:

He got done for speeding. He got a £300 fine.
He got done for tax evasion. He got three years for it.

3 Speaking

Discuss these questions in groups.

1. How do you feel about speed cameras and CCTV? Is there much use of these in your country?
2. How do people generally view the police in your country? Have you ever had any dealings with the police? Why? How did you find them?
3. Would you ever intervene in a crime? Why? Why not?

4 Using grammar: passives

Look at the examples below. Which are passive sentences?

a. I had my car broken into last week.
b. My car got broken into while I was in the shop.
c. They must've broken into the car in a matter of seconds.
d. They think they've found the culprit.
e. Two men have been arrested in relation to the robbery.
f. I had to get the car repaired after I got it back.

For more information on how to use passives, see G19.

Complete the sentences with the verbs in the correct form. Some are passive, some are active.

Conversation 1

impose realise release tow away

A: Did I tell you I (1) .... my car .... last week.
B: You're joking? Where was this?
A: It was down by the park. They've (2) .... new parking restrictions down there and I (3) ....
B: What a pain! So how much did it cost to (4) .... it .... from the pound?

Conversation 2

beat up hospitalise keep mug steer clear

A: I'm thinking of going to Ballack's Cross later.
B: Really? I'd (1) .... of there if I were you. It's quite a notorious area for thieving and the like. I know a couple of people who (2) .... down there. One of them (3) .... quite badly. He (4) .... for about a week.
A: That's terrible. Thanks for the warning. I'll (5) .... an eye out for any trouble.

Conversation 3

do get off imprison leave
do go through knock down

A: Did you see that that footballer (1) .... for reckless driving? It looks as if he's going to (2) .... They reckon he might get as much as one year.
B: Only a year? He (3) .... lightly, if that's the case. He (4) .... a woman, didn't he?
A: Yeah, apparently she (5) .... paralysed. He (6) .... 60 miles an hour in the city centre and (7) .... two red lights.
B: It's disgraceful. He would've got a lot longer than that if he wasn't so rich.

5 Practice

Think of three crimes that have been in the news or have happened to you or someone you know. Spend five minutes planning what you're going to say about them. Write a question you could use to start the conversation. Be prepared to explain what happened and / or comment on what you think of the crime.

In pairs, have conversations about the crimes like those in Activities 2 and 4.

6 Crime idioms

Discuss with a partner what you think the idioms in red mean.

1. She's too soft with her son. She lets him get away with murder.
2. Let's walk. It's murder finding a parking space at this time of the day.
3. I could've murdered her when I found out she'd lost our front door keys.
4. I need a lie-down. It was murder in the shop today.
5. I could murder a cup of tea. I haven't had one all day.
6. £4 for a cup of coffee, it was. Honestly, it's daylight robbery.
7. I can't believe we lost. Honestly, we were robbed.
8. Millions of pounds' worth of food is never sold. It's a criminal waste when there are people starving in the world.

Discuss these questions with a partner.

a. Do you know anyone who gets away with murder?
b. Have you ever felt you could've murdered someone – metaphorically speaking, of course? Why?
c. Have you seen any sports matches where a player or team was robbed? What happened?

Writing: Giving instructions and advice

1 Speaking

A cheap way to go on holiday is to do a house swap. A family in one country comes and stays in your house while you go and stay in theirs. There are a number of firms on the web that offer to put people who want to swap in touch with each other and to vet participants.

What do you think of this idea? Would you do it? Why / why not?

Look at the following possible house swaps. Who would you most like to swap with? Why?

1. A slightly run-down one-bedroom loft apartment in Brooklyn, New York.
2. A two-bedroom cottage in a remote village in Scotland.
3. A tenth-floor three-bedroom flat on the outskirts of Barcelona.
4. A spacious family bungalow close to the beach and 1.5 hours' drive from Auckland, NZ.
5. A charming two-bedroom apartment in the heart of Brussels.
6. A five-bedroom traditional house with large grounds in a town in Germany, close to the Swiss-French border.
7. A three-bedroom terraced house in the suburbs of London, 8km from the centre. Pet cats.
8. A two-bedroom luxury penthouse with a roof terrace and city views, Guadalajara, Mexico. No pets.

How would you describe your own house / flat?
Now write a description of your own house / flat in a similar style.

2 Reading

You are going to read a letter with instructions and advice to people doing a house swap. Complete each gap with one word.

Dear Olivier,

Thanks for your letter with all the details about your house and area. Just one small thing – you mentioned we could use your car, but you weren't absolutely clear about the arrangements (1) .... regard to sorting out insurance, etc. Will you do it and, if so, what details do you need (2) .... me? Apart from that, everything looks fine. So, as promised, here are all the things you need to know about our place.

Getting in

I've arranged to leave keys with two of our neighbours – in (3) .... one of them is out – Dorothy at number 3, and Vince and Duncan at number 4. They're all very friendly and will help you out if you have any problems with anything. When you come in, you'll have to turn off the burglar alarm, which you'll find in the cupboard under the stairs. The code is 6711. Again, I've told Dorothy and Vince to (4) .... you in, so you shouldn't have any problems the first day. Make sure you set the alarm when you go out, though. Close all the doors downstairs and then press AWAY and then ARM. You then have ten seconds to close the door.

The rest of the house

I think everything is fairly self-explanatory and I've left notes where you may need help. The only thing I should warn you about is that the oven is a bit temperamental. I'd keep an eye on anything you put in there, (5) .... you want it burnt to a crisp.

Shops and places to eat

We'll leave you something to eat in the fridge for when you arrive. If you've got any special requests, let us know! For the basics, like bread and milk, there's a small shop in the village, but for anything else you're (6) .... going into Skipton. There are a couple of supermarkets and on Tuesdays there's a street market. If you want to eat out, the *Six Trees* does very good food, although it is a bit pricey. The pub in the village serves a decent Sunday lunch. There are also a couple of good places in Skipton. If you like Indian food, *Shariff's* is particularly good and very reasonable. I (7) .... steer clear of *Moretti's*, the Italian on the main high street, though. We had a very bad experience when we went there last time.

Places to see

Obviously, the main attraction round here is the walking. You must go to Malham Cove and if you're feeling particularly energetic, you could try the Three Peaks. The idea is to do the 25 mile-walk, climbing all three peaks, within 12 hours. You get some fantastic views from the top. If the weather gets the better of you, you could visit the castle in Skipton or, if you don't (8) .... a bit of a drive, there's The National Museum of Film and Photography in Bradford, which is fantastic. There are a number of leaflets and maps in the cupboard and drawers in the living room. I (9) .... to admit, there's not a great deal specifically aimed at teenagers. You might be tempted by the ads for Dalesville you will see, but I really wouldn't bother. It tries to sell (10) .... as a theme park, but the rides are very small and more suited to young children. The rest of it is just a glorified farm really.

Anyway, that's about it. Obviously, if there's anything else you need to know, just get in touch.

Marjorie

Real English: The oven is a bit temperamental

If you say a mechanical device is a bit temperamental, it means that sometimes it works OK, sometimes it doesn't. If a person is temperamental, their mood can change very suddenly. For example:

The boiler's quite temperamental. Sometimes it just switches itself off for no apparent reason.

Have you got anything temperamental in your house?

Do you know anyone who can be a bit temperamental sometimes?

3 Speaking

Discuss these questions with a partner.

1. Would you like to stay in Marjorie's house? Why / why not?
2. Do you know what a typical Sunday lunch involves in the UK? Does your family have a typical Sunday lunch?
3. Does the idea of the Three Peaks walk appeal to you? Have you done anything like that before?

4 Clarifying

Match each sentence with two clarifying statements or questions.

1. You mentioned there's a swimming pool, ☐ ☐
2. Did you want us to feed your dog ☐ ☐
3. Are you definitely coming to stay in the summer ☐ ☐
4. Have you got any bicycles we could use ☐ ☐

a. or have you decided to stay put?
b. but you didn't say if it was heated or not.
c. or have you sorted out someone else to deal with it?
d. and, if so, how long for?
e. and, if not, would it be possible to hire any?
f. and, if so, can you leave instructions about its requirements?
g. and, if so, how many?
h. but I wasn't clear if it's just for the use of people from your apartment block.

Now write two different ways you could clarify each of these general statements or questions.

5. Is there anywhere to hire a car near you?
6. You mentioned there's a language school nearby.
7. Is there anywhere to buy food near you?
8. Did you want me to send you some cash for things in advance?

5 Using grammar: giving advice

Complete these pieces of advice with a modal verb and / or the correct form of the verbs in brackets.

1. I .... (steer clear) of the town centre on a Friday as it .... (get) absolutely packed and the traffic's horrendous.
2. If you .... (be into) windsurfing, you're best .... (head) to the north coast of Cornwall.
3. If you .... (never go) camping before, I .... (not recommend) going to Scotland as the weather can be quite unpredictable. Mind you, Scotland is well worth .... (visit).
4. I .... (not bother) going to that museum unless you .... (be) particularly interested in Roman artefacts.
5. If you .... (fancy) a wild night out, you .... (try) the Chocolate Factory just outside town. It's an arts complex.
6. I .... (give) the wax museum a miss if I .... (be) you unless you .... (enjoy) standing around in queues all day.
7. You absolutely .... (go) on a boat trip down the river. You .... (regret) it.
8. .... (not be tempted) by any of the 'girlie' bars in Soho. You .... (get ripped off), I promise you.

For more information on ways of giving advice, see G20.

6 Planning a letter

You are going to write a letter to one of the people whose house is advertised in Activity 1. With a partner, decide which one.

What extra information would you like to know from the house owners?

Think of where you live. What places would you recommend for shopping, eating and spending your time on holiday?

Write a letter to the owner of your chosen house. Use the letter in Activity 2 to help you. Try to use as much language from these two pages as you can.

Review: Units 13–18

1 Adjectives

Complete the sentences with the adjectives in the box.

chronic	devoted	grave	irreverent
continual	fanatical	impressive	subtle

1. He's absolutely .... to his wife and kids. It's quite touching to see – in this day and age!
2. I've got .... doubts about the whole idea. I just don't think it's feasible.
3. Oh, it's a lovely wine – quite rich and fruity, with a .... hint of chocolate.
4. She's absolutely .... about yoga and aerobics!
5. There's a .... shortage of doctors in the more rural areas.
6. There just seems to be a .... stream of people coming and going next door. It's starting to drive me mad!
7. She was unlucky to lose. It was a very .... performance for such a young player.
8. As a writer, he's always had a very .... attitude towards the establishment – and I guess that's why they've had him arrested!

Now discuss these questions with a partner.

a. Do you know anyone who's absolutely fanatical about something?
b. Can you think of any writers, musicians or directors who have an irreverent attitude towards the establishment? Do you like their work?
c. Do you have grave concerns about anything at the moment?

2 Adjective–noun collocations

Match the adjectives to the nouns they collocate with.

1. disastrous ☐ a. face
2. post-traumatic ☐ b. hatred
3. racial ☐ c. policy
4. straight ☐ d. stress

Now match these adjectives to the nouns they collocate with.

5. critical ☐ e. side
6. full-scale ☐ f. acclaim
7. subliminal ☐ g. messages
8. funny ☐ h. riot

Which verb(s) could you use with each of these adjective-noun collocations? Write an example sentence for each. Compare your sentences with a partner. Whose are more useful?

3 Passives

Complete the sentences with the correct form of the passive verbs in the box.

be coerced	be cremated	be detained
be hailed	be convicted	be denied
be diagnosed	be indicted	

1. He .... with cancer a few years ago and passed away last September. He .... and his ashes were scattered at sea.
2. It was really frustrating. I .... by customs officials for hours on end and then eventually I .... entry to the country.
3. It was awful! She .... into signing a confession and .... then .... of murder – and yet she was totally innocent!
4. Oh, the irony! They went in there expecting to .... as liberators and then their president ends up .... for war crimes!

Now complete these sentences with the correct form of the passive verbs in the box.

be arrested	be buried	be invaded
be released	be beaten up	be hospitalised
be occupied	be suspected	

5. The country .... by the Romans in AD 43 and .... then .... for four hundred years.
6. I'm going to visit my granddad's grave tomorrow. He .... in a graveyard quite near here.
7. It was quite strange. He .... of being a member of the mafia for years. Then a few weeks ago he ...., but a couple of days after that, he .... just .... without charge.
8. He got caught up in a pub fight and .... so badly that he ended up having to .... with three broken ribs.

Discuss these questions with a partner.

a. Has anyone famous been arrested recently? What for?
b. Do you know where any of your relatives are buried – or where they were cremated?
c. Has anyone you know ever been beaten up? What happened?

4 Verbs

Complete the collocations with the verbs in the box.

combat	exercise	get	open	take
contest	foil	have	slash	twist

1. .... a gas attack / a plot to bomb the city
2. .... revenge on him / me for granted
3. .... his wardrobe / his wrists / prices
4. .... fire on demonstrators / talks
5. .... the AIDS problem / terrorism
6. .... what I said / the truth / my knee
7. .... abducted / withdrawal symptoms
8. .... a do / compulsory military service
9. .... the fine / the charges / the will
10. .... your imagination / your brain

Spend one minute memorising the collocations above. Then cover the activity. Your partner will read out the ten verbs. How many collocations can you remember?

5 Grammar

Complete the sentences. Write ONE word in each space. Negatives such as *don't* or *aren't* count as one word.

1. I was .... thinking of maybe going out somewhere tonight. I don't .... anyone fancies coming with me, do ....?
2. We actually managed to meet the deadline – no mean feat .... how little time we actually had!
3. A: I really should get going.
   B: Why? It's not .... though you have to work tomorrow.
   A: No, I know. It's just .... it's late – and I want to sleep in my own bed tonight!
4. Can I call you back after 9? I'll .... finished this by then.
5. I quit my job last year – and .... looked back since!
6. If she sees something she likes, she'll buy it – .... much it costs!
7. The dinner party went pretty well, all things ....
8. It's not surprising the course didn't run, when you consider how .... people study Old German these days.
9. You .... have told me about it earlier. I .... have helped you move if I'd known.
10. If you ask me, they .... cut taxes. If they did, it .... encourage people to save more.

Compare your answers with a partner and explain your choices.

6 Look back and check

Work in pairs. Choose one of these activities.

a. **Look back at the three conversations in Activity 4 in Unit 18 on page 105. Ask your partner about any words you've forgotten. Then repeat Activity 5 on page 105, but this time, talk about three different crimes to the ones you discussed last time.**

b. **Look back at Activity 5 in Unit 13 on page 79. Check you remember all the vocabulary. Then repeat the practice at the end of the Activity, but this time, talk about two different films to the ones you discussed last time.**

7 What can you remember?

With a partner, write down as much as you can about the texts you read in Unit 14 and Unit 15.

Unit 14: Us and them?

Latent conflict and emergence

Escalation

Stalemate

De-escalation

Dispute settlement and peace building

Unit 15: We are all different, we are all the same

Which text did you enjoy more? Why?

8 Compound nouns

Make ten compound nouns by matching the first and second words.

1. an initiation		a.	politics
2. a registry		b.	office
3. guerilla		c.	provider
4. mood		d.	casualties
5. an Internet		e.	ceremony
6. conflict		f.	installation
7. border		g.	skirmishes
8. civilian		h.	warfare
9. a video		i.	swings
10. identity		j.	resolution

Discuss these questions with a partner.

- Can you remember five other kinds of ceremony?
- Do you know anyone who's prone to mood swings?
- Is identity politics much of an issue in your country? What kind?
- Have you ever been to see a video installation? What was it like?

9 Idioms

Complete each idiom with a noun. The first letters are given.

1. She spoils that kid terribly. Honestly, she lets him get away with m.. .
2. Once you start restricting political speech, it's a slippery s.. and pretty soon you could end up with awful censorship!
3. The fire was actually a bit of a b.. in disguise. I mean, the insurance payout was really useful!
4. I think you should ignore what your parents think is right. Stick to your g.. and do what's best for you.
5. Make sure you read that contract carefully. It's a potential m.. . You'll have to really watch your step with it.
6. When I told my dad I'd crashed his car, he really hit the r.. .
7. God, you've changed your t..! A week ago you never wanted to see me again, and now you suddenly want to get married!
8. He was asking £85 per ticket! Honestly, it was daylight r..!

Now discuss these questions with a partner.

a. What was the last thing you saw that you thought was daylight robbery?
b. Have your parents ever hit the roof? Why?
c. Has anything ever happened to you that you later came to see as a blessing in disguise?

10 Word building

Complete the sentences with the correct forms of the words in brackets.

1. I'm sorry, but I'm not prepared to sit here and listen to all these horrible .... jokes! (sex)
2. He had a breakdown last year and has been on anti-.. ever since. (depressed)
3. She went right up in my .... after she told the boss to get lost! (estimate)
4. My fear is that racist attacks will just lead to increased .... of certain communities. (ghetto)
5. They're developing a new .... for Alzheimer's. (treat)
6. We were held up at .... It was terrifying! (gun)
7. Let him watch it if he wants to. There's nothing wrong with a bit of harmless ...., is there? (escape)
8. I just think there's an .... on oil, that's all. (rely)

11 Vocabulary quiz

Discuss these questions in groups of three.

1. How could you obstruct the course of justice?
2. When might you be in hysterics?
3. Can you think of any up-and-coming young bands / young athletes / areas?
4. How could someone be libelled?
5. What age group often sniggers? What at?
6. What's the difference between a massacre and genocide?
7. What does someone do if they are a guinea pig?
8. What kind of things could be a front for the mafia?
9. When might someone be left seething? And left destitute?
10. Why might you chuckle to yourself?
11. When and how does collateral damage occur?
12. What's the difference between being convicted of a crime, being arrested for it, and being charged with it?
13. Why would a couple have a shotgun wedding?
14. When might you pass your condolences on to people?
15. What's the problem if a film is a bit soppy? And if it's really gory? And if it's a bit convoluted?
16. What can you rustle?
17. What's the difference between a terminal condition and a chronic one?
18. What do you want if you're a bit peckish?
19. When might you squirm?
20. What kind of ceremony might be lavish? And what kind might be solemn?

Writing

1 Grammar

Complete the second sentence so that it has a similar meaning to the first sentence, using the word in brackets.

1. If I were you, I wouldn't go to that museum – unless you're particularly interested in art and design.
   I .... to that museum – unless you're particularly interested in art and design. (bother)
2. If I were you, I wouldn't go to the Italian restaurant in town.
   If I were you, I'd .... (miss)
3. You absolutely must go on a boat trip down the river. I'm sure you'll enjoy it.
   You absolutely must go on a boat trip down the river. You .... (regret)
4. If I were you, I'd give all the bars in the town square a miss.
   .... any of the bars in the town square. (tempted)
5. The countryside to the north of the city is really amazing.
   The countryside to the north of the city is well .... (visit)
6. If you're into cinema, you really should head for the Curzon in Mayfair.
   If you're into cinema, you .... the Curzon in Mayfair. (best)
7. If you've never been hill-walking before, you're best avoiding the hills in the south of the country.
   If you've never been hill-walking before, ... the hills in the south of the country. (recommend)
8. Hever Castle is well worth visiting.
   You .... Hever Castle. (absolutely)

2 Adjectives

Complete the sentences from film reviews with the adjectives in the box.

controversial	intricate	puerile	underrated
devastating	preposterous	riveting	witty

1. This film is a real gem, though clearly very .... for it remains relatively unknown in this country.
2. The film proved highly .... upon its release and was banned in several countries.
3. The film purports to be a comedy, but seems .... and offensive in the extreme to this viewer.
4. It is an absolutely .... thriller. I was gripped from beginning to end.
5. The plot is complex, ... and full of twists and turns.
6. The ending is one of the most emotionally .... scenes in the history of cinema.
7. The whole plot is so far-fetched and .... , I turned it off after the first half hour.
8. The dialogue is sharp, fast and very, very ....

3 Describing visual information

In most lines of this piece of writing, there is one unnecessary word. It is either grammatically incorrect or does not fit in with the sense of the text. Some lines are correct. Cross out the words you think are unnecessary.

1. *This graph shows the health problems were reported in the*
2. *last year by people working 48 hours a week or more than.*
3. *Perhaps unsurprisingly, over the half of all people questioned*
4. *claimed to be suffering from mental exhaustion, whilst 43%*
5. *said they were having difficulty for sleeping. A slightly*
6. *lower percentage (40%) stated that they sometimes felt*
7. *unable to cope with, whilst just under a quarter of all*
8. *respondents suffered from chronic headaches. Anxiety and*
9. *depression afflicted just little under a fifth of those*
10. *questioned (19%), whilst 14% felt their sex drive had been*
11. *negatively affected. Both of heart and blood problems and*
12. *diarrhoea hit 12% of respondents, whilst only a small*
13. *percentage (5%) had had the ulcers and an almost*
14. *insignificant number (2%) reported alcohol or drug problems.*
15. *As it can be seen from these figures, the current culture of*
16. *overwork is taking a serious toll on those are involved in it.*
17. *These findings suggest a need for further thought for to be*
18. *paid to ways of reducing working hours, because thus helping*
19. *to improve the health of the nations' workforce.*

Compare your corrections with a partner. Did you cross out the same things?

It's not the winning, it's the taking part. • The result sparked a riot. • It's time I got rid of some of this flab. • What's your handicap? • It's mind-numbingly boring. • It's been hailed as a great victory, but I'm not so sure. • We're not competing on a level playing field. • It's just banter. • They use so much foul language. • They're role models. • It really is a cut-throat business. • It was a salutary lesson. • He must be on something. • He blew it big time. • That's a nasty challenge. • What're the odds of that happening? • Pretty slim, I would've thought. • They didn't create any clear-cut chances. • He's past it. • He's trying to rejuvenate his career. • She doesn't pull her punches, does she? • In all likelihood, they'll win. • They only just scraped through.

19 Sport and fitness

Reading

1 Speaking

Read these statements and decide how far you agree with each. Then discuss your ideas with a partner.

1. All children should participate in competitive sport.
2. Sport helps to teach valuable lessons in life.
3. Sporting competition creates divisions.
4. There is no such thing as non-competitive sport.
5. Sport distracts people from focusing on more important issues like poverty.
6. International sport breeds an unhealthy kind of nationalism.
7. It's not the winning, it's the taking part.
8. Violent sports like boxing have no place in civilised society.

2 Before you read

You are going to read an article exploring various reasons for liking and disliking sport. Match these verbs from the text with the words they go with.

1. heal	☐	a.	drama and tension
2. prevent	☐	b.	rifts
3. boost	☐	c.	civic pride
4. offer	☐	d.	people together
5. bring	☐	e.	serious matters from being discussed
6. fuel	☐	f.	tensions

Now match these verbs with the words they go with.

7. spark	☐	g.	a competitive edge
8. pick yourself up	☐	h.	a mind-numbing effect
9. use	☐	i.	sport as a conversational crutch
10. dominate	☐	j.	after a defeat
11. have	☐	k.	violence
12. foster	☐	l.	the media

Which of the 12 expressions explain why people like sport and which explain why people dislike it?

Compare your ideas with a partner.
How many other reasons for liking and disliking sport can you think of?

3 While you read

As you read this article, think about these questions.

1. Are any of the reasons for liking and disliking sport you thought of mentioned?
2. Are any other reasons mentioned?
3. Which reasons do you agree / disagree with? Why?

Keeping the sports-haters onside

PERHAPS unsurprisingly, the news that London had won its bid to host the 2012 Olympic Games was not met with universal delight. Whilst the city's mayor hailed the victory as a great moment and one which would boost civic pride, increase tourism and employment opportunities, and result in better housing, sporting and transport facilities, a significant proportion of the British population greeted the news with a mixture of cynicism and dismay. Of course, this was partly down to purely selfish reasons. Fears of a massive hike in council tax were rife and pessimists pointed to the mountain of debt that Montreal was saddled with after it hosted the 1976 Olympics: over $1 billion, a sum the city was still paying off more than 25 years after the Olympic flame had been extinguished!

However, the voices of dissent also had other issues apart from the drain on public resources, and many of them revolved around a general dislike of sport. It is undoubtedly true that sport has come to dominate the media in an absolutely unprecedented manner and, should you desire to do so, it would be quite possible to spend almost all of your waking hours channel-surfing from one sporting event to the next.

4 Speaking

Discuss these questions with a partner.

1. What major sporting events has your country hosted? Were they worth it? Why / why not?
2. Do you follow any local sports team? Do you ever watch any of your national teams or athletes competing?
3. Can you think of any recent news that's been greeted with …
   - cynicism?
   - widespread joy?
   - universal outrage?
   - astonishment?
4. Did you know any of the sports idioms mentioned in the article? Can you think of any other sports idioms like this?

Whilst football rules the roost on terrestrial TV, cable and satellite bring everything from trampolining to archery to the 'world's strongest man competition' into living rooms across the land – and many fear the Olympics will just lead to complete and utter saturation coverage with wall-to-wall sport for weeks on end. Some point to the mind-numbing effect this will have on viewers: non-stop sport tends to mean other issues fail to grab the public's attention and this can prevent far more serious matters from being discussed, or even thought about.

Others, however, lament the ruthless, competitive edge that the generally male-dominated world of sport helps foster in the young. Some women see sport not only as a pathetic conversational crutch which their male counterparts use to get them through day-to-day social exchanges, but also as a more malign influence. The combination of cut-throat big business muscling in on sport, athletes being portrayed as heroes and a win-at-any-costs mentality is seen as deeply unsavoury. Indeed, today's generation of young footballing superstars have been blamed for everything from foul language in schools to binge-drinking and even to an over-emphasis on consumerism.

Despite all this, sport's ever-increasing popularity is obviously not for nothing. Whether as a viewer or as an active participant, sport offers drama, tension, escapism and release for countless millions around the world and can provide salutary lessons in life: how to be a good loser, how to pick yourself up again after defeat, how to focus on a long-term goal. On top of this, whilst sport can obviously fuel tensions and spark violence, it can also serve to bring disparate groups of people together and heal long-standing rifts. Furthermore, as anyone who's ever been abroad equipped with almost none of the local language, but with a basic knowledge of the game can tell you, perhaps even more than English, it is football that is truly the global language now. Taxi rides and train journeys from Moscow to Mozambique have been enlivened by little more than shared smiles and the words 'Pele', 'Maradona' or 'Zidane'!

However, there is a further, far less obvious reason for keeping at least one eye on the world of sport and that is the vast impact sport has had on the English language. A whole area of metaphorical and idiomatic language has moved from a sporting context into much broader usage. For instance, **in the run-up to** an election, the opinion polls may show two parties **running neck and neck** – both polling very similar high percentages. Another idiom taken from the field of horse-racing is **horses for courses** – meaning you need to choose the right people for particular activities because everyone has different skills. Boxing fans are more likely to understand that when you **throw in the towel**, you admit defeat and that if you manage to escape from an unpleasant situation at just the right moment, you're **saved by the bell**. Similarly, keen swimmers are far more likely to grasp that being **out of your depth** means things are too difficult for you, whilst **swimming against the tide** involves refusing to do what everyone else is doing and trying to come up with your own way of doing things instead. Surely for these reasons, if for no others, sport is worthy of our attention.

5 Idioms

Complete the idioms with the words in the box.

bait	belt	court	playing field	sights
base	course	goalposts	punches	water

1. They still subsidise their farming industry really heavily and we don't, so we don't have a level ………………………… to compete on.
2. Our daughter's 16 now and she's got her ………………………… set firmly on becoming a doctor. I can't believe how focused she is!
3. A turnout of around 50% at elections seems to be par for the ………………………… now.
4. I'll say one thing for her. She's very direct. I mean, she says exactly what she thinks. She doesn't pull any ………………………… .
5. We've told them what we're willing to offer, so now the ball is in their ………………………… . It's up to them to decide what they want to do.
6. I met every single sales target the boss set me, but he just kept moving the ………………………… and changing what he wanted me to do!
7. I don't mind him criticising me, but when he called me a moron, well, I thought that was a bit below the ………………………… !
8. My landlord put my rent up last year and since then I've been struggling to keep my head above ………………………… .
9. Chris is over from Boston next week. It'll be good to touch ………………………… . It's been quite a while since I saw him last.
10. There's no point laughing at my team. I'm not going to rise to the ………………………… and start arguing with you about it!

Underline the whole idiom in each sentence. Which sport do you think each idiom comes from originally?

Now discuss these questions with a partner.

a. Have you ever felt completely out of your depth? When?
b. Do you know anybody who doesn't pull any punches? Does it bother you that they're like that?
c. Have you got your sights set on anything at the moment? What?
d. Is there anyone you need to touch base with at the moment?

Conversation

1 Discussing players and teams

Discuss with a partner which of these sentences you think are positive and which are negative. Explain your decisions.

1. She just lacks a certain self-belief.
2. He's gorgeous!
3. He's all power and strength, and no touch.
4. He's the weak link in the team.
5. He's a really nasty player.
6. They have too many off days.
7. He must be on something.
8. He's an up-and-coming player. He's the new Pete Sampras.
9. He's got such drive and intensity.
10. She's quite underrated.
11. He's past it.
12. They've never quite fulfilled their potential.
13. He went off the rails.
14. He's trying to rejuvenate his career.
15. He's a gutsy player. He never gives up.
16. He can't handle it when the pressure's on.

Make a list of five sportsmen, sportswomen or teams which you could use some of these expressions to describe. Talk with a partner about the players you chose. Has your partner heard of them? What do they think of them?

2 Listening

You are going to listen to three people – Lee, Terry and Grace – talking about a game. Listen and answer these questions:

1. What was the score?
2. What is each person's view of the game?

Are you similar to either the men or the woman? In what way?

3 Listen again

Discuss which person said the following and what they were talking about.

1. It was miles offside.
2. Talk about a waste of money!
3. All they do is boot it up the field.
4. Can he keep it up for a whole season?
5. The likelihood is you'll get relegated.
6. It's just a bit of friendly banter.
7. That old chestnut!
8. It's so tribal.
9. That lot are not exactly models of good behaviour.
10. That's got to be the most feeble argument I've ever heard!

Listen again and check your answers.

Now look at the tapescript and underline five useful collocations or expressions you would like to remember.

Real English: That old chestnut

An old chestnut is a story, joke, argument or excuse which has been repeated so many times that you are bored of it, or – in the case of arguments or excuses – you just don't believe anymore.

A: *Sorry, I haven't got my homework. My dog ate it!*
B: *Oh, not that old chestnut again! Do I look stupid?*

4 Speaking

Discuss these questions with a partner.

1. Do you know any teams who have been in financial difficulties? What happened?
2. Have there been any problems with hooliganism recently?
3. Do you think there is much racism in sport?
4. Do you agree that football supporters are different to other kinds of sports fans? Why / why not?
5. Does 'bad behaviour' by sports people bother you?

5 Expressing degrees of certainty

Choose the two correct forms in each sentence.

1. A: I *bet / guess / hope* they do better than they did last year.
   B: *Fat / No / Impossible* chance!
2. A: The British guy doesn't have *a chance / an opportunity / a hope* of winning.
   B: I don't know. I think he's got *a similar / an even / a reasonable* chance.
3. There's a *definite / really / distinct* possibility that they'll call an election some time this year and the *likelihood / possibility / probability* is that the Conservatives will win.
4. The chances of Leeds ever winning the title are pretty *slender / slim / skinny*.
5. The *odds / chances / possibilities* are I won't get into Cambridge University, but it's worth a try.
6. You shouldn't worry about it so much. I mean, what are the odds of any of us actually getting killed in an aeroplane? Pretty *low / little / slim*, I would've thought.
7. I'll do my best to finish the report by Friday, but in all *likelihood / chance / probability*, it won't be ready till Monday.

Real English: The odds

When you make a bet in a bookmaker's (or 'bookies'), you look at the odds – the chances of something happening, expressed as a number (10 to 1, for example). In spoken English, we often use the odds to mean the probability of something happening – or not happening.

A: *What're the odds of Iceland actually winning?*
B: *About a million to one, I would've said.*

Now complete these sentences with your own ideas.

a. The chances of me getting married in the next few years are ....
b. There's .... chance .... will win the league this year.
c. If there was an election this year, the likelihood is ....
d. There's a .... possibility I ....
e. What are the odds of .... ?

Discuss what you have written with a partner.

For more information on expressing degrees of certainty, see G21.

6 Talking about sports and keeping fit

Complete the texts with the words in the box.

challenging	dribbled	hacked
off-piste	charging	drown
kickabout	undertow	dragged under
flipped	obsessive	virgin

1. I guess I'm a bit (1) .... about it. I go most weekends to a resort near our town, but the runs aren't that (2) .... and there isn't much in the way of (3) .... stuff. I went to Colorado last year, where there was loads of (4) .... snow. It was incredibly exhilarating.
2. We were just having a (1) .... in the park really, but this one guy was taking it all really seriously, (2) .... around like a lunatic and screaming at his team-mates if they didn't pass. Anyway, at one point I (3) .... past him and he tackled me – or rather (4) .... me down – and he managed to break my leg!
3. It was quite frightening actually, because one wave (1) .... me over and I could feel there was a really strong (2) ...., and I had to kick really hard to stop myself being (3) .... I did think for a moment I might even (4) ....

Now complete these texts with the words in the box.

beat	calls	fade	paced
blasted	collapsed	fell apart	play-off
blew	dropped	get	whacking

4. It was great. I think I (1) .... my personal best by about 10 minutes! I felt so strong all the way round and I didn't (2) .... towards the end like I normally do. I think I (3) .... myself a bit better – didn't set off so fast. Last time, I really hit the wall and nearly (4) .... in exhaustion.
5. She was playing really well, but then she had a couple of bad line (1) .... at crucial moments, and I think she let it (2) .... to her and her whole game just (3) .... She just kept (4) .... it out of the court or netting it. It was just embarrassing!
6. He completely (1) .... it. I think he (2) .... five shots over the last three holes. He could've still got into a sudden-death (3) .... right at the end, but he (4) .... it right over the green and took three to get down from there.

Which sports are being discussed in each of the six texts?
Do you ever watch – or take part in – any of these sports?
Have you ever seen any of the things described happen – or have they ever happened to you?

20 Belief

My folks are quite devout. • I'm fasting at the moment. • I'm a lapsed Catholic. • I attend church regularly. • He converted to Judaism. • I only go for the hymns. • They don't moralise about how I should live my life. • It commands us to give to charity. • You should judge things on their merits. • Ours is a very secular society. • I'm a bit sceptical about that kind of thing. • She's very evangelical about it. • May the force be with you! • I don't believe in reincarnation. • It draws on pagan mythology. • He's dabbled in Buddhism. • It's been entirely discredited. • It's verging on genius. • It's helped to centre me. • They celebrate the winter solstice. • You have to live with the consequences. • It's a rather misguided belief. • That's bad karma, man! • Personally, I swear by it. • It's been blown up out of all proportion.

Conversation

1 Talking about religion

Complete the conversations with the words in the box.

agnostic	brought up	meditates	practising
atheist	converted	mosque	pray
became	higher power	out there	supposed
believe	Mass	practise	

1. A: Are you religious at all, Marie?
   B: Yeah, kind of. I was (1) .... as a Catholic. My folks are quite devout, so we used to go to (2) .... together at least once a week, but I don't really (3) .... anymore. I mean, I stopped going to confession years ago and I don't really (4) .... much anymore. I do still go to church when I visit my parents, but that's about it.
2. A: Are you religious at all?
   B: No, not really. I mean, I do believe there must be something (1) .... , you know, some kind of (2) .... , but I don't know if I'd call it God or what. I suppose I'd have to say I'm (3) ....
3. A: Are you religious at all, Ron?
   B: No, not even in the slightest. To be honest with you, I don't (1) .... in God at all. I'm a complete (2) .... Religions have caused so many wars, I'd rather just believe in people instead.
4. A: Have you seen much of Will since university?
   B: Yeah, I have, actually. Did you know he (1) .... a Buddhist? He (2) .... a couple of years ago and he's really serious about it now. He (3) .... for about three hours a day. He's like a completely different person.
5. A: What religion are you, Budi?
   B: I'm Muslim.
   A: Oh right. (1) .... ?
   B: Pretty much, yeah. I don't eat pork or drink. I go to the (2) .... on Fridays, but I'm not as devout as some people. I mean, you're (3) .... to pray five times a day, but I just don't have the time.

Real English: My folks

This is an everyday way of saying my parents. However, folk is also often used to mean people (in this case, it is an uncountable noun). We can also address groups of people by saying Folks.

I've got my folks coming down for the weekend.
We met some nice folk there.
OK, folks. Is everybody ready? OK. Let's get started.

2 Speaking

Discuss these questions with a partner.

1. Do people ever ask you about your religion? Would it bother you if someone did?
2. Do you know anyone who's quite devout?
3. Do you know anyone who's converted? Why?

3 Practising your faith

The sentences below refer to beliefs and practices of different religions (shown in brackets). Look at the words in red. Do you know what they mean? Check with a partner.

1. My daughter's got her confirmation soon. (Christianity)
2. I've given up chocolate for Lent. (Christianity)
3. Is there a halal butcher's anywhere in town? (Islam)
4. She doesn't wear a full veil – just a headscarf. (Islam)
5. I'm fasting at the moment. (Islam)
6. My son had his circumcision ceremony recently. (Judaism)
7. There's a synagogue just round the corner. (Judaism)
8. Do you know if this meat is kosher? (Judaism)
9. I believe in reincarnation. (Buddhism)
10. She wears a bindi. (Hinduism)
11. We've got a little shrine in the garden, where we burn incense and leave offerings. (Hinduism)
12. The indigenous tribes there still worship the sky and the sea and the volcanoes. (Animism)

Now discuss these questions with a partner.

a. Do you know if any other religions have any of these practices or beliefs?
b. Do you know anyone who follows any of these beliefs or practices?
c. Do you know anything else about the beliefs and practices of the different religions mentioned?

4 Listening

Three colleagues – Arthur, Gary and Jamelia – are talking about their plans for the Christmas holidays. Jamelia is a Jehovah's Witness.

Before you listen, tell a partner what you know about Jehovah's Witnesses.

Now listen and note down anything new you learn about Jamelia's beliefs and practices.

5 Listen again

Listen to the conversation again and try to answer these questions.

1. How does Gary's wife feel about her parents coming down for the holidays? Why?
2. How do Gary's kids feel about it? Why?
3. What's Gary's main goal for the holidays?
4. What's Arthur up to over Christmas?
5. What four reasons does Jamelia put forward for not celebrating Christmas?
6. How does Arthur take the mickey out of Gary?
7. In what way does Gary rub Jamelia up the wrong way?
8. How does Jamelia usually spend her weekends? Why?

Discuss your ideas with a partner.

Now look at the tapescript on page 159 and underline three words or expressions you'd like to know more about. Ask some other students for help. Then ask your teacher if you need to.

6 Speaking

Discuss these questions with a partner.

1. How would you have reacted to Jamelia's comments about Christmas? Why?
2. How do you feel about evangelical religions?
3. The American Constitution enshrines the principles of freedom of religion and freedom of worship. Do you think this is a good idea?
4. The American Constitution also argued for a secular state: the separation of church and state. Do similar arguments exist in your country?

7 Using grammar: verb patterns

In the conversation, Jamelia said that Jesus 'never commanded anyone to celebrate his birth'. Complete these sentences by putting the verbs in brackets into the correct form. Some sentences require a negative. You may also need to add prepositions.

1. He's quite devout, but what I really admire about him is the fact that he refuses .... about the way other people choose to lead their lives. (moralise)
2. I went to confession and confessed .... money from my brother. It was a real weight off my shoulders. (steal)
3. I think most religions warn their followers .... drunk, don't they? (get)
4. The Holy Book urges you .... for yourself. (think)
5. My RE teacher at school once accused me .... about my true religious feelings! He couldn't accept I was an atheist! (lie)
6. I still don't get why you insisted .... your daughter baptised if you're not really all that religious. (have)
7. I used to really object .... my religion printed on my ID card. (have)
8. I didn't grow the beard for religious reasons or anything like that. It was really just because my wife nagged me .... it. (try)
9. The priest managed to persuade her .... an abortion. (have)
10. I believe that God has commanded us all .... even our enemies. (love)

For more information on verb patterns, see G22.

Now discuss these questions with a partner.

a. What was the last thing you were nagged into doing?
b. Have you ever been accused of something you didn't do?
c. What kind of things did your parents and teachers warn you not to do? Did you heed all of their advice?
d. Is there anything you object to? Why?

Reading

1 Speaking

Read these ten statements and decide whether you agree with them or not, and to what extent.

1. When people stop believing in God, they don't believe in nothing – they believe in anything. (G. K. Chesterton)
2. Any belief that helps centre people is a good thing.
3. Most people today don't have a coherent system of beliefs.
4. If you believe in science, you can't believe in religion.
5. There are all kinds of strange phenomenon in the universe which science can't explain.
6. There must be life on other planets.
7. We all need some kind of faith to help us get through.
8. Religious people have always produced the best art.
9. It's not religion that causes wars – it's politics.
10. Religion stops people thinking for themselves.

Discuss your ideas with a partner.

2 Before you read

You are going to read an article about contemporary attitudes to religion. To help you understand the article better, here are a few definitions.

A census is an official count of the number of people living in a country. It also obtains other information about people – such as their age, religion, etc.

The Jedi are a fictional religious group featured in the *Star Wars* films.

Taoism is an ancient Chinese belief system that says people should try to lead a simple, natural life.

Crop circles are parts of fields where crops have been flattened – often in the shape of a circle. Some people believe they are made by aliens.

New Age beliefs reject many modern Western values in favour of an eclectic approach to spirituality that incorporates many ancient and non-Western ideas.

Had you heard about Jedis, Taoism, crop circles or New Age beliefs before? What else do you know about them?

3 While you read

Now read the article. As you read, think about the degree to which the writer would agree with the ten statements in Activity 1.

When you have finished reading, discuss your ideas with a partner. Find a new partner and discuss to what degree you agree with what the writer says.

Feel the force!

The rise of Jedism

The most recent census of the British population revealed that the fourth-largest religion in Britain – with 390,000 followers – is Jediism. That is Jediism as in the film *Star Wars*, as in 'May the force be with you!' When I first heard this, I thought it must be some kind of joke, and indeed closer inspection revealed that the figures had been inflated by the circulation of a chain e-mail, which claimed that if 10,000 people identified themselves as Jedis on the census form, the 'faith' would be officially recognised as a legal religion. However, doing a search on the Internet uncovers over 35,000 hits and several of the sites dedicated to 'believers' seem to be fairly serious. Here, for example, are some extracts:

> 'Many religions started with a scripture. Jedi's just happened to be written on a strip of celluloid. Like all religions, we should be judging it on its merits and relevance to our own lives, not by the medium by which it is conveyed.'

and

> 'I had a friend who practised Jediism. Of course, from what he explained to me about his beliefs, it sounded more like a *Star Wars*-ish form of Taoism than a separate belief system, but it really seemed to centre my friend and give him strength, so I said, more power to him.'

Shopping for a god

Of course, the last speaker is not far off when she says Jediism is connected to Taoism. The director and writer George Lucas used a mixture of ancient and pagan myths, which he had learned about in the writings of Joseph Campbell, to create his new fictional religion. That this has been actually adopted by some people is perhaps not that surprising, as a similar kind of pick 'n' mix belief system appears to be becoming increasingly prevalent. People pick and choose aspects of different religions and customs. While many people still like to be baptised, get married in church and have a religious funeral with prayers and hymns, relatively few actually bother to attend church on any kind of regular basis – except for a nice sing-along at the Christmas carol service. Furthermore, among these

people, you're likely to find a few who dabble in a bit of meditation and Buddhism or have environmental beliefs that verge on animism!

Science and mumbo-jumbo

It may also seem ironic that a science fiction film should spawn this kind of anti-scientific thinking, but again this kind of confusion is everywhere. Churchgoing in Britain has been in decline, due in part to the rise of science and technology, and yet at the very same time there has been an explosion of interest in all kinds of things which have, at best, only a tenuous scientific basis. I know people who variously swear by taking large amounts of vitamin supplements to stave off colds, visit homeopaths, carry crystals in their bags to give them confidence, have horoscope readings done, feng shui their home, and believe in crop circles and alien abductions. Some of these things haven't been fully tested, although logic may dictate they can't be true. Others have been discredited by science and yet still people believe in them.

The wiser choice

It seems as if we almost need some kind of faith as humans. While we can see that science works and brings technological and health benefits, we also recognise that it doesn't deal very well with our emotional or spiritual lives or answer the big questions such as 'Why are we here?' Feeling bereft and lost without a religion, many turn to the rather more commercial battery of self-help books and courses which promise to 'transform your life'. While many of these use pseudoscientific language, you nevertheless need faith to believe they really will work.

If faith, then, is a matter of choosing between one of the ancient faiths and these pick 'n' mix beliefs, I would take one of the older faiths any day. They have produced better art, more beautiful buildings and better music than any of these New Age self-help cults. And they also have the benefits shown by a recent scientific study – people with a religious faith are generally happier and live longer!

4 Word check

Complete these sentences with the correct form of the verbs in the box.

reveal	dedicate	adopt	swear
inflate	judge	pick	verge

1. You can't just .... and choose the bits you want to believe in. You have to take it as a whole.
2. Personally, I .... by this shampoo. It certainly got rid of my dandruff!
3. I don't want to be treated differently to anyone else just because my dad's the boss! I want to be .... on my results.
4. A recent survey has .... that the traditional British nuclear family is less and less common.
5. I work for a charity .... to helping people with learning difficulties.
6. That film is amazing! It's .... on genius!
7. I don't know why, but my son has recently .... all these horrible American slang words!
8. If you ask me, the media have .... the number of deaths. They always blow things up out of all proportion.

Now look at the article again and find these eight verbs. Underline the words they went with. Using your dictionary, try to find at least one more useful collocation for each verb.

Now discuss these questions with a partner.

- Which musicians / films do you think are verging on genius?
- Has anyone made any decisions recently that you think are verging on madness?
- Are there any brands you swear by? Why?

5 Speaking

Do you believe in any of these things?
Do you know anybody who does?

conspiracy theories	out-of-body experiences
feng shui	palm reading
fortune telling	reincarnation
ghosts	telepathy
karma	the power of crystals

Discuss your ideas with a partner.

Writing: Making requests and enquiries

1 Speaking

Have you ever had to write and request or enquire about any of these things? Tell a partner.

1. a refund
2. the correction of a billing error
3. an estimate
4. a copy of an official document
5. a discount or a free product sample
6. information from a government agency
7. information from a school or university
8. acknowledgement of receipt of something

2 Stating your purpose

When we write e-mails to people we know relatively well, the language we use is very similar to everyday spoken English. Letters to people we know less well are much more likely to be formal.

Circle the words in red which are more appropriate for the context.

a. Hi Jamir. You couldn't just quickly send / forward me a note saying you've received that cheque, could you?
b. I am writing to request / ask for a complimentary copy of *Practising English Writing*, as advertised in your sales brochure.
c. I am writing to inform you of the fact / tell you that in a recent statement I was overcharged by thirty pounds / ripped off.
d. I am writing to request that you reimburse me / give me back in full the amount sent with my recent order from your company.
e. Hi Mike. Just a quick one to ask if you could let me know / inform me how much the tickets will be.
f. I am writing to request further information regarding / more info about the current situation in Sierra Leone and to see / determine whether the Home Office is currently telling people not to / advising against travel to the country.
g. I would be most grateful if you could / Can you forward me details of your course fees and dates for the next academic year.
h. I am writing to enquire about the chances / possibility of acquiring / getting hold of a replica of my birth certificate.

Now match these lines to the eight different kinds of letters and e-mails in Activity 1.

3 Using grammar: softening

We sometimes use past forms to show politeness, but more generally we extend the questions using some typical starters. These forms make it easier for the person we're writing to to say no.

Complete the questions with these polite starters.

Could you do me a favour	Would it be at all possible
Do you know	Would you mind
I was wondering	You couldn't
Is there any way	You wouldn't happen

1. .... if you and Jan would like to come over for dinner on Friday?
2. .... and just quickly fax me over the Burns report?
3. .... to have a copy of the FR30-L7 form lying around, would you? If you do, could you get it couriered over to me asap?
4. .... re-send the link for that Dutch news site, could you?
5. .... you could forward me a list of the names and addresses of all those involved in the incident?
6. .... to get a copy of our rental agreement sent to me at this e-mail address?
7. .... asking Mr. Lewis if he'd mind having a brief look at a manuscript I would like to submit in the near future?
8. .... what time Mr. Wang will be arriving, by any chance?

Can you put these words into the correct order to make one very long polite request?

me / I / you / your / you / huge / don't / favour / possibly / a / suppose / do / and / me / laptop / could / could / lend? I'd be incredibly grateful!

4 Listening

The polite ways of starting questions in Activity 3 are also common in spoken English.

Listen to eight questions. You will also hear the answers. Which two are sarcastic?

Now write five questions of your own. Ask other students in the class. They can reply as they wish.

5 Practice

Re-write these questions using the word in brackets, so they sound more polite.

1. Whereabouts in Venice is he staying? (happen)
2. Could you check this letter for me? (favour)
3. Could you possibly send me over some of that saffron from Tehran? (couldn't)
4. Could you get the report back to me by Friday? (possible)
5. Is it OK if I don't pay the bill till next month? (would / mind)
6. Can you pass my name and address on to him? (any way)
7. Do you want to write an article for our magazine? (wondering / like)
8. When is the delivery due? (know / chance)

Now work with a partner and write short two- or three-line replies to these questions.

'Yes, sir. The prices are given on request. However, all requests must be in writing.'

6 Speaking

Discuss these questions with a partner.

1. Have you ever been on a school exchange trip to another country? Where did you go? What was it like?
2. Have you ever been abroad to study a foreign language? How long for? Did you enjoy it?
3. What kind of factors are important for you when choosing a place to study?

7 A letter of request

Complete the letter with one word in each space.

Via Principe Amedeo 141,
Bari 70121
Italy

22nd May 2006

The Carnaby School of English
42 Carnaby Road
Hull HU1 9QV

Dear Sir / Madam,

I am writing to enquire (1) .... the English courses offered at your school as I am currently (2) .... to send my 17-year-old daughter, Lucia, to England for two months this summer.

I would be most (3) .... if you could forward me details regarding the levels, times and cost of classes offered. I am keen for Lucia to study at (4) .... three hours a day, if that is at all possible. I was also (5) .... if your school offers any kind of social programme, as I am sure she would be (6) .... in exploring the city and getting the chance to meet other students.

Finally, would it be at all (7) .... to forward me details of accommodation for students that is available in Hull. If possible, I would like my daughter to stay with an English host family as I feel that would help her integrate whilst also ensuring she has the opportunity to practise her English on a daily (8) .... Does the Carnaby School arrange any form of home stay itself, by any (9) .... ?

I look forward to hearing from you soon and thank you in (10) .... for your help,

Yours faithfully,

Marcello Lupoli

Marcello Lupoli

8 Writing your own e-mail

Read the advertisement below. You are going to write an e-mail to Davy enquiring about the tuition he offers. Underline or make a list of the expressions from this unit that you'd like to use in your e-mail. Remember that e-mails are closer to spoken English than formal written English.

Cover the expressions and write your first draft. Then check that you used the expressions correctly and write a second draft.

The hubcap fell off. • Just stick it in the boot. • Open up the bonnet and I'll have a look. • He clipped it when he went past. • I stalled in the middle of this big junction. • I had a gut feeling something was up. • You wouldn't want to bump into him on a dark night. • It just wouldn't budge. • Are you going away? • It rather shattered my illusions. • We dragged the kids round the museum. • They were in a right sulk. • We had a slap-up meal. • It was just a wild goose chase. • I wouldn't bother. • I agree with you up to a point. • He's a bit of a xenophobe. • I think he just said it out of ignorance. • I just go out of habit these days. • We got completely fleeced. • OK, let's put you out of your misery, then. • She just wouldn't let it lie.

21 Travel and tourism

Conversation

1 Different kinds of vehicles

What are the advantages of each of these different kinds of cars? Discuss your ideas with a partner.

an automatic	an estate	a hatchback	a limo
a convertible	a 4 × 4	a manual	a sports car

Now discuss the advantages of these kinds of vehicle.

a camper van   a folding bike   a moped   a van

Can you think of any downsides to owning any of these vehicles?

Real English: a limo

Limo is the usual everyday way of saying limousine. Limos are usually driven by a chauffeur, whereas buses, trains and taxis are driven by drivers. Very long limos are usually called stretch limos.

We hired a chauffeur-driven limo for my birthday and got driven round the city centre all evening!

Have you ever been in a limo? When?

2 Speaking

Discuss these questions with a partner.

1. Have you ever owned any of the vehicles in Activity 1? What were they like?
2. Do any particular cars hold any special memories for you? Why?
3. If money was no object, what kind of car would you most like to own?
4. Are there any cars you wouldn't be seen dead in? Why?

3 Parts of a car

Label the picture with the words in the box.

headlights	number plate	windscreen
bonnet	tyre	windscreen wipers
bumper	indicator	wing mirror

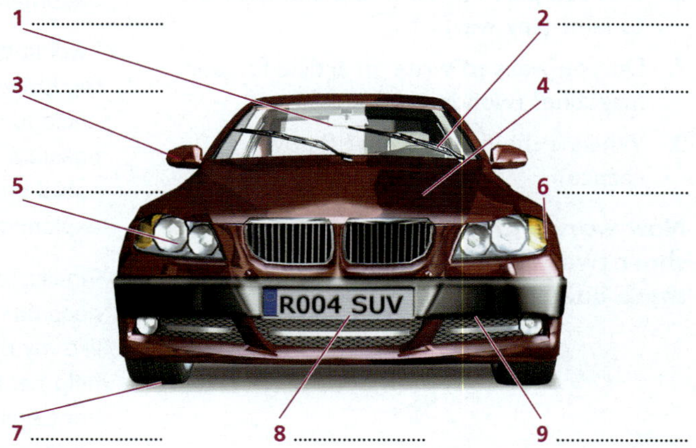

Now label this picture with the words in the box.

accelerator	clutch	gear stick
horn	steering wheel	brake
dashboard	handbrake	

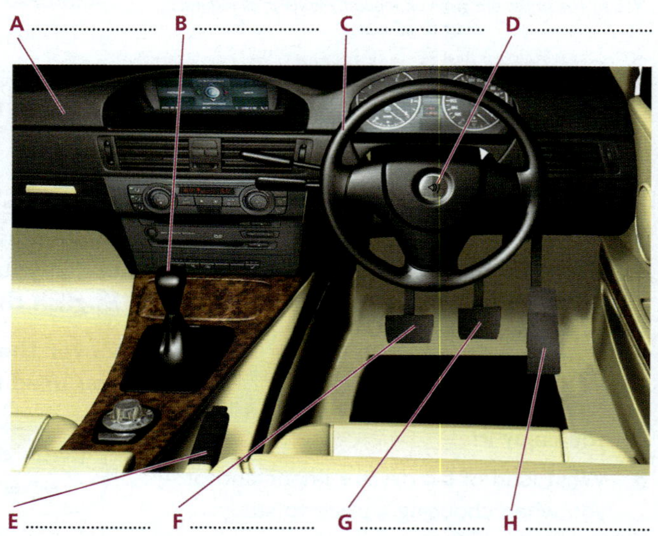

Work with a partner. Take turns to show your partner one of the pictures above, but with the box covered. How many words can your partner remember?

4 Talking about cars and driving

Complete the sentences with nouns from Activity 3.

1. The guy coming towards us didn't dip his .... , so I was dazzled for a minute and nearly drove off the road!
2. Some idiot knocked my .... off yesterday. He must've just clipped it when he went past. I'd better get it sorted quickly. I don't want to get stopped by the police.
3. I was driving my mum home when some little monster threw a stone from a bridge and it completely shattered my ....
4. I need to get someone to look at the .... It keeps slipping and I can't use the gears properly.
5. This red light on the .... came on and then it just wouldn't stop flashing for ages! It was really distracting!
6. I was reversing into a parking space and somehow managed to step on the .... instead of the .... ! I went crashing into the car behind!
7. It was bucketing down and the .... wouldn't work, so I couldn't see a thing. We had to pull over and wait for the rain to stop.
8. I must've forgotten to put the .... on when I parked, because the car rolled down this slope and into the lake!

Have you ever had any of these problems?

Have you ever had any other problems with any of the other things in Activity 3?

5 Listening

You're going to hear four people – Julie, Mandy, John and James – talking about bad experiences in cars. Listen and answer these questions about each one.

a. What was the problem?
b. Who was driving the car?
c. What happened in the end?

Discuss which person said the following and what they were talking about.

1. I really thought we were goners.
2. We were obviously completely at his mercy.
3. It was much posher than our old heap.
4. I just kind of went with the flow.
5. I needed to fill up.
6. I was such a bag of nerves.
7. He then proceeded to completely fleece us.
8. My concentration went to pieces.
9. I stalled.
10. It was all starting to look ever more like a wild goose chase.
11. He put me out of my misery.
12. I had a gut feeling something was up.

Listen again and check your answers.

6 Speaking

Discuss these questions with a partner.

1. Have you ever had any bad taxi experiences?
2. Have you passed your driving test? If you have, did you pass first time?
3. What would you say are your strong points and weak points as a driver?
4. Have you ever thought you were a goner? When? What happened?

7 Using grammar: *wouldn't*

In the fourth listening, James said that 'No matter how I twisted it or pulled it, it just wouldn't come off'.

Read the information on how to use *wouldn't* in G23 on page 170. Then divide these sentences into four groups of two, according to the different uses and meanings of *wouldn't*.

1. They promised me it wouldn't cost more than a hundred.
2. I tried to talk him out of it, but he wouldn't change his mind.
3. You wouldn't want to bump into him on a dark night!
4. Sorry I'm late. My car wouldn't start!
5. It wouldn't have made any difference even if I had braked harder.
6. It gives me no pleasure to say this, but I did tell you we wouldn't win!
7. I wouldn't have said he was arrogant – but he is very self-confident.
8. If it hadn't been for her, I wouldn't have lost my job.

Compare your ideas with a partner. Explain your decisions.

8 Practice

What do you think happened in each of the situations reported in these sentences?

1. They just wouldn't let me in.
2. He just wouldn't believe me.
3. It just wouldn't budge.
4. She just wouldn't accept my apology.
5. He just wouldn't leave me alone.
6. He just wouldn't let it lie.

Have you ever had any of these problems?

Tell a partner what happened.

Reading

1 Speaking

Discuss these questions with a partner.

1. Have you travelled much?
2. What's your favourite place you've been to on holiday? What was the most disappointing place? Why?
3. Do you know anyone who never goes away on holiday? Why don't they?
4. Do you live in a tourist area? Is this a good or bad thing?
5. Have you heard of any arguments put forward against travel and tourism? Think in terms of culture and society, economics and the environment.

2 As you read

You are going to read an article by the father of a family that never goes away on holiday. Read and find out why. As you read, also decide which of the words in red means:

1. a huge argument
2. achievements
3. a feeling of being unable to think clearly
4. angry and silent because you didn't get your own way
5. make me annoyed
6. ripped off
7. occasional
8. required for a particular purpose
9. do unimportant things in a leisurely way
10. look for customers
11. push and knock against people in a crowd
12. spend lots of money on something extravagant

When you have finished reading, cover the text and discuss the reasons the father gives for not going on holiday.

Can you remember all the words in red and how they were used?

3 Comprehension

Which of these statements about the text do you agree with?

1. The writer is just tight-fisted.
2. The writer is basically just a bit of a lazy slob.
3. The writer is too soft on his children.
4. I feel the same way about sightseeing as he does.
5. I think the writer's a bit xenophobic.
6. He must've just been unlucky with problems on holiday.
7. None of those things have ever happened to me.

Have a break from holidays

While many of our friends are on holiday in exotic far-flung places this summer, our family will be staying at home to get away from it all, as we have done for the last five years. We generally just potter about at home; catch up with some reading; do a spot of gardening – nothing too strenuous – just mow the lawn or do a bit of pruning – that kind of thing. The kids are old enough to go off on their own and often go to the local park or open-air pool. We often have visitors and this year we've got some friends coming over from the States, so we might go on the odd day trip somewhere – visit a stately home or something like that. On the whole, though, we don't bother going much beyond our local area. It's a pattern we're going to stick to for the foreseeable future for a number of reasons.

First and foremost, it's just much more relaxing. You don't have any of the inconveniences and annoyances which are so often associated with travelling: endless queuing at airports; getting fleeced by taxi drivers and souvenir sellers; getting an upset stomach from dodgy food and the local tap water. And that's not to mention the kids whinging 'Are we there yet?' every two minutes; 'Do we HAVE to go to the museum?'; endless choruses of 'BORING!' Honestly, there's nothing like dragging a couple of sulky teenagers round some Roman remains to put you off that kind of thing for life. All this whining would inevitably wind me up, which in turn would lead to a blazing row where I would rant and rave about how ungrateful they were, and how anyone else would leap at the chance to see the places we were taking them, and then I'd threaten them that next time we'd just stay at home! Well, finally I carried out the threat – and everyone's far, far happier, not to say better off! By saving money on travel, we can afford to splash out on a slap-up meal in a decent restaurant and get the best seats in the house if we go to the theatre, which, by the way, is of greater benefit to our own economy.

If the truth be told, I can't say I ever *really* enjoyed going sightseeing anyway. I think we were going on holiday simply out of habit and going sightseeing out of some weird sense of duty. I felt it was what you ought to do when you go abroad and that it would be educational for the kids. Most of the time, though, these places actually just left me cold. I wandered through them in a slight daze, took the requisite photos, made the required comments about how fascinating it was, but essentially felt nothing! Even the really big monuments, which are genuinely impressive, didn't move me in the way I expected. Take the Pyramids. I'd always wanted to go and see them. I'd imagined myself trekking through the desert on a camel to reach them, the sun beating down on my back. The reality, when I finally went there, was that I only had to trek through the streets of Cairo in a taxi to reach them. Far from being in the middle of the desert, they are surrounded by the slightly run-down suburb of Giza. While they are hugely impressive feats of engineering, you have to jostle with hoards of tourists to get anywhere near them, fighting off the crowds of locals as they tout for business, hassling you to change money or to take a camel ride. I don't blame these people – they're just trying to earn a living – but frankly, I could've done without it and, for me at least, it meant the Pyramids didn't live up to my expectations. And that's it. I've come to realise that famous places are just so much more enjoyable in anticipation than in reality, so it's best not to shatter your dreams and simply never visit them!

4 Debating

Look at the following conversations:

A: Staying at home is just a lot less stressful than travelling!

B: I know what you mean in a way, but don't you find it's easy to get drawn into doing work-related things when you're at home?

A: I just think all the construction work connected with tourism is putting a terrible strain on local services.

B: Fair enough, but it's also boosting the local economy and providing employment.

We often partially agree or concede a point before we go on to disagree or put an alternative argument forward. We use several fixed expressions to do this.

Put the words in order and make complete expressions.

1. know / I / mean / what / you
2. way / true / that's / a / in
3. that / is / truth / some / in / there
4. fair / I / that's / a / comment / guess
5. with / point / agree / up / you / to / a / I
6. suppose / argue / I / that / you / could
7. you're / can / I / see / at / what / getting
8. that's / certain / a / up / only / point / to / true

Now practise saying the expressions.

5 Practice

You are going to debate the idea that we should all travel less and restrict the growth of tourism. Student A should agree with this statement and Student B should disagree.

Spend two or three minutes thinking about what you are going to say and then have the debate with your partner. Make sure you have at least five points to support your argument. Try to use some of the expressions from Activity 4.

6 *Out of habit*

Look at this sentence from the text.

We were going on holiday simply out of habit and going sightseeing out of some weird sense of duty.

Out of + a noun shows the reason for doing something.

Complete the sentences with the nouns in the box.

anger	curiosity	frustration	respect
boredom	desperation	loyalty	spite

1. I think a lot of these kids get involved in vandalism just out of sheer .... There's so little to do round there.
2. He knew the treatment would be risky, but he had it out of .... He'd tried everything else.
3. Just out of .... , who did you vote for?
4. They had two minutes' silence out of .... for the victims of the disaster and the bereaved families.
5. I think a lot of the rioters were acting out of .... and .... because the government wasn't addressing their needs in any way.
6. He lied to the police out of a false sense of .... to his friends.
7. He sold his story to the papers simply out of .... , because his ex had dumped him.

Have you ever done anything for any of the above reasons? What?

What kind of things might you do for the following reasons?

out of a sense of obligation
out of fear
out of gratitude
out of guilt
out of ignorance
out of love
out of pity
out of sympathy

The baby's a bit clingy at the moment. • She's a typical stroppy teenager. • He's had a few scrapes with the police. • He just sits in his room and reads angst-filled books. • Her dad's a bit over-protective. • You're grounded! • Don't be so earnest about everything. Lighten up a bit! • I just wanted to melt away into the background. • Don't you feel the teeny-weeniest bit guilty? • No wonder she hasn't got any friends! • I've got absolutely no desire to have kids. • There's no sign of him getting a job. • My granddad's a bit stuck in his ways. • My gran's getting a bit doddery now. • It's the fastest-growing demographic group. • They just threw him on the scrap-heap. • Honestly, I was livid.

22 Youth and experience

Conversation

1 Role play

Imagine you have a colleague at work and you have heard she is pregnant. Think about how you would bring up the subject when you see her next. Think of five questions you might ask her. Write them down and try to remember them.

With a partner, role-play the conversation you think you would have.

Now imagine you meet your colleague for the first time after she's given birth. She is with her baby. What would you say? Think of five questions you might ask.

With your partner, role-play the conversation you think you would have.

2 Listening (1)

Listen to a conversation between a woman – May – and a colleague of hers – Esther – who has just recently had a baby. As you listen, take notes about the birth and the baby.

Compare what you heard with a partner.

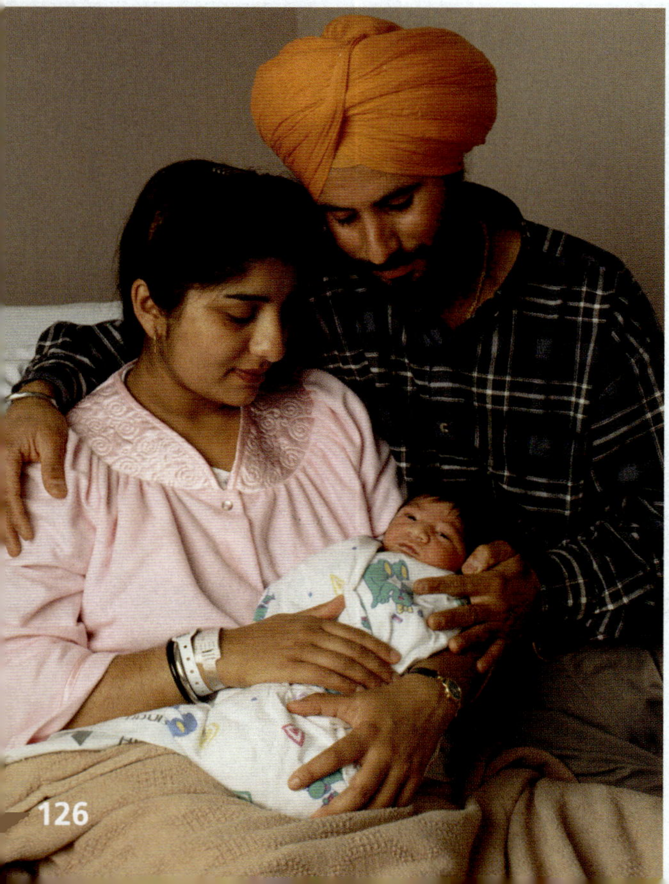

3 Describing people at different ages

Complete the sentences with the words in the box.

angst	chubby	gives in	shot up
authoritarian	clingy	handful	smothers
brat	got in	patronising	stroppy

1. She's a real .... She's got bags of energy and she can really wear you out – especially when she throws one of her tantrums.
2. She's a right spoilt .... She gets everything she wants and she gets away with murder sometimes.
3. He's very .... at the moment. I can hardly put him down without him crying. It's really wearing.
4. She just won't let go. She doesn't give him any space to breathe. She just .... him.
5. Oh, he's so cute. Look at those lovely little .... cheeks.
6. She can be really .... sometimes. She gets in a mood and then locks herself in her bedroom for hours on end.
7. It's incredible! He's just .... over the last year. He's gone all thin and gangly, and his voice seems to have broken overnight.
8. He's so soft. He just .... to her as soon as she makes a fuss.
9. He's pretty wild, really. He's .... with the wrong crowd and he's had a few scrapes with the police.
10. She's just really .... She talks to them like they were still two years old.
11. He's going through a bit of a phase. You know, he's the typical ....-ridden teenager. It's all 'What's the point? We're all going to die anyway' at the moment.
12. He's quite .... They've got a lot of really strict rules they have to stick to.

Which of the sentences above describe the following?

a. a baby / toddler
b. a teenager
c. a parent

Look at the words in the box. Which of them might you use to talk about each of the three kinds of people above?

cheeky	encouraging	puerile	sweet
crawl	out of control	rebellious	supportive
earnest	over-protective	snigger	teething

Use some of the words above to tell a partner about any toddlers, teenagers and parents you know.

4 Listening (2)

You are going to listen to two conversations. While you listen, think about the following questions.

1. Which language from Activity 3 would you use to describe the parents and toddler discussed in Conversation 1 and the father and son speaking in Conversation 2?
2. Can you think of any other words to describe the people you heard about?

Discuss your answers with a partner.

5 Vocabulary focus

Match the verbs with the words they were used with in the conversations.

1. run	☐	a. blue murder
2. throw	☐	b. him be
3. scream	☐	c. into the background
4. melt away	☐	d. circles round my brother
5. leave	☐	e. your mind to mush
6. turn	☐	f. himself on the floor

Now match these verbs with the words they were used with in the conversations.

7. answer back	☐	g. people at face value
8. show	☐	h. authority
9. take	☐	i. a little more respect
10. question	☐	j. your anger
11. challenge	☐	k. the way that you did
12. express	☐	l. assumptions

Listen again to check your answers.

6 Speaking

Discuss the following questions with a partner.

1. How do you relate to people a lot younger or older than you?
2. Have you ever been in a similar situation to the one described in the first conversation? What happened?
3. What do you think is the best way to discipline children?
4. Do you think it's good to bring children up to question authority?

7 *No wonder*

We often make comments starting with No wonder to mean 'In that case, it's not surprising that ...'. For example:

A: My brother always gives in to my nephew's every demand.
B: No wonder the kid's such a brat!

Write what you think was said to elicit each of these comments.

1. No wonder their children are so fat!
2. No wonder he hates his dad!
3. No wonder she hasn't got any friends!
4. No wonder he's so popular!
5. No wonder she left him!
6. No wonder it's taken you so long!
7. No wonder I couldn't find them!
8. No wonder it's not working!

Work in pairs. Student A – read out the things you wrote. Student B – respond with one of the No wonder comments.

8 Using grammar: Expressions with *no*

Complete the sentences with a noun from the box and the verb in brackets in the correct form. You also need to add a preposition in sentences 5–10.

chance	desire	good	need	recollection
choice	excuse	intention	point	sign

1. Personally, I have no burning .... (get married)
2. There's no .... to persuade him. He's not going to change his mind. (try)
3. There's no .... me. I was just doing my job. (thank)
4. It's no .... him. It just goes in one ear and out the other. (nag)
5. There's no .... like that, however upset he was. (swear)
6. I'm sorry, but I have absolutely no .... for what I said, because it's true. If they don't like it, that's their problem. (apologise)
7. I have absolutely no .... that film, but Barry insists I saw it with him, so I must've done, I suppose. (see)
8. There's no .... them ever .... a baby. (have)
9. We did try IVF, but it didn't work out, so we had no .... but .... (adopt).
10. The economy's been in a mess for a while now, and there's no .... things .... just yet. (pick up)

Now complete these sentences in ways that are true for you.

I've absolutely no desire ... .
There's no point ... .
There's no excuse ... .
I've absolutely no doubt ... .

Reading

1 Talking about elderly people

Make sure you understand the words and expressions in red. Tick the sentences that describe elderly people you know.

1. He's quite hard of hearing now.
2. She has to wear a hearing aid now.
3. She's getting on a bit now.
4. He's a bit stuck in his ways.
5. He's a bit of a bigot.
6. She can't really get around without her Zimmer frame.
7. Her memory's not what it used to be. She's going a bit senile.
8. He's getting a bit doddery now.
9. He's still very sprightly.
10. She had a stroke a few years ago and now she's paralysed down one side of her face.
11. She's doing really well, all things considered.
12. He's still got all his faculties. He's as sharp as he ever was.
13. His eyes aren't what they used to be.

Tell a partner which sentences you have ticked and who they describe.

2 Listening

You are going to listen to two friends – Mary and Roy – talking about their grandparents. As you listen, try to answer these questions.

1. What problems do Roy's grandparents have?
2. How does he get on with them? Why?
3. What are Mary's grandparents like?
4. How does she get on with them?

Discuss your answers with a partner. What do you think about their attitudes towards their grandparents and towards growing old?

Real English: the good old days

People talk about the good old days and say Those were the days about times in the past that they remember with affection. The implication is that things have gone downhill since! The expressions are also used sarcastically.

I remember the good old days when petrol was only 60p a gallon!

A: *We used to be able to smoke wherever we wanted in here.*

B: *Those were the days, eh! How we miss you inflicting your stinking cigarette smoke on us all.*

3 Before you read

You are going to read an article about elderly people in Britain. Complete the introduction with the words in the box.

canvas	demographic	ratio	sharp
comprehensive	massively	respectively	suggests
contrasts	parallel		

Pensioners: the new generation

New research (1) .... that Britain's population may well be ageing even faster than had previously been believed. Life expectancy for both men and women has continued to rise. Average life expectancy at birth now stands at 81 for females and 76 for males. This (2) .... dramatically with 49 and 45 (3) .... at the turn of the last century. Indeed, the number of centenarians is expected to rise (4) .... over the next few decades due to a combination of medical advances, improved standards of living, better diet and more (5) .... care for the elderly.

Running (6) .... to these trends is a (7) .... fall in the birth rate, as women are tending to wait longer and longer before having children. One result of all this is that the (8) .... of people working to people who have retired is shrinking year on year, a fact that has serious implications for the social security system.

We were curious to see what today's pensioners make of being part of Britain's fastest-growing (9) .... group and thus set out to (10) .... opinion. Here's what six over-70s told us:

How similar does this situation sound to the one in your country?

4 While you read

Now read what the six people had to say. As you read, decide which – if any – of the people in the article you think each of these sentences describes.

1. .... sounds particularly livid.
2. .... seems to have almost given up on life.
3. .... comes across as being very considerate – perhaps a bit too considerate for his / her own good, in fact!
4. .... sounds like he's / she's looking at things through rose-tinted glasses a bit.
5. It sounds like .... is getting to reap the rewards of all his / her hard work earlier on in life.
6. .... seems to really be living it up.
7. .... seems to be more or less living on the breadline.
8. .... sounds all bitter and twisted to me.
9. .... comes across as being remarkably well-balanced.

Discuss what you have written with a partner. Explain why you agree or disagree with your partner's choices.

Edna

I'm 73 and I only stopped working last year. I've found retirement quite hard to cope with. It's only over the last year that I've come to see what a massive investment I'd made in my career – emotionally and psychologically. I spent nearly 50 years teaching and loved every minute of it and now I've stopped, I feel like I'm just biding my time till I go. I've tried applying for work as a supply teacher, but no-one will touch me because of my age. I don't like to make a big song and dance about the ageism thing, but it does get to me. There seems to be a total lack of appreciation of all the experience I've accrued. We're just thrown onto the scrap-heap and left to rot!

Harold

I'm sure you've heard about the power of the grey pound, haven't you? Well, I'm one of the beneficiaries of all that! I was always quite careful when I was working. I put a little by every week and built up quite a nice little nest egg for when I retired, and now I'm having the time of my life. We went cruising down the Nile last year and we're now thinking of having a Jacuzzi put into the bathroom. Well, you can't take it with you when you go, can you?

Rosie

I wouldn't want to be young today, I really wouldn't. Society's gone to the dogs, if you ask me. I'm glad I won't be around that much longer to have to witness it all. Now, back when I was young, in the good old days, we had respect for older people and we all had proper manners too. Nowadays, though, all that's gone out the window. It's all dog-eat-dog and Me Me Me today.

Dorothy

I've never felt as happy as I do now, it might surprise you to hear. My daughters and granddaughters all work, and it makes me ever so proud to see how well they're doing. They've been able to take advantage of all the opportunities my generation were denied. Because we're a close-knit bunch, and we all live within spitting distance of each other, I help out with my great-grandchildren. It's nice to feel needed – and it keeps me young at heart, being around the kids.

Callum

I'm doing as well as can be expected, I suppose. I moved into an old people's home a few years back – well, sheltered accommodation is what they call it, but it boils down to much the same thing – and I can't complain. I do have children of my own, but I wouldn't want to be a burden to them or impose myself on them, so I guess this will have to do. I do get slightly lonely sometimes though, especially now that my darling wife has gone.

Kelvin

I worked for forty years as an engineer, helping build this country's infrastructure, only to end up being sold down the river by the powers that be! I only get a pittance of a pension because the firm's pension fund collapsed the year I retired. They'd invested in some high-risk, high-return markets and lost pretty much everything. The government refused to bail them out, meaning I'm now left having to live on a shoestring budget. It really makes my blood boil when I think about how much I gave and what scant reward I get in return!

5 Vocabulary check: idioms

Complete the sentences with words from the article.

1. I don't want to make a big song and .... about it.
2. I was just thrown onto the .... and left to rot!
3. I managed to build up quite a nice little .... egg.
4. I'm having the time of my ....
5. Society has gone to the ....
6. That's all gone out the ....
7. We all live within .... distance of each other.
8. It helps keep me young at ....
9. I don't want to be a .... to my children.
10. They sold me down the ....
11. I'm having to live on a .... budget.
12. It really makes my blood ....

Which of these sentences do you think you're most likely to use? Which might the elderly people you know use? Why?

6 Speaking

Discuss these questions with a partner.

1. Do you agree with Rosie that society's going to the dogs? Why / why not?
2. Do you think ageism is much of a problem in your country? How do you feel about it?
3. Would you feel OK about putting your parents into an old people's home? And if you had kids yourself, would you be OK about moving in with them when you get older?
4. Do you think people should be able to rely on getting a state pension or should they expect to have to top it up with a private pension scheme?
5. Have you heard of the grey pound before? What about the green pound or the pink pound? Are any of them strong in your country?

Writing: Reports

1 Speaking

Discuss these questions with a partner.

1. Have you ever taken part in or conducted a survey? What was it about?
2. Do you ever read or write the following kinds of reports? Why? What's usually in them?

Accident reports	Progress reports
Annual reports	School reports
Departmental reports	Scientific reports
Financial reports	Weekly reports

2 Topic sentences

The first sentence in a paragraph usually shows the general 'topic', which is then fleshed out in more detail in the rest of the paragraph.

What do you think will be the details in the paragraphs following these topic sentences in a report?

a. This report provides a summary of the findings of a customer satisfaction survey which was carried out during the week of 24th to 30th March.

b. Given the tight budget, we are restricted in what we can do to improve the areas highlighted by the survey.

c. The customer evaluation of staff was very mixed.

d. Overall, customers were positive in their views of our products.

e. One issue which emerged from customer responses was the poor organisation of stock and lack of clear signage.

3 Reading

Read the report and match the topic sentences to the correct paragraph. Were your ideas in Activity 2 correct?

Discuss these questions with a partner.

1. What kind of shop do you think Gadfly's is?
2. From what you read, do you think you would shop there? Why / why not?
3. Do you think the recommendations will work? What would you recommend?

1 .... The survey was a mixture of just over 100 evaluation forms, which customers filled in at home, and subsequently returned by post, as well as 20 face-to-face interviews conducted in-store. While the survey showed reasonable levels of satisfaction with the range and value of our products, there were serious issues raised regarding service and layout of the store.

Products

2 .... Price-wise, they rated our store very highly, with some 87% stating Gadfly's provided equal or better value on designer and home brand lines. There were similar results with regard to the variety of stock available in store, although, as we shall see, there were a number of people who stated that the range of products could be organised better.

In-store layout

3 .... While many recognised that Gadfly's provided a good range of products – clothing in particular – they were frustrated by the fact that they had to search for the correct sizes. They also disliked the fact that different designer brands were frequently lumped together.

Over 15% complained that shelving and rails were too close together, so that it was uncomfortable to move round and browse. 'It's a constant jostle' and 'far too cramped' were not untypical comments. One man who was interviewed said, 'I find the whole experience hell! If I can persuade my wife to go elsewhere, I will.' Even though this may be expressed in rather extreme terms, it does illustrate that this is a real problem that is putting off customers and it is something that needs addressing.

Service

4 .... While customers were very positive about staff in terms of attitude and politeness, as far as efficiency and knowledge were concerned, staff scored very badly. Customers felt that staff – particularly those dealing with electrical goods – were not very well-informed about the products they were selling.

Several customers said they had been left waiting for 15 minutes or more while staff checked in the stock room. Some of the comments were damning: 'my five-year-old could tell me more about the computers'; 'the guy just smiled like a village idiot'; 'the girl did her best and was very apologetic, but her best just wasn't good enough.'

Recommendations

5 .... Staff should be provided with bullet-pointed lists of key features of products. I would also strongly recommend moving two members of staff from the tills and detailing them to regularly tidy up and reorganise clothes on shelves and racks. I suggest we introduce an Employee of the Month award to back up these changes. In the long term, we should seriously consider a full re-fit, although this obviously has huge cost implications.

Real English: price-wise

We often add -wise to a noun to mean *regarding* or *concerning*. Some of these -wise words, like price-wise and business-wise, are quite common, but this is something which people sometimes do inventively. For example:

Service-wise, the restaurant is improving.
The car scores well efficiency-wise, but is very slow.

4 Referring to things

We often refer to a particular area dealt with in a report using words and expressions such as 'regarding'. Complete the sentences with one word in each space. The first letter is given.

1. As f.................................. as the price of the course was c.................................., there were few complaints and we were compared favourably to our competitors.
2. Overall, the results of the survey were quite discouraging, although there were more favourable responses with r.................................. to pricing.
3. In t.................................. of price, customers rated the school very highly.
4. P.................................., the food in the canteen was rated very highly and it was generally felt it was cheaper than in the nearby restaurants.
5. While the store scored well on pricing, several respondents made negative comments c.................................. quality.
6. The company was ranked in the top five best tour operators in the country when it c.................................. to value for money.

5 Rating things

The verbs below summarise how respondents rate businesses in customer evaluation surveys. Match the verbs with the words they go with.

1. be praised	☐	a. for its attention to detail
2. be compared	☐	b. for praise
3. be ranked	☐	c. badly on quality
4. be singled out	☐	d. the experience very highly
5. not rate	☐	e. the company down on service
6. score	☐	f. unvafourably to others
7. mark	☐	g. bottom out of 500 schools
8. make	☐	h. negative comments

Now imagine you're writing a report based on a survey of a restaurant you know. Write sentences like those in Activity 4 using the verbs above. Write about:

the atmosphere	the drinks	the parking
the building	the food	the service
the décor	the opening hours	

6 Making formal recommendations

Complete these sentences with the verbs in brackets in the correct form.

1. The school should seriously consider .... a wider variety of courses. (offer)
2. The décor desperately needs .... (update)
3. The company urgently needs .... some more experienced staff. (recruit)
4. I would strongly recommend that the department .... more rigorous security procedures. (institute)
5. At the very least, a permanent fan should definitely ....(install)
6. I would certainly suggest that less money .... on photocopying. (spend)

Underline all the adverbs and the verbs they collocate with.

7 Reporting people's responses

In reports, we often summarise comments people have made that seem quite similar to us.

Summarise in one sentence the pairs of comments using the words in brackets.

1. I was worried that the kids weren't properly supervised.
   I felt the kids were left to their own devices too much. (voiced concerns)
2. I'd like to see a greater range of facilities provided. Why don't you provide a crèche and baby changing facilities? (expressed a desire)
3. Four hours a day in one class is too long.
   I just couldn't really concentrate by the end, I was so tired. (it was felt)
4. We had to queue up for both drinks and food.
   Not only do you have to wait for ages to order, you then have to queue up to pay! (disliked)

8 Planning a report

You are going to write a report on a shop or school that you know. In pairs, discuss what headings you will use for the report. What points would you raise under each of these headings? Invent some comments from a survey to include.

Write your report (300 words or so). Remember to start each section with a clear topic sentence. Try to use as much language from these two pages as you can.

You're treading on thin ice there. • It's a bit of a minefield. • I just made some throw-away comment. • No sooner had I said it than I regretted it. • I was mortified when I found out. • It's a major faux pas, apparently. • I think it's de rigueur to buy your teacher a present, isn't it? • She's a bit blasé about the dangers. • He was effing and blinding. • I won't repeat what he called me. • It actually refers to a man's private parts! • I don't think many people would take offence at that. • It's blasphemous. • This kind of thing is just dumbing down our culture.

23 Taboos and embarrassing situations

Conversation

1 Using vocabulary: awkward situations

Put the words in brackets in order to make five common idioms.

1. I just made some throw-away comment about how much he smokes, but I think .... because he got really defensive. (nerve / I / have / a / hit / must / raw)
2. It was stupid, really – just .... I called her Liz instead of Lisa, but she went crazy! (the / slip / of / tongue / a).
3. Then he started asking me how long we'd been going out together and I realised he'd .... Honestly, I don't know where he got THAT idea from! (of / stick / got / the / end / the / wrong)
4. A: I don't think you look fat in it at all. Anyway, there's nothing wrong with being a BIT overweight.
   B: Watch what you're saying! .... here. (are / ice / treading / you / thin / on)
5. .... I asked her if she had any kids! How was I supposed to know she couldn't have any! (my / it / I / foot / really / put / in)

Can you translate these idioms? Do you use similar ones in your language?

Now complete these sentences with the words in the box.

faux pas	mortified	no-no	taboo
minefield	mouth	steer clear	tread

6. I've learned from bitter experience that politics is a bit of a .... subject in their house. It's best just to .... of it altogether.
7. The whole subject of race is a potential .... on my degree course. You have to .... very carefully indeed with it.
8. I committed a bit of a .... by making a joke about the king and then laughing my head off – only to realise everyone was just looking really, really annoyed! Me and my big .... , really!
9. I left my chopsticks pointing up in the bowl once I'd finished, but apparently that's a real .... in Japan.
10. When I realised my zip had been open all that time, I was absolutely ....

2 Speaking

Discuss these questions with a partner.

1. Have you ever really put your foot in it – accidentally said something that annoyed or upset someone?
2. Are there any subjects you find it's generally best to steer clear of?
3. What advice would you give to foreigners visiting your country about things that are real no-nos?
4. Have you ever committed any real faux pas when you've been abroad?
5. Have you ever felt absolutely mortified? Why?

3 While you listen

You are going to hear Erica talking to her friend Kirsten about a recent visit to her in-laws in the Ivory Coast. As you listen, try to answer these questions.

1. How does she get on with her in-laws?
2. What happened during the meal out?
3. How does she put her foot in it at the end of the conversation?

4 Vocabulary focus: collocations

Match the adjectives to the nouns they were used with in the conversation.

1. this icy ☐ a. look
2. the pecking ☐ b. faux pas
3. an awkward ☐ c. habit
4. small ☐ d. silence
5. a major ☐ e. order
6. this annoying ☐ f. talk

Now match the adverbs to the verbs.

7. I innocently ☐ g. coming to terms with it
8. They started shifting ☐ h. said
   i. uncomfortably in their seats
9. I was silently ☐
10. They're gradually ☐ j. getting my head round it
11. I'm slowly ☐ k. mouthing.

Look at the tapescript on page 161 and underline the sentences with these collocations. Try to notice any other words which are used with them.

5 Using grammar: *No sooner had … than …*

In the conversation, Erica said 'No sooner had I finished the sentence than this awkward silence fell.' We often use this structure when we're telling stories to emphasise the fact that the second action happened very quickly after the first.

Notice that we invert the subject and the auxiliary when we start the sentence or clause with No sooner. This adds emphasis.

For more information on how to use *No sooner*, see G24.

Rewrite these sentences using *No sooner*.

1. It was awful! We got to the check-in desk and then I suddenly realised I'd left the tickets at home.

   ....
2. I felt awful! I did it and then I immediately realised I'd made a terrible mistake!

   ....
3. It was typical! We offered the unions a decent pay rise and then the very next day they called a strike.

   ....
4. It was weird! About half an hour after I booked an appointment with my doctor, the pain just disappeared.

   ....
5. It was such a stressful evening! First my ex-wife rang and then about five minutes later my lawyer called.

   ....

6 Using vocabulary: loan words

In the conversation, Erica said she 'committed a major faux pas.' The expression faux pas is originally French, but was borrowed by English and is now a normal part of the language.

Look at these other French words which are often used in English. Then discuss the questions with a partner.

1. Have you ever heard any of these words before?
2. Do you use any of them in your language?

au fait	coup	en route
au pair	cuisine	en suite
avant-garde	déjà vu	fiancé
blasé	de rigeur	genre
buffet	double entendre	laissez faire
camouflage	duvet	matinée
c'est la vie	élite	nouveau riche
chic	en masse	risqué
cliché		

Tell your partner how you think the words above are pronounced – in English.

Now listen to the tape and practise saying the words.

Complete 1–8 below by adding words from above:

1. There was a military .... there last year and the army have been in power ever since.
2. He went to a very .... school. It must cost at least twenty thousand a year to go there.
3. It's already become a bit of a .... to describe Paris as the most romantic city in the world – but it's still true!
4. I couldn't believe it! He told this really .... joke – in front of my mother! She looked mortified!
5. He's quite .... about speaking in public. He doesn't seem to get worried about it at all.
6. It's a big tourist resort. People flock there .... every summer.
7. I heard she's got engaged. Have you met her .... yet?
8. A: Can you help me install this?
   B: Sorry, but I'm not very .... with these new computers.

Now discuss these questions with a partner.

a. Do you know any words from your own language that are now an everyday part of English?
b. How many English loan words can you think of in your language?
c. Are you sure they mean exactly the same thing in your language as they do in English?

Reading

1 Speaking

Discuss these questions with a partner.

1. Do you swear in your own language? When?
2. Why do you think people swear?
3. How do you feel when you hear foreigners swearing in your language?
4. Do you know any English swear words? How did you learn these words?

2 Reading

You are going to read a text about the way public reaction to swearing has changed in Britain. As you read, try to answer these questions.

1. What has been the public reaction to the opening of the French Connection store?
2. What three major changes in attitudes towards swearing are outlined?
3. What kind of language do the majority of people still find shocking?

After you finish reading, discuss your answers to the questions with your partner.

Taboo or not Taboo?

IT'S THE END OF CIVILISATION as we know it – or so it must seem to some now that French Connection UK (or FCUK as the clothing firm is more commonly known) has set up shop right across the Brompton Road from Harrods – that most conservative and most English of department stores. In reality, however, it is perhaps only a small minority who will truly feel a sense of shock at the opening. To the vast majority, the company's supposedly risqué use of an acronym so closely resembling the f-word has actually become a tired and tedious cliché, more likely to bore than to outrage!

Much of this, of course, is down to the fact that the way in which society perceives – and uses – swear words has changed radically over the years. Of course, the use of so-called bad language has a long and noble tradition in English with literary greats such as Chaucer and Shakespeare liberally sprinkling their works with taboo words and dirty jokes. More recently, it has not been uncommon for prize-winning novels to contain plentiful examples of the f-word in its many different grammatical shapes and forms.

However, five hundred years ago it was religious language used in blasphemous contexts that shocked people most. This was an age in which the majority were devoutly religious and firmly believed in God. Over the centuries, religion and the church slowly lost their grip on the popular imagination and today it is only a small minority who still feel offended by expressions such as 'Oh my God!' or 'God only knows!'

By the 1800s, as the conservative Victorian era got underway, words describing sexual acts, sexual organs and bodily functions became the new taboos. In the name of taste and decency these words can obviously not appear in English-language coursebooks, but they have doubtless been encountered by many foreign-language learners on the streets or in movies and songs. Indeed, since the critic Kenneth Tynan first uttered the f-word on British television in 1965 – an incident which sparked public outrage and a huge flood of complaints and even had one Member of Parliament suggesting Tynan be hung – it has become so incredibly common-place that for many it has become debased and has lost its power to shock. As a case in point, the repeated use of the euphemism 'feck' in the Channel 4 comedy show *Father Ted* prompted barely a trickle of letters of complaint.

Given this, it is perhaps not surprising that in a post-political-correctness Britain, the last taboos now seem to be insults based on race, gender, sexuality or disability. In a recent survey, over three-quarters of those polled said they had no problem with swearing on TV after the 9pm watershed so long as it was in context – used, for instance, to express shock – though most also disliked gratuitous swearing – swearing for its own sake. However, what the majority found truly offensive was directed abuse – swearing AT people as opposed to WITH them – abuse of minorities and racial abuse. This is perhaps a reflection of Britain's growing multi-racialism and tolerance towards alternative lifestyles. Whilst there are undoubtedly still some who lament what they see as the dumbing down of the English language and the way in which 'the language of the gutter' has infiltrated all aspects of modern life, this shift in attitudes towards swearing could also be seen as a very good thing. It seems to suggest that we now worry less about words describing what our bodies do – and more about words which hurt and wound – and surely that can only be a good thing.

3 Word building

Complete the sentences with the correct form of the word in the box.

suppose	liberal	disabled	doubt
radical	body	offend	shift

1. Swearing and violence are .... closely related, but I personally fail to see a clear connection.
2. There's been a huge .... in attitudes towards women over the last decade or so.
3. Racism is .... the biggest social problem facing our country now. It's doing untold damage.
4. I think people who have physical and learning .... are still seriously marginalised in our society.
5. Sex and sexual images are now used far too .... in advertising. Most of the time it's just gratuitous.
6. The way our parents viewed sex and swearing was .... different to ours. The sexual revolution of the 60s and 70s changed everything.
7. I don't understand why people are so embarrassed about .... functions. It's all natural.
8. I personally find sexist language deeply ....

Discuss with a partner if you agree with the statements above.

4 Using grammar: *Given*

In the following example from the text what does *this* refer to? Look back and check if you need to.

Given *this*, it is perhaps not surprising that in a post-political-correctness world, the last taboos now seem to be insults based on race, gender, sexuality or disability.

We often use *Given* at the start of a sentence to show that because of a particular fact, this is my opinion.

Match the sentence beginnings and endings.

1. Given the amount he eats,
2. Given the traffic,
3. Given the personal problems he's having,
4. Given the time,
5. Given the political situation,

a. the government's advising people to leave the country.
b. I think we'd better skip the next exercise.
c. we were lucky to get here when we did.
d. it's amazing he stays so cheerful.
e. it's amazing he's as thin as he is.

5 Practice

Complete these sentences with your own ideas.

1. Given our financial situation, ...
2. Given her age, ...
3. Given what we paid for the car, ...
4. Given the fact that I've only been learning for six months, ...
5. Given the state of the house when we bought it, ...
6. Given ...., ...

Real English: In view of

In more formal, written English, we often use In view of (the fact) instead of Given.

In view of our tight budget, some very tough decisions will need to be made.

In view of the fact that the country has contravened UN regulations, the imposition of sanctions should now be considered.

6 Euphemisms

We use euphemisms to avoid what some people see as embarrassing or impolite words.

Complete the sentences with the correct euphemism from the box.

dirt	eff off
powder my nose	relieving himself
effing and blinding	passed away
privates	sugar

1. I kicked the ball right in his .... The poor guy was in agony.
2. Do you know where the little girl's room is? I just need to ....
3. I came out of my house yesterday and there was this guy just .... in the street. It was disgusting. When I said so, he just started .... at me.
4. His wife .... three years ago, but he still hasn't got over it.
5. Honestly, he was so rude to me I just felt like telling him to ...., but you can't do that to your boss, can you?
6. Oh ....! I've stepped in some dog .... Honestly, these dog owners should be fined for not clearing it up!

Do you have any similar euphemisms in your language? Do you use them? Do you know any others in English?

He was the golden boy of British tennis. • He was dogged by injury. • He starred in a couple of B-movies. • She's just another wannabe model. • He went off the rails. • She tried to resurrect her career. • He just vanished off the radar. • I read all the trashy tabloids. • I wasn't really reading it. I just had a quick flick through. • I just happened to see it. • He's a complete nobody. • I have penned the odd song myself. • I'm a sucker for any soppy romantic film. • You didn't fall for it, did you? • Oh, so you know George Clooney, do you? • Apparently, their marriage is just a sham. • She's in rehab now. • This all just appeals to the lowest common denominator. • He took out an injunction to stop the story coming out.

24 Celebrity and scandal

Reading

1 Speaking

Discuss these questions with a partner.

1. Who do you think the most globally famous person from your country is? What're they famous for? Are you a fan?
2. Are there any famous foreigners living and working in your country? How do you feel about them? Why?
3. Have you ever seen or met any famous people? Who? Where?

2 Describing why people were famous

Complete these sentences with the words in the box.

caps	fling	host	rails
soap	contestants	glamour	kiss-and-tell
runner-up	wonder	famous	golden boy
launched	smash		

1. She was one of the .... in the first ever 'Big Brother' reality TV show.
2. She was a famous .... model and pin-up girl.
3. He was this one-hit .... in the 80s. He had a single called "Don't Forget Me" that was a .... hit all over Europe.
4. I never really knew what she did. She just seemed to be famous for being ....
5. She had a .... with some government minister and then sold her .... story to the tabloids.
6. He was a child star on TV in the 70s and then went completely off the .... when he hit adolescence.
7. He was .... in the Tour de France in the mid-90s.
8. He was the .... of English football – for a few months. He won a couple of .... for the national team.
9. He used to be a late-night chat-show ....
10. She was a .... star in the 90s and then she got out of that and .... a fairly disastrous singing career!

3 Practice

Think of three people you could describe using some of the language from Activity 2. Describe the people in as much detail as you can to a partner, but don't mention their names. Can your partner guess who you're describing?

4 Before you read

You are going to read about what happened to the four people in these photos after their moments of fame.

First, discuss these questions with a partner.

1. Do you recognise any of these people?
2. Do you know why they were famous?
3. Do you have any idea what happened to them next?

Decide which photos you think these words go with.

an eco-warrior
did stints as a bouncer
endorse a brand of diet products
feel hard done by
leaked recordings of telephone conversations
pursued a sideline career as a rapper
sent home in disgrace
went solo

Compare your decisions with a partner.

5 While you read

The class should now split into two groups. One group should read the text on this page. The other group should read the text on page 176.

Read your text and find out if you matched the words in Activity 4 with the correct photos.

Once you have finished reading, compare your findings with someone from the other group. Find out as much as you can about each person.

Where are they now?

Andy Warhol once claimed that everybody will get their fifteen minutes of fame – and it is certainly starting to look that way! We now have celebrity chefs and celebrity gardeners, fly-on-the-wall TV shows about celebrity love islands and celebrity detox camps, plus countless celebrity gossip magazines and web sites. Celebrity scandal is splashed all over the tabloids, and in our subsequent conversations many of us talk as if we are on first-name terms with the Justins, Kylies, Leonardos and Christinas of this world.

Yet what happens when the limelight fades and the crowds move on to the next sensation? Here, we track the twists and turns in the lives of four ex-celebs now residing in the 'where are they now?' file.

Andrew Ridgeley

As half of the duo – Wham! – that propelled George Michael to superstardom, Andrew Ridgeley enjoyed a string of Top Ten hits in the mid 1980s, culminating in the mega-million-selling smash, 'Last Christmas'. The pair appeared in the first Live Aid concert at Wembley Stadium and were the first western group to play in China.

However, by 1987 it was all over. George went solo and Andrew was left to get over being known as the lesser talent and "the other one in Wham!" He then seemed to vanish off the radar, spending part of his fortune on an ill-fated attempt at becoming a racing driver, and trying his hand at restaurant ownership. A comeback LP, 'Son of Albert', flopped and Andrew is now a partner in a surfing firm and something of an eco-warrior, lobbying the government as part of the Surfers Against Sewage group.

Ben Johnson

When the naturalised Canadian sprinter Ben Johnson won the 100 metres in the 1988 Seoul Olympics, he was hailed as the world's fastest man. However, a mere three days later, he was stripped of his medal and sent home in disgrace. Johnson's crime was testing positive for a banned steroid. It was an ignominious end to what had been a glittering rise to stardom – and one that denied Johnson the chance of cashing in on his success and earning millions from endorsements.

Johnson was born in Jamaica, but emigrated to Canada aged 14 and made his Olympic debut in Los Angeles in 1984, winning bronze. Three years later, he set a new world record of 9.83 seconds, a figure he himself bettered in South Korea, where he ran an incredible 9.79.

Johnson attempted a comeback in 1991, but received a life ban in '93 after failing another drug test. He then drifted from one strange career move to another, briefly acting as a trainer for Argentinian football legend Diego Maradona and then helping coach the son of Libyan leader, Colonel Gaddafi. He was last heard of living back with his mother in a relatively impoverished state, reduced to racing against horses and cars for publicity.

Today Johnson perhaps has good reason to feel hard done by – four of the other seven sprinters from Seoul subsequently also failed drugs tests – including the man who took his gold, Carl Lewis!

6 Comprehension check

Work with your partner. Decide if these statements about the four celebrities are true or false. Can you remember the exact words in the text?

1. Andrew Ridgeley's career as a racing driver wasn't very successful.
2. His solo album sold well.
3. Ben Johnson came third in the Los Angeles Olympics 100 metres.
4. Ben Johnson is still quite well-off.
5. Monica Lewinsky used to tell her secrets to Linda Tripp.
6. She started knitting because she didn't really enjoy being in the public eye.
7. Mr. T is now Laurence Tureaud's official name.
8. Mr. T's videos encourage kids not to get involved with crime.

Now look at the text again and underline the exact words.

7 Speaking

Discuss these questions with a partner.

1. Which of the four people do you think seems most well-adjusted nowadays? And who seems least well-adjusted?
2. Did any of the four stories remind you of any other celebrities? In what way?
3. Why do you think President Clinton's popularity ratings actually went up in the wake of the Lewinsky scandal?
4. Why do you think so many celebs end up with drink or drug problems, or else embroiled in endless litigation?

Conversation

1 Speaking

Discuss these questions with a partner.

1. Do you ever read any gossip magazines?
2. Do you ever get stories about celebrities' private lives in any of the serious papers?
3. Do you know any stories about celebrities in the news at the moment? Do you have an opinion about them?

2 Listening

You are going to listen to three people talking about gossip magazines and celebrities. Listen and answer these questions.

1. How many of them like reading gossip magazines?
2. Why do they like / not like celebrity gossip?
3. Which celebrity story do they mention?
4. Why were the celebrities mentioned famous?

3 Listen again

Can you remember what was said in each of the gaps below? There is more than one word missing in each sentence.

Compare your ideas with a partner.

1. I was just having .... – just keeping myself up to date with the latest celebrity gossip
2. I bet you've got a full ....
3. Have you ever seen anything .... ?
4. She was, I don't know, some reality TV .... or something.
5. Yeah? Probably. .... There always seems to be one celeb or other getting treatment for some addiction.
6. No, I didn't. I'm with you. .... for any of those glossy gossip mags and trashy tabloids.
7. I just happened to switch over and .... of it.
8. We're just becoming obsessed with celebrities and .... our whole media culture.
9. We build these people up and say how wonderful they are just so we can ....
10. They all employ publicists and .... and libel actions at the first whiff of scandal.
11. It just appeals to the ....
12. You are just .... , aren't you? You don't really believe that, do you?

Now listen again and complete the gaps.

Which of the arguments about celebrities and gossip magazines do you agree with? Would you like to be a celebrity?

Real English: an old fogey

An old fogey is someone who has old-fashioned views and doesn't like change. You don't need to be old to be one!

A: *I don't know! Young people today don't have any respect.*
B: *Oh, don't be such an old fogey! You're only 33!*

4 Speaking

Discuss these questions with a partner.

1. Do you subscribe to any magazines, journals or papers? Which ones? Why?
2. Is there anything you're a real sucker for?
3. Do you know anyone who picks arguments for the sake of it or deliberately winds people up?

5 Changing word class

Look at this sentence from the listening:

Her only talent seems to be for bedding B-list celebrities.

Bed here is used as a verb rather than its more common use as a noun. It means 'to have sex with'.

This change in word class is quite common in English, although it's sometimes difficult to know what's possible and what's not.

Which two words in red are not possible in the word class they are used in below?

1. He's a complete nobody. I don't know why he's a famous.
2. Apparently, the club was just a front for the local mafia.
3. There was a big celebrity awards do on in the centre of town.
4. We had to elbow our way through the crowd to get near the stage.
5. I tried to be as nice as possible, but I obviously didn't word it right because she actually kneed me!
6. I can't meet you today, but I'll pencil you in for Friday.
7. He was this rabidly anti-gay MP – until he was outed in the press by his secretary.
8. I'm hoping the company will up its offer. Otherwise, I'm just going to leave.
9. I'm sure Chris will have some ideas about how to improve things. He's very switched-on.
10. He was completely whiskied. He must've downed six or seven drinks while we were at the party.

Use your dictionary to find the meaning of the following nouns when they are used as verbs. Write example sentences for each.

brick	circle	foot	ground	sellotape
bus	floor	gas	pen	table

6 Using grammar: question tags

We often use question tags to show surprise or incredulity.

You are just winding us up, aren't you? It's got to be a joke.

It was him, was it? I might've known!

Show your surprise by adding a question tag to one or both of the sentences in each of the ten examples below.

1. Nobody really believes that. Everybody knows it's all just about the money.
2. So it's my fault. I don't think so!
3. You don't really believe that. You can't do.
4. I don't have to come with you. Do you really need someone to hold your hand?
5. You didn't fall for that old trick. That's the oldest one in the book.
6. She didn't. She wouldn't really do that.
7. They can't really expect us to pay for this. It's outrageous.
8. So it was easy. Is that what you think?
9. You didn't think he'd actually do it. It was a joke.
10. She's not going to marry him. That would be such a disaster.

Listen to check your answers. Notice the intonation. Practise saying the sentences in pairs.

For more information on how to use question tags, see G25.

7 *It's a scandal*

Complete the sentences below with the verbs in the box in the correct form.

accept	chuck	dump	out
admit	collapse	expose	sleep
batter	cover up	kerb-crawl	snort

1. His wife's .... him out because she found out he'd been having an affair with the kids' nanny.
2. Apparently, the marriage was a sham to .... the fact that he's gay.
3. There was some exposé in the paper about him .... with call girls.
4. He was picked up by the police for .... in the red light district.
5. Apparently, he didn't even bother to tell her face-to-face it was over. He actually .... her by e-mail.
6. He was filmed .... a bribe to throw the game.
7. She claimed she was a qualified doctor, but she was .... as a fraud.
8. She's always denied taking class-A drugs, but then they caught her on camera .... coke.
9. Apparently he's been .... to rehab for addiction to heroin.
10. He made his fortune through various dodgy dealings and his whole business empire .... when it was exposed.
11. He's got this wholesome, goody-goody image, but apparently he .... his wife and he's just a really nasty piece of work.
12. She denied she was a lesbian, but she was .... in the paper by an ex-lover.

Now discuss these questions in groups:

a. What do you think is the most scandalous story above? Why?

b. Do you think any of the stories above have no place in a newspaper? Why?

c. Have you heard of any of these – or similar – scandals? Who was involved? What happened?

Writing: Giving presentations

1 Speaking

Discuss these questions with a partner.

1. Have you ever seen anyone give a presentation – or had to give a presentation yourself? When was it? Who was it to?
2. How long was the presentation? How did it go?
3. Was Powerpoint or an OHP used?
4. Were there any handouts?
5. Were questions taken from the floor?
6. Have you ever seen anyone have any problems whilst giving a presentation?

Real English: OHP

OHP stands for overhead projector. The plastic sheets you use with an OHP are called OHP transparencies.

2 Dealing with problems

Complete these sentences with the words in the box.

backtrack	clip-on	mike	slide
bag	give	place	smudged
bear	make that out	sharper	train

1. Can you hear me OK at the back? I'm afraid the ....'s not working.
2. .... with me a minute. That's the wrong ....
3. Can you .... OK, or is it a bit too small?
4. It's quite fuzzy, isn't it? Is there any way you can make it a bit .... ?
5. .... me a minute. I've lost my .... of thought.
6. Sorry. Bear with me. I've lost my ....
7. Oops! Let me just .... a minute. I've missed a bit out.
8. Oh, sorry. That transparency's got all .... Can you still read it OK?
9. Have you got a .... mike I can use, or are they all hand-held?
10. You'll have to excuse me. I'm a .... of nerves up here!

In which 2 sentences above is the speaker talking to a technician?

'And that's why we need a computer.'

3 Preparing your presentation

Discuss with a partner how far you agree with each of these pieces of advice about giving presentations.

a. Don't read your presentation off a piece of paper.
b. Tell some jokes.
c. Use Powerpoint or an OHP.
d. Write the whole presentation out as you would say it.
e. Don't be afraid to ad-lib.
f. Signpost the presentation clearly.
g. Just be yourself, be natural.
h. Record your presentation before you give it.
i. Don't allow interruptions or questions till the end.

4 Listening

You're going to hear a brief talk by one of the authors about how he prepares for presentations.

Listen and answer these questions:

1. Which of the tips in Activity 3 does he mention? To what extent does he agree with them?
2. What does he say is the most important thing to bear in mind when giving a presentation?

Is there anything you heard that you disagree with?

Read the first paragraph of this talk on page 162. Decide where you think the speaker paused. Listen again to check your ideas. Practise reading the paragraph out.

5 Connecting with your audience

In Activity 4, you heard that it's important to make sure your audience relate to what you're saying. There are lots of expressions good presenters use to do this.

Make complete sentences by matching the beginnings with the endings.

1. As I'm sure many of you already know,
2. I can see some of you
3. I would imagine I'm not alone
4. We all know what that means,
5. Now I know what you're thinking. You're thinking:

a. don't we? It means an economy that's stuck in recession!

b. have clearly had a similar experience. Not nice, is it?

c. the story of *Apocalypse Now* is based on Joseph Conrad's novel *Heart of Darkness* – only set during the Vietnam War.

d. why should I care about a thing like that? Well, here's why.

e. in thinking this. I'm sure the thought has crossed some of your minds too, hasn't it?

Now make complete sentences by matching these beginnings with these endings.

6. It might well be that you think
7. But that's just where
8. I'm sure all of you in this room
9. I'm sure you don't need me to tell you
10. I can't be the only person alive who

f. believes this isn't a conspiracy theory – it's the truth!

g. you know all there is to know about the subject.

h. you'd be wrong!

i. have heard of sushi, right? Well, here's something you maybe didn't know about it.

j. what an incredible writer Dostoevsky is.

Underline all the parts of the sentences above you think you could re-use in a presentation of your own.

6 Writing your presentation

You are going to give a five-minute presentation to some other students in the class. First, choose a topic you'd like to talk about. It should be something you know more about than other students. It could be something you have talked about in public before, something connected to your work, or a hobby. It could be a report on a book or an article you have read, or an overview of a topic that interests you. The more specialized your subject, the better!

Spend 20 minutes writing what you're going to say. Make sure you signpost the presentation clearly and try to use some of the language from Activity 5 to help other students relate to the topic.

7 Asking for clarification

Complete these questions using the verbs in the box.

dealing	give	quoted	said
talking	describing	made	referred
say	elaborate	mentioned	run
showing			

1. When you were .... about the political situation in Guam, you .... the relationship with Japan. Could you .... a bit more about that?
2. When you were .... us the statistics for deforestation, you .... some figures from a survey carried out by Greenpeace. Have you got any more information on that?
3. When you were .... the way bridges are usually constructed, you .... to a process called destructive testing. Could you .... through that again?
4. When you were .... with the issue of police corruption, you .... reference to a case involving the London Metropolitan police force. Could you .... on that a bit?
5. When you were telling us about how the fishing unions defend their rights, you .... something about trade agreements between ASEAN countries. Could you .... us a few more specifics on that?

8 Giving your presentation

Look back at the presentation you have written. Work in groups of four or five. Take it in turns to give your presentations to the group. Take notes as other students talk. After each presentation, there should be questions from the floor.

Try to ask questions like those in Activity 7.

Review: Units 19–24

1 Adjectives and nouns

Put the words and expressions in the box into four groups of four.

a brat	doddery	past it	sulky
cheeky	evangelical	practising	underrated
confession	hyper	senile	a weak link
devout	gutsy	sprightly	a zimmer frame

children	old people	religion	sports players
....	....	....	....
....	....	....	....
....	....	....	....
....	....	....	....

Add two more words you learnt in the last 6 units to each list.
Work in pairs.
Student A: Explain five of the words above.
Student B: Close your book and guess the words.
Then swap roles.

2 Vocabulary quiz

Discuss these questions in groups of three.

1. What do you do if you have a kickabout?
2. What's the difference between a headscarf and a veil?
3. Can you think of two events that have had saturation coverage?
4. What kind of person has a tantrum? What do they do when they have one?
5. What's the difference between an atheist and an agnostic?
6. What happens if a car stalls?
7. If someone is effing and blinding, what are they doing?
8. Can you think of three things you launch?
9. Why is it bad not to dip your headlights?
10. What happens when a CD, film or product flops?
11. What do you do if you fast? Why does someone fast?
12. If you're xenophobic, what don't you like?
13. Can you think of three things that can be rife?
14. Where are the bonnet, dashboard and bumper on a car?
15. What do you find at the end of a wild goose chase?
16. What happens if someone goes off the rails?

3 Verbs

Complete the collocations with the verbs in the box.

flip	grab	lose track	rejuvenate	shatter
fulfil	hurl	proceed	run	verge on

1. .... your illusions / the windscreen
2. .... counter to your intuition / circles round him
3. .... madness / genius
4. .... your attention / a seat
5. .... your career / your skin
6. .... abuse / stones at the police
7. .... a coin / channels
8. .... of time / of what's happening in the news
9. .... your potential / the entry requirements
10. .... with a plan / to tell everyone about her problems.

Spend one minute memorising the collocations above. Then cover the activity. Your partner will read out the ten verbs. How many collocations can you remember?
With your partner, think of one more collocate for each verb.

4 What can you remember?

With a partner, write down as much as you can about the listening in Unit 21 and the text in Unit 22.

Unit 21: Four bad experiences in cars

Unit 22: Pensioners: the new generation

Which did you enjoy more? Why?

5 Grammar

Complete the second sentence so that it has a similar meaning to the first sentence, using the word in brackets.

1. As soon as I pressed the send button, I regretted ever writing it.
   No .... I began to regret ever writing it. (than)
2. If you don't like walking, then it's not the best place to visit.
   I .... you're really into walking. (bother)
3. Basically, the only reason I did it was because I was bored.
   I just did it .... , to be perfectly honest.(out)
4. You can never be sure, but the odds are that they'll win.
   In .... , but you can never be sure. (all)
5. Many people said they wanted more information before the course started.
   Many people .... more information before the course started. (a desire)
6. The only option we had was accepting the pay-off.
   We had .... accept the pay-off. (choice)
7. The lack of fully-qualified staff really needs addressing.
   The company .... employing more fully-qualified staff. (seriously)
8. I don't suppose you could tell me what time the film starts.
   You .... what time the film starts, would you? (happen)

Have you ever immediately regretted doing something?
Have you ever been left with no choice but to do something you didn't want to do?

6 Grammar and vocabulary

Complete the short text with ONE word in each space.

Flicking (1) .... the glossy magazines in the dentist's waiting room the other day, I couldn't (2) .... noticing the number of articles which (3) .... to alternative medicine or some kind of new age healing. One was about some celebrity who apparently swears (4) .... having hot cups put on her back; another celeb proclaims that eating three pounds of raw carrots a day will stave (5) .... cancer; a third tells the story of how an out-of-body experience with a shaman helped her to pick herself (6) .... from deep depression. And of course, along with the articles come adverts with people touting for (7) .... and trying to cash in (8) .... each New Age fad. (9) .... the advances in science and technology, it seems strange that people still look for these most unscientific methods to cure our ills. Certainly we should try and (10) .... any proposed cure or belief on its merits, but most of these things are (11) .... no real benefit. At best they may offer false hopes but at (12) .... they may cause real damage. A case which has recently been highlighted was of a woman who was suffering from cancer. She (13) .... been persuaded from taking proven conventional treatments into taking an alternative treatment consisting of herbs and fruit juices.

Tragically, the woman died. (14) .... view of such cases, the government should consider (15) .... far more to regulate and control this kind of 'healing'.

Have you tried any alternative or complementary medicines?
Do you agree with the writer of the article?

7 Word building

Complete the sentences with noun forms of the words in brackets.

1. The main .... of the tax cuts will be married couples. (benefit)
2. I wasn't asking for any particular reason, just out of .... (curious)
3. I don't think she meant to insult anyone. She just said it out of .... of the situation. (ignore)
4. We were invited to his .... even though we aren't Christians ourselves. (confirm)
5. I have to say, I'm not getting much .... from my life at the moment. (fulfil)
6. He was never religious before, but then he went through this great .... and he's become a born-again Christian. (convert)

8 Look back and check

Work in pairs. Choose one of these activities.

a. Look back at the vocabulary in Activity 5 in Unit 19 on page 113. Ask your partner about any words you've forgotten. Then re-do the discussion after the activity with a new partner.

b. Look back at Activity 4 in Unit 21 on page 125. Spend a few minutes thinking about arguments for and against globalisation. With a partner, debate the idea that globalisation is generally of benefit to the world and should be encouraged. Try and use the expressions in Activity 4.

c. In pairs, how many French words that we use in English can you remember? Make a list of them. Which pair has the most in the class? Look back at unit 23, Activity 6 on page 133. Were there any you'd forgotten?

9 Idioms

Complete each idiom with a noun. The first letter is given.

1. We did exactly what our clients had asked for, but then at the last minute they moved the g.................................. and asked for something else.
2. A: You've completely ruined it! It's a write-off.
   B: Keep your h.................................. on. It's only scratched and slightly dented!
3. Now I've lost my job all my plans for buying a house have just gone out of the w.................................. .
4. With all the subsidies they get from their government, we're just not competing on a l.................................. playing f.................................. .
5. A: Honestly, the way people just chuck litter out of their car window makes my blood b.................................., it really does!
   B: Andrew, give it a r..................................! I've heard it all before.
6. With the recession the way it is, our company's just struggling to keep its head above w.................................. .
7. I'm afraid bad service is just par for the c.................................. with that company.
8. I don't really have any plans. I'm just happy to go with the f.................................. .
9. A: Do you know the answer yet?
   B: No, just put me out of my m.................................. and tell me what it is.
10. I just don't understand why he would do something so stupid. I just can't get my h.................................. round it.

Can you think of any situations from the past when you could've used any of these idioms? Tell a partner.

10 Passives

Complete the sentences with the correct form of the passive verbs in the box.

be adopted	be fazed	be saddled with
be chucked out	be fleeced	be splashed
be discredited	be grounded	be stripped of

1. I don't really want to do a degree at the moment, because I don't want to .... all that debt for years after I finish.
2. They caught him using drugs and he .... of school.
3. It was quite a nice hotel and generally the service was great, but we .... absolutely .... for the telephone calls we made. They charged us £16 for six calls.
4. After the failed drugs test, he .... his world records.
5. The claims that the therapy offers a breakthrough in treatment for cancer .... largely ....
6. His picture .... all over the papers after he won the lottery, but he didn't seem to .... by any of the publicity.
7. The human rights charter .... by our country in 1987 after successful lobbying by a number of NGO's.
8. After my parents found out I'd been smoking, I .... for a week.

11 Adjective–noun collocations

Match the adjectives with the nouns they collocate with.

1. an off		a.	car
2. a flashy		b.	population
3. a cut-throat		c.	excuse
4. the indigenous		d.	day
5. an ignominious		e.	link
6. a feeble		f.	business
7. a rebellious		g.	group
8. a disparate		h.	end
9. a tenuous		i.	career
10. a glittering		j.	teenager

You can find out how common a collocation is by doing a search on the internet. Put the words in quotation marks like this: "the indigenous population". Try changing words, for example people / tribe / group to see which is more common.

Were you a rebellious teenager? Do you know anyone who was? In what way?

Writing

1 Requests

Put the words in order to make sentence starters for softening requests.

1. if / you / all / mind / at / would
2. huge / me / you / a / do / could / favour
3. be / possible / at / it / all / would
4. could / suppose / I / you / don't
5. to / wouldn't / happen / know / you
6. there / wondering / way / was / if / I / any / was

Now make complete requests by matching the sentence starters with the endings.

a. who I need to contact regarding scholarships and grants.
b. courier over the reports I left in your office, could you?
c. you would re-consider your decision over the compensation?
d. we postponed the meeting to discuss the finance figures till next week?
e. to put me up for a few nights while I'm in Berlin?
f. and cover my shift for me tonight? I'd make it up to you.

Ask and answer the questions above in pairs.

2 Formal vocabulary

Rewrite the underlined sections to make them sound more formal by using the verbs in the box in the correct form. You may need to make other changes.

acquire	elaborate on	identify	propose
request	await	forward	inform
reimburse	submit		

1. I am writing to ask for an application form for the post of admin manager advertised in today's *Guardian*.
2. Could you send on my enquiry to the relevant person.
3. Thank you for your application. We will let you know our decision shortly.
4. The report singled out one particular cause for concern.
5. The report puts forward a number of solutions.
6. The report recommended that we should consider getting a major shareholding in one of our competitors, HYDET.
7. The report was short on detail so I have asked him to tell us more about certain areas.
8. We will naturally give you all your money back.
9. The report was handed in some time ago, but we are still waiting for a response.

3 A report

The report below was written by a student. Her teacher has underlined eighteen mistakes. Try to correct them with a partner. The first one is done for you.

This report provides a summary of the student feedback on the trip to Corfe Castle and Studland, which ~~it~~ was organised by the school on the weekend of the 19th and 20th of June. The feedback was conducted through a form which was filled in by the participants a week later their return. On the whole, students enjoyed their weekend and stated that they thought the area was well worth visiting. On the contrary, there were some serious issues which were raised and they need to address should the school decide to run this trip again.

Accommodation

The major complaint was the accommodation. While students didn't have any objections to camping in principal, the vast majority of those who gave feedback singled out the campsite for criticism. It was felt that the facilities were simply inadequate: the showers were cold; there were insufficient toilets so there was often a queue; and, in general, the washing area was dirty. Two people voiced concerns that the place was a risk of health. One said, and I quote, "I won't even let my dog stay here!" In addition to this, several people felt the campsite was too isolated, as it was some way from the nearest village.

Entertainment

According of the daytime activities, most people were very happy. People rated the day at the beach very high – especially because of the unusually hot weather – and they also enjoyed the castle visit and cream tea. However, when it's coming to the evening, there were a lot of negative comments. It was generally felt that the evening was rather aimless and boring and several people said a desire to some kind of organised activity such as a campfire sing-along or a visit to a local pub.

Recommendations

The school should seriously consider finding an alternative campsite. Concerning the price, people were quite happy and said they would be prepared to spend a little extra for a site with better facilities. There are several in the area and I would heavily recommend one near a village to allow for an evening visit to a typical English country pub.

You are going to report on an event which was held to celebrate the end of year at the place you study or work at. There were some problems with the venue and the entertainment provided. Other aspects were better. Write a report of around 300 words giving your recommendations.

Tapescript

Unit 1

3 Listening (page 10)

P: It was a coffee you wanted, wasn't it?
Z: Yeah, thanks.
P: Do want a piece of chocolate?
Z: No thanks. I'm trying to watch my weight.
P: Yeah, I should try to lose a bit, but I just find it hard to stick to any kind of diet. Anyway, life's too short to be worrying about your weight all the time.
Z: Yeah, you're probably right. Go on, give us a bit, then.
P: You know it makes sense.
Z: I don't know about that … Mmm, it's lovely. What kind is that?
P: Green and Black's. I think it's organic.
Z: Let's have a look at the packet. Well, it's gorgeous. I'll have to get some of that.
P: Go on, have another piece.
Z: Cheers.
P: So what do you think of the class?
Z: It's alright, actually. I like Marie Therese. She's a lot better than the teacher we had last term.
P: Well, that wouldn't be difficult. Pierre was such a bore – all he did was ramble on about grammar all the time. We hardly got to say a word.
Z: I know. That's why I stopped going towards the end of term. Mind you, it's a bit difficult to get a word in edgeways now with that guy, Tony, around. What's his problem? The guy never shuts up.
P: Tell me about it! He's such a know-all as well. Have you seen the way he corrects everybody else?
Z: Oh God, I know. It's so annoying, the way he interrupts you.
P: Still, at least we get to talk in pairs and practice things a bit.
Z: That's true. Mind you, I was stuck next to that guy, Al.
P: Oh yeah. He's a bit of a weirdo, isn't he? He never seems to look you in the eye.
Z: And you can't ever hear what he's saying. He just mumbles to himself and fiddles around with his pens and papers.
P: Yeah, I've noticed that. Very odd. Do you think he's got some kind of obsessive-compulsive disorder?
Z: I don't know. Maybe. Whatever it is, it's a bit disconcerting. Have you spoken to that Welsh guy, Gareth, yet?
P: Yeah, we had a chat last week. He seems quite a nice bloke. Why?
Z: I just wondered. I haven't actually spoken to him, but, you know, he seems … nice.
P: What? You're not telling me you fancy him.
Z: No, don't be ridiculous. Anyway, what if I do?
P: Well, he's a nice guy and everything, but he looks like Mr. Bean!
Z: No, he doesn't!
P: He does! And anyway, you're married.
Z: Yeah, so? There's no harm in looking.
P: You're such a hypocrite! I bet you wouldn't say that if it was me looking at a woman
Z: Fat chance of that!
P: You know what I mean. You always used to complain about your old boss – whatsisname – because he was always eyeing you up and down.
Z: Oh, come on! I mean, there's looking – and there's looking. He was just always looking down your top when you were talking to him. It gave me the creeps. He was so smarmy as well.
P: Well, maybe you give Gareth the creeps.
Z: Please! It's not the same at all – and you know it.
P: I know. I'm just winding you up. Don't take any notice.
Z: You're such an idiot sometimes.
P: Oh well, let me make it up to you. I'll get you some more of that chocolate.
Z: Can you get me some water as well? Cheers.

Unit 2

5 Listening (page 15)

R: Hello?
L: Oh hello, Rachel. It's me – Lynn.
R: Oh hiya. How're you?
L: Dreadful, since you ask! My new job is turning out to be a bit of a nightmare, as it happens. It's really getting me down.
R: Oh no. How come? What's the problem?
L: How long have you got? Honestly, I don't know where to begin! It's been hell from the minute I started there.
R: But I thought this was supposed to be the one – you know, your big break.
L: Yes, well, so did I, so did I. But they keep changing what they want me to do. It's like they can't make up their minds what my actual job description is. I thought I was being employed as a PA, but I seem to spend half my time being the office dogsbody. I mean, all I seem to do most days is make the tea and do the photocopying and then the rest of the time I spend finishing off reports and proposals that the boss is supposed to have done himself! I've told him I don't think half of this stuff is part of my job description, but he just laughed and said it always takes his new PAs a while to find their feet! I mean, what on earth is THAT supposed to mean? How many PAs has he had!
R: It does sound a bit worrying, I have to admit.
L: He seems to think I'm some kind of miracle-worker! I've been sweating blood for him these past few weeks, and he STILL seems to think I'm not pulling my weight! I don't know what he expects, I really don't!
R: Have you tried having a little talk with him … tell him how you're feeling? That might help.
L: You're joking, aren't you? He's really, really moody, very up-and-down and I'm terrified I'd catch him on the wrong day and he'd just really lose his temper. Really ... if things don't get better soon, I'm going to have to start thinking about looking for something else.
R: Oh no. Lynn! This is awful! I'm so sorry it's not working out for you. I wish there was something I could say to make things better, but …
L: No, no. It's OK. It's not your fault, is it? Anyway, listen. I'm sorry to go on about it all. I just needed to let off a bit of steam.
R: That's OK. That's what friends are for.
L: Anyway, how're you? Sorry – I haven't even asked you yet, have I?
R: That's OK. I'm pretty good, actually. I don't know if you'll want to hear this now, but I've actually just got promoted at work.

1 Vocabulary and listening (page 16)

The family of a black man who committed suicide after being subjected to constant racist bullying have agreed an out-of-court settlement from his employers. Julian Smith hanged himself at his family home two years ago and his mother subsequently sued the company for racial discrimination on behalf of her son.

The company conducted a thorough internal investigation, which revealed that white colleagues had consistently undermined Julian in his work and ostracised him following an initial complaint he had made to management about abuse and name-calling.

In a statement the company expressed deep regret at its handling of the affair and stated that it was instigating sweeping changes to ensure that all discrimination is stamped out.

In another hearing a woman has been awarded £22,000 in compensation for sex discrimination after she was denied the opportunity to work part-time when she returned to work following the birth of her first child.

The company is going to appeal against the decision. In a statement they said the decision restricted its flexibility as a business and that it would make the company uncompetitive.

Writing: An introduction

2 Listening (page 18)

I'm sometimes amazed at the difference between students' writing and speaking. Some students are quite fluent – even quite sophisticated – in their use of language when speaking, but then you see a piece of writing and it's a bit of a mess. Then there are others who are quite quiet or faltering when speaking, but then turn out to be pretty good at writing. I guess it just goes to prove that writing and speaking are very different skills. But I think it's also because of the kind of language different students have met. The language we speak in English and the language we write is often quite distinct both in terms of the grammar and the vocabulary we use. For example, words like 'moreover' and 'nevertheless' are far more common in written English than in spoken English, and passives are more common in scientific writing, for example, than in normal speech, while something like inversion is much more common in writing than speaking. Similarly, while speech is obviously governed by grammar and you will see examples of the same tenses and structures in both speaking and writing, it'll often be used in slightly different ways, or with different vocabulary because in spoken English we are interacting with another person more directly than in written English.

It's not surprising, then, if students have been fed a diet of grammar exercises and vocabulary closer to examples of written language and have then had little chance to practise speaking, that their ability in writing outstrips their spoken English. Alternatively, other students who have learnt English just through talking – often outside the classroom and in an English-speaking environment – frequently find their written English isn't up to the same standard.

The relationship may be compared to the difference between two distinct sports – at an extreme, say, between football and tennis. Being good at one may help you to be a little bit better at the other in simple terms of fitness, co-ordination, etc, but to become proficient in both you have to practise both and practise the different skills of both. From that point of view, you also need to remember that not all kinds of writing are the same. Again, there may be common elements to all writing – good spelling and punctuation, for example – but, what you write in a university essay and what you write in a job application letter will be quite different in terms of vocabulary, grammar and the way they are organised.

A different analogy might be to compare writing to cooking. Different dishes require different ingredients and techniques, and you may have to practise making each dish a number of times to get good enough to be able to make it without looking at the recipe book or to develop your own successful variations!

To improve either your writing or speaking you need good models, and you need to practise structures and vocabulary as they are used naturally in either speaking or writing. That's why in this level of *Innovations*, we look at the written language and written grammar in these writing sections, whilst in the main body of the book, there's a greater focus on spoken language. It's also why we focus on the structures and vocabulary closely associated with each type of writing. We hope it works for you.

Unit 3

2 Listening (page 20)

Conversation 1

(M = Matt, R = Ruth)

M: So, do you have any previous teaching experience?

R: Yes, I do. A bit. I spent a couple of years working for VSO, doing volunteer work in a remote part of Sierra Leone, in West Africa.

M: Oh really? What was that like?

R: It was incredible, it really was. I was living in a coastal region and there were little villages scattered all over the place, up and down the coast, so I used to ride up and down on my motorbike and hold classes in these ramshackle little schools. It was amazing how motivated everyone seemed, considering how remote from their experience most of the material I was using with them was and how cut off from the English-speaking world they were.

Conversation 2

(J = Jeremy, H = Holly)

J: Hey, did I tell you? I saw Neil and Becca the other day. I went round to see them in their new flat.

H: Oh yeah? How are they? What's their new place like?

J: They seemed pretty good. A bit worn-out after all the house-hunting and then the D-I-Y, but they were in good form. The flat's OK as well – a bit bigger than their old place, with a little garden and everything.

H: Yeah? And what's the area like round there? It's not a part of town I'm familiar with.

J: No, I wasn't either. It's OK, I suppose – if you like that kind of thing. I mean, personally, I found it a little bit bland and suburban, you know. They're right out in the commuter belt, so it's what you'd expect for that kind of area, I guess. Lots of tidy front lawns and dads washing their cars and families with a couple of kids.

H: Sounds like my idea of hell.

Conversation 3

(P = Paul, J = Jane)

P: The Baltic States are hot news this season and British tourists are flocking to them in their droves. Many budget airlines now offer cut-price deals to the capitals and the countries are slowly developing a more sophisticated tourist infrastructure. Jane Peel is fresh off the plane from Tallinn, the historic capital of Estonia, so let's hear what she has to say about her trip there. Jane.

J: Thanks, Paul. Yes, for once all the hype seems to be true. The Baltics really are as good as everybody says they are. Tallinn is a wonderfully compact little city and if you stay centrally, everything is very accessible. The city centre is a conservation area and so all the buildings are protected. It's an area steeped in history and the skyline is amazing – all soaring church steeples and old rooftops.

P: It all sounds rather wonderful, Jane. So were there any downsides?

J: No, not really. I've been told that visiting in the winter is a bit of a no-

no as the days are short and bitterly cold, and I guess the food still leaves a bit to be desired – it tended to be quite stodgy and there wasn't a huge amount of choice, but otherwise, I certainly had nothing to complain about.

P: And what struck you most about the city, Jane?

J: The nightlife, without a doubt. The Estonians party like there's no tomorrow and are nowhere near as dull as their southern neighbours would have you believe! If anything, the opposite is true! On Fridays, downtown Tallinn is party central. Trust me!

7 Pronunciation (page 23)

1. I get anxious about everything.
2. I suffer from anxiety attacks.
3. There was a big controversy around the incident.
4. It was a really controversial decision.
5. It's one of the country's main exports.
6. We export them all over the world.
7. I'm in charge of finance.
8. It was a purely financial decision.
9. It was a rather insulting offer.
10. Don't take it as an insult, but it's not very good.
11. I'm not very good at photography.
12. I'm not very photogenic.
13. There's no such thing as bad publicity.
14. They didn't publicise the event very well.
15. I'm not responsible for your things.
16. I've got a lot of responsibilities now.

Unit 4

3 Listening (1) (page 24)

S: Hello. Thomson Learning, Saroj speaking. How can I help you?

N: Hiya, Saroj. It's me, Natalie.

S: Hiya!

N: You're back then.

S: Yeah, yeah. I got back on Monday.

N: So how was it?

S: Oh, the holiday itself was great, but getting there was a bit of a nightmare, to be honest. They've tightened up so much on security – it's such a palaver – they must've searched my bag about ten times. Can you believe they confiscated my tweezers? They said they could be used as an offensive weapon.

N: You're joking. That's so over-the-top! What did they think you were going to do – pluck the pilot to death?!

S: They said they were too sharp – I could stab someone with them.

N: Oh please! That's ridiculous. Honestly, you must've been furious. I would've kicked up a right fuss.

S: I know, but there's no point making a scene. They can make things really awkward for you, you know. As it was, we only just got to the boarding gate on time – they were sending out announcements telling us our bags were going to be taken off the plane.

N: Oh no. You made it in the end, though.

S: Yeah, just about. I think we were probably the last ones on, though. We got a few dirty looks when we got on. And then at the other end we had all the hassle of passport control there – you know they take your fingerprints and there's lots of questioning – it's quite heavy. And I'm sure they pick on me more. They really make you feel unwelcome.

N: That's awful. The whole thing's gone too far. I know we've got to guard against terrorist attacks and all that, but it's so over-the top now – people are just paranoid. It's scary.

S: I know, but you know …

N: I was watching this programme about the new terror laws they've introduced. They're outrageous!

S: They are bad.

N: They can basically arrest people and hold them without trial for as long as they like and without any evidence – it's such an infringement on civil liberties.

S: Yeah, I did actually see this great film the other day. It's a bit complicated. I won't go into the whole story, but basically it's about this Muslim woman and she ends up being interrogated by the police because they're questioning some other guy she knows. Anyway, the policeman goes to her 'Tell us what you know about him'. And she says 'I don't know. What am I supposed to know?' And the policeman goes 'I don't know. That's why I'm asking you' and she's like 'Well, how am I supposed to tell you something I don't know when you don't know what it is that I don't know'. And the policeman just says – 'Well, that's your problem' and they lock her up in the cells. It was so absurd – you know – a complete Catch 22.

N: Well, that's it and apparently that's more or less how this new legislation works. Honestly, it's frightening. It's bound to lead to miscarriages of justice.

S: Yeah.

N: Anyway, listen, I didn't mean to get into a conversation – strictly speaking I shouldn't be using this phone for personal calls. So, anyway, I was just wondering if you wanted to meet up later? Are you around after work?

S: I am, actually. Shall I meet you in the usual place around six?

N: Yeah, great. We can catch up a bit more then.

S: Yeah, I'll look forward to it. See you.

N: Yeah, bye.

6 Listening (2) (page 25)

N: Hi there. Sorry I'm a bit late. I got held up at the office.

S: That's OK. I've only just got here myself.

N: Where do you want to go?

S: I was thinking of Andretti's – we haven't been there for a bit.

N: Yeah, OK. Actually, somebody told me it's changed hands. I don't know what it's like now.

S: Oh right? Well, are you sure?

N: Yeah, yeah, yeah. It'll make a change, but we can always go somewhere else if it doesn't turn out to be very good.

S: Yeah.

N: I just need to pop to the cash-point first, though.

S: OK. It's more or less on the way. So how are you? I didn't ask when you rang earlier.

N: No, I'm sorry if I was a bit abrupt, but our boss gets a bit funny about us making personal calls. It's bad enough with him breathing down our necks all day, but he'd just popped out of the office.

S: Don't worry about it. I know how it is. So anyway, apart from that, how're things?

N: It's been a bit weird actually. We were burgled while you were away.

S: No, you're joking! When did that happen?

N: Last Sunday night. We were actually asleep upstairs.

S: You're joking! That's awful! Did they wake you up?

N: No, fortunately. I don't know what I would've done if they had.

S: No, absolutely. You don't want to have to confront some stranger in the middle of the night. You don't know what they might do. They could be armed or anything.

N: Well, this is it. Anyway, what happened was I just came down in the morning and I noticed that all the drawers in the kitchen were open and then I noticed the radio CD thing was missing.

S: Oh no. That's awful! Did they take anything else?

N: Not much. A bit of money, some bits of jewellery nothing particularly valuable. Apparently, there's been a spate of them. The police reckon it's probably drug addicts – they just look for portable things and stuff they can sell quickly.

S: Right.

N: According to the police officer that came round, about 80 per cent of all the burglaries they have round our area are junkies trying to fund their habit.

S: That's shocking! They should do something about it.

N: Well, apparently they are having a bit of a crackdown, but unless they're actually caught in the act, it's difficult to gather enough evidence and then when they are caught, they just reoffend as soon as they come out of prison because they still haven't kicked the habit.

S: Really? It's amazing that some people think it should be legalised when there's such a problem.

N: Yeah, well – you know – I guess they should just set up more rehabs to help people get off drugs.

S: Mmm. So anyway how did they break in?

N: I don't know. There was no sign of any break-in – they hadn't forced the lock or anything. I might've left one of the windows unlocked. The police said they might've just lifted the front door keys off the hook we have by the door. Apparently, they just put a long stick through the post box and unhook it that way.

S: Really? God, it must be really unsettling for you.

N: Yeah, it is. I really feel my home's been violated.

S: I can imagine. It's dreadful.

6 Lawyer jokes (page 27)

1. How can you tell when a lawyer is lying? His lips move!
2. What's the difference between a lawyer and a vampire? Vampires only suck your blood at night!
3. What do lawyers use for birth control? Their personalities!
4. What's the difference between a lawyer and God? God doesn't think he's a lawyer!
5. What do lawyers have in common with rhinos? They're both thick-skinned, short-sighted – and always ready to charge!
6. How do you stop a lawyer from drowning? Take your foot off his head!

Unit 5

4 Listening (page 30)

(R = Robin, S = Sharon)

R: So what do you think about the first one, the Mexican chicken mole?

S: Sounds interesting, doesn't it? It's quite an unusual combination, meat and chilli and chocolate.

R: Yeah, quite an off-putting one, I'd say. I do like chocolate, but not with meat and garlic and stuff. I just imagine it'd be a bit sickly. The idea of it really puts me off, to be honest.

S: God, you're so unadventurous in your tastes. I think all the different contrasting flavours could be really nice. You never know, do you? The only worry I'd have would be the Mexican chillies. They can be really hot sometimes, those things. So what about this second one? The West Beach diet thing?

R: I suppose it sounds all right, but it's not exactly filling, is it? A bit of spinach and a couple of oranges. It's not really a meal, is it?

S: It depends, doesn't it? I mean, it IS a diet. I imagine it'd be quite nice in the summer or if you're trying to shed a few pounds.

R: I can't keep track of all these different diets. And anyway, they never work, do they? Where IS West Beach anyway?

S: I don't know, but the Atkins diet works, doesn't it? I did it once and lost loads of weight.

R: Yeah, and then put it all back on again once you came off it.

S: Oh, thanks a lot!

R: Well, anyway, it's definitely more of a snack than a meal.

S: Yeah, maybe … but I'd give it a go. I like any kind of salad, really.

R: Oh well. Each to their own … which brings us to the real winner! Liver! Mmmm!

S: Are you serious? How can you eat that stuff? It's disgusting?

R: God, I love it! It's delicious and I like the idea of the marinade as well. It sounds lovely. My mouth's watering just thinking about it.

S: Ugh! I can't stand liver, kidney, anything like that. I can't stand the texture. It's all so rubbery. I wouldn't touch it if you paid me!

R: Well, I'd have no problems whatsoever with it myself.

S: Ugh! Rather you than me.

R: Oh well. It's your loss.

5 Listening (page 33)

S: Anyway, Just to change the subject, have either of you seen that Jamie Oliver programme about school dinners?

M: No, but someone at work was talking about it today.

N: It's unbelievable! You must watch it.

S: Yeah, it was awful. It's just the amount of crap children eat and that they serve for school dinners. It's no wonder so many of them are suffering from obesity. They showed these kids having lunch and it was all just chips, chicken nuggets and burgers. And it wasn't even fresh meat – you know – it's all this processed stuff, with loads of additives and salt and rubbish. Honestly, some of the kids had never even eaten salad.

M: Yeah, yeah. This woman at work was saying that some of them didn't know what a courgette was.

N: That's right! It was amazing. He showed them all sorts of vegetables and they didn't know what any of them were. He'd hold up a leek and ask them what it was and they'd say 'Is it an onion?'.

S: Yeah, do you remember one of them said it was a kiwi!

M: That's awful. I'm sure my kids aren't that bad. Mind you, it's very difficult to get them to eat any vegetables.

L: They eat quite a lot of fruit, though.

M: I guess so.

N: No, this was REALLY bad. I mean, he spoke to this nurse who ran a constipation clinic and she said they had kids there who hadn't, you know, done one for six weeks because they don't have any fibre in their diets. Six weeks without a …

S: … Yeah, OK Nigel. I think they get the picture! I was going to edit out that bit.

N: What? I was only going to say can you imagine what it must be like when they finally do!

S: OK. OK. You'll put everyone off their dinner!

M: Honestly, men! They have to bring everything down to basics!

L: That's a bit unfair. I didn't say anything. Anyway, what are we having for the next course? I'm still starving. I've hardly eaten all day.

Unit 6

4 Listening (page 35)

Text 1

A: Did you see that thing on the news last night about the twister in Sussex?

B: In Sussex? You're kidding!
A: No, really! I couldn't believe it either, but apparently England is particularly prone to them, they said. There's something like 35 a year, but most of the time they happen in really remote, cut-off areas so nobody really gets affected by them.
B: Really? I thought they only happened in Tennessee and places like that. So was it bad?
A: Yeah, pretty bad. It only lasted a few minutes, but it caused a lot of damage. It ripped through a residential area and some houses had their roofs blown off, a few garden sheds were blown to pieces, lots of windows got blown out.
B: God! Was anyone killed?
A: No, but a few people ended up in hospital with cuts and bruises from all the flying debris. Oh, and there was a cow involved as well! It got sucked up and dumped about a mile away in a supermarket car park!
B: Oh! I bet that made a right mess. I'm glad it wasn't me that had to clean that up!

Text 2

A: Hiya. Did you have a good Christmas?
B: Yeah, it was great, thanks. We only got back last night, actually.
A: Oh right. Where was it you went again? It was Asia somewhere, wasn't it?
B: Yeah, we were in Nias in Indonesia. It's this island off the south coast of Sumatra. It's a big surfing place. The waves there are amazing.
A: Wasn't that one of the places that got hit by that tidal wave the other year?
B: Yeah, it was. I think something like a thousand people died there and half the villages were wiped out. We were staying right on one of the beaches that got hit by it. It was a pretty sobering experience, really. I mean, they've done a lot of reconstruction work and everything, but there were still bits they haven't really managed to rebuild yet and almost everyone we met had been affected by it all in some way or another.
A: Yeah, I bet.
B: The guy who ran the hostel place we were staying in actually lost his brother and was left homeless for weeks afterwards. It was just incredible how upbeat he seemed – given the circumstances.
A: Well, people are pretty resilient, I guess. You just have to pick up the pieces and move on – get on with rebuilding your life after something like that happens.
B: No, I know. I know. The people there just seemed very pragmatic and realistic about things, but some people still seemed a bit angry about aid not always getting through.
A: Oh really? How come?
B: Oh, it's hard to know, really, but I think some people felt some of it might've vanished along the route, you know.
A: Yeah, I suppose there's always the risk of that happening.

Text 3

A huge earthquake has hit south-eastern Iran. At least fifteen thousand people are feared dead and the death toll is expected to rise in the days ahead. The quake had its epicentre near the ancient city of Bam and many of its buildings have been totally flattened. Many people are believed to be buried under the rubble and President Khatami has spoken of a 'national tragedy' and has urged all Iranians to help the victims. A big relief operation is under way with many foreign countries sending supplies and rescue workers to Iran. The quake occurred at 5.28am local time and it is thought that many people were crushed as they slept. There have been scenes of intense grief in the city with survivors weeping next to corpses wrapped in blankets. Emergency centres set up in makeshift buildings are now trying to care for the tens of thousands who have been injured. The Red Crescent is setting up tents to house those left homeless by the quake. A telephone hotline for donations is being launched today. More details will follow.

Unit 7

3 Listening (page 44)

Conversation 1

A: Is that you?
B: Yeah.
A: Oh my God! You're so different! Look at that hair!
B: It used to take me about an hour to get it spiked up like that.
A: And what happened to the pierced nose?
B: The same as the rest. Work, life. You can't go into a classroom with ripped jeans and spiky green hair.
A: I suppose not, but don't you think it's a shame?
B: No, not at all. Those days are long gone. Wearing a suit and tie is much easier.

Conversation 2

A: Oh my God! What HAVE you done to your hair?
B: It was only supposed to lighten it a little.
A: It's almost orange! I told you not to! What did you use?
B: It's this stuff I got from the chemist.
A: Let's have a look. They shouldn't have sold it to you! You're only 13. You're too young to be dyeing your hair. So how long did you leave it in for?
B: An hour.
A: An hour! No wonder it's come out the way it has. You're meant to rinse it out after 15 minutes.
B: Are you?
A: Yeah, it says here. Didn't you bother to read the instructions?
B: No, but I wish I had. I look like a complete idiot!

Conversation 3

A: So why did you have it done?
B: Various reasons, really. The summer's coming and it'll be hot and I'm bound to be going swimming more. It's just a pain to be washing and drying it all the time and, you know, it gets all tangled. It's just more manageable with it short.
A: I know what you mean.
B: But the other reason was I just had the feeling – well, it may sound silly – but that I was being pigeonholed a bit, maybe held back a bit at work.
A: Yeah?
B: Yeah. I've overheard the odd comment – you know, about dizzy blondes and that. I just feel I'm not always taken seriously. People like to put you in a box, don't they?
A: Well, that's their problem. You should just ignore them.
B: It IS their problem, but at the same time it does affect me and what I get to do, so if a change of style helps me get ahead in the company a bit more, why not? Anyway, as I said, I was ready to have it chopped off.
A: Fair enough.

Conversation 4

A: So how's the chemo going?
B: We'll just have to wait and see. They seem happy enough with the results so far. In the meantime, I'm trying to put it to the back of my mind.
A: I'm sure. It must be difficult.
B: Yeah. The worst part about it at the moment is my hair.
A: Oh dear, is it falling out?
B: Honestly, there are whole clumps of it when I wash it.
A: Oh Paula, I am sorry.
B: Yeah, well. I'm trying to see it as an opportunity. I'm thinking of getting a wig.
A: A wig? I don't see that as much of an opportunity. I think I'd feel a bit self-conscious wearing one.
B: Oh, I wouldn't – and I've always fancied having thick blonde hair. I think I could pass for a bit of a Marilyn Monroe.
A: Hah, yeah. I can see that. I'll come and help you choose one, if you like.

B: Great. It'll be a laugh and I need a bit of cheering up.

Conversation 5

A: So what else did you get?
B: Well, Colin bought me a day at this health spa.
A: Really? That must've cost him.
B: Yeah, but he did owe me something special after my last birthday.
A: Oh yeah, he completely forgot, didn't he? So what are you going to do while you're there?
B: Well, all sorts. There's a steam room, which I love.
A: Mmm, so do I.
B: And I'll probably have a massage and that, but they also have this envelopment treatment.
A: Oh yes? What's that?
B: Oh, it's this thing where you have your whole body covered in mud and then you're wrapped in these kind of hot sacks. It's supposed to leave your skin incredibly soft and sensitive.
A: Oh, so is that why Colin bought you it?

Unit 8

2 Listening (page 48)

H: Did you see that party political broadcast by the Conservatives yesterday, Abigail?
A: Yeah, I caught the end of it.
H: That guy Peter Green, honestly, he gives me the creeps. He's so smarmy.
A: I don't find him that bad. He's just very smooth in front of the camera, you know. He's just got slick presentation skills.
H: Yeah, well, it's a fine line between smooth and smarmy, I guess. Anyway, what really annoyed me was their stance on immigration. Although actually, it's just the whole negativity of their campaign. They don't seem to be putting forward any real policies. Did you see it, Miriam?
M: No, but I know what you mean. It's quite off-putting really.
A: Well, Labour haven't exactly been running a positive campaign. They've said some pretty strong things themselves.
H: Well, I didn't say I was going to vote for them. I've had enough of them as well – especially after what they've done with education, putting up university tuition fees and involving all these private companies in schools.
M: I have to say, the private companies don't bother me so much. I mean, they're only involved in a tiny proportion of schools. What concerns me in education is the increase in faith schools. I just don't think religious organisations should run schools.
A: Why not? I went to a catholic school. It was a really good school.
M: I'm not saying there aren't good religious schools, it's just that I worry that, you know, we're living in a multicultural country and you get all these different religions and their kids are being educated in their separate little worlds. I just don't see it helping integration. You know it would just make more sense if the whole thing was secularised.
A: So who are you going to vote for?
M: Well, having said that, I'm probably going to stick with Labour. They've basically done all right since they've been in power. And I quite like Frank Black as a leader and, you know, it's the economy, isn't it.
H: I find him a bit shifty myself. The guy just never gives a straight answer. You should vote for the Lib Dems.
A: You reckon? They're a bit lightweight, aren't they?
H: No, not at all. I mean, I think Jimmie White's quite down-to-earth and that. I don't think he's the most charismatic politician ever, but, you know, he tells it like it is and they've got some serious policies.
A: Don't you think it's a bit of a wasted vote, though, especially round your way? Your MP's got a pretty big majority, hasn't he? They're never going to get in.
H: Well, if you take that attitude, you might as well not bother at all. Toby, you've been very quiet. What do you think?
T: Oh, I haven't got a clue – I keep out of all of it, if I can help it. They're all as bad as each other. I wouldn't trust any of them as far as I could throw them.
A: You're such a cynic!
H: Well, you're not giving much away either. You're not going to vote Conservative, are you?
A: I'm not saying. I haven't decided.

Unit 9

2 Listening (page 54)

Conversation 1

A: You're back home early, love.
B: Yeah, I know. It was rained off. The pitch was completely waterlogged, so it was too muddy to play on. It was like a mud bath! They've postponed it till near the end of the season.
A: Oh well, never mind. Do you want a cup of tea?
B: Oh, yes please. I could do with warming up a bit.

Conversation 2

A: I thought they said it was supposed to be nice and sunny today.
B: I know. It's started spitting outside. It's going to bucket down any minute. I can't see them having the reception in the garden if it stays like this.
A: Me neither. Do you think they'll have enough room if they have to move everything indoors?
B: I don't know. We'll have to wait and see, I guess.

Conversation 3

A: So how was Malaysia? Did you have a good time?
B: Yeah, it was amazing. Well, I enjoyed it anyway. I'm not sure my mum would want to go there again, though.
A: Oh no! How come?
B: She just really couldn't handle the heat. I mean, it is a bit much, to be honest. When you first get off the plane, it's like walking into a wall. You start sweating like a pig almost at once!
A: Ugh! That doesn't sound much fun.
B: No, I know. You have to wear really light clothes and shower every few hours or so. My mum started getting a heat rash too, which was pretty much the final straw for her! Apart from that, though, it was amazing!

Conversation 4

A: Hello. Johnson Learning.
B: Oh hi, Stef. It's me, Richard. Listen. I'm stuck in Amsterdam. My flight's been grounded. It's been blowing a gale for hours and they've just put out an announcement saying it's delayed indefinitely, so could you let whoever was supposed to be picking me up from Heathrow know. And I'll call you when I hear more news, OK.
A: OK. Sorry!
B: Oh well, there's nothing you can about it, is there? Anyway, listen, I'm almost out of money, so I'd better go. See you. Bye.

Conversation 5

A: What happened to your face?
B: Oh, nothing much. Just a few cuts and bruises. I was involved in a minor car crash.
A: You're kidding? How did that happen?
B: It was coming back from up north last weekend. It'd been snowing for ages and then it dropped to minus God knows what during the night and by morning all the roads were thick with ice. Anyway, this cab driver came to pick us up and take us to the airport and I don't know if he'd been drinking or not …
A: It's always possible, up there!
B: Yeah, or if it was just because the roads were so slippery, but about five minutes after we set off we went

skidding off the road and through all these bushes and we ended up in this field. We were lucky no-one was really hurt. We could've been killed!

Conversation 6

A: The 16.42 service to Oxford will be delayed for up to half an hour due to leaves on the line.
B: Oh, that's bloody typical!
C: Because of what was it? Did he say there was something on the line?
B: Yeah, it'll be leaves on the line.
C: Leaves? From trees? You're joking, aren't you?
B: No, it's not uncommon at this time of year. The leaves fall off the trees, land on the line and then get turned into a kind of slimy mush, which makes the line really slippery. When the driver tries to brake, the train just carries on! It's really dangerous. And some leaves are worse than others – so the joke among passengers if a train is late is – it must be the wrong leaves again!
C: I've heard everything now! In Germany this would be impossible! Leaves on the line! You know this could only happen here in England!
B: Listen, I'm not proud of it, OK!
C: Leaves on the line! Wait till I tell my friends back home! Nobody will believe me!
B: OK, OK. You've made your point, Jurgen. There's no need to rub it in! I never said it was perfect here!

5 Using grammar: conditional sentences (page 57)

A: Have you seen this article in the paper about the effect the increase in air travel's having on the atmosphere?
B: Yeah, I read it this morning. It's dreadful. I don't know why they don't just put up taxes on all air tickets. You know, like £300 minimum to take the plane.
A: They can't do that. There'd be a riot. People just wouldn't stand for it. I mean, so many people travel now. People have just got used to it, haven't they?
B: I know, but it's just totally unsustainable. If they don't do something fairly drastic, the situation's just going to deteriorate.
A: Yeah, but putting up prices … it's unfair, isn't it? It's such a crude way to do things. It's always ordinary people who get hurt.
B: Well, what do you suggest?
A: I don't know. Maybe they should just ration the journeys – you know, three journeys a year each or something like that.
B: I don't know. I don't think it would work. People would just find ways of getting round it.
A: Mmm, maybe, but it'd be better than pricing us out of the sky!

Unit 10

5 Listening (page 60)

Conversation 1

A: Excuse me. Do you work here?
B: No, I don't, no.
A: Oh sorry. I didn't mean to suggest … Well, anyway, you wouldn't happen to know if they sell adaptors for foreign plugs here, would you? You see – like for this one. It's different to the ones we have – it's Japanese.
B: I doubt it. I mean, ask one of the staff, but I would've thought you'd need a specialist electronics store.
A: Yeah, I HAVE had a look. I don't suppose you know if there's a place round here.
B: Sorry. Not as far as I know.
A: Oh well, thanks anyway. You've been very helpful.

Conversation 2

A: There you are! I thought I'd lost you. Have you paid?
B: No, I got a bit distracted. I was just looking at these MP3 players. They're quite cool.
A: Well, take your time! We're only supposed to be at the station in five minutes.
B: Yeah, OK. You were the one who went to the toilet. Now where's the assistant? She was here a second ago. Honestly, they're never here when you want them.
A: Oh, this is just great! We're going to miss this train. I know we are.

Conversation 3

A: What do you think of this?
B: Yeah, it looks fine.
A: You always say everything looks fine. You just want to get home and watch the football.
B: There ISN'T any football on and I think it looks fine. What do you want me to say?
A: I don't know. Just take more interest. Anyway, you don't think it makes my bum look big?
B: No, it's fine. It looks normal.
A: Normal? That's VERY flattering, that is.
B: Oh, for goodness sake! It's gorgeous. It's a wonderful dress. It shows off your backside to the fullest potential and you have a bum J-Lo would be proud of.
A: Well, you're just being stupid now. Honestly, I can't have a sensible discussion with you!

Writing: Letters of complaint

2 Listening (page 62)

E: How was it in Birmingham? You went to see your parents, didn't you?
D: Oh, Birmingham was fine, but it was an absolute nightmare getting there and back.
E: Really? I heard there was some disruption on the line.
D: Yeah, just a bit! We had to come back by coach in the end because there were no Goldlink trains running on the Saturday.
E: What? None?
D: Well, we could've got a train with another company, but they had engineering works, which meant we'd have to get a bus part of the way, so it was going to take over four hours.
E: Four! It's only supposed to take an hour and three quarters normally, isn't it?
D: Yeah, and get this – we would've had to upgrade our tickets. We would've actually had to pay £10 more.
E: That's outrageous! Didn't they warn you that this was going to happen?
D: Well, this is it. When I bought the ticket I said we were coming back on the Saturday, but they didn't say anything. It was lucky I rang up to check the train times on the Saturday morning. Otherwise, we would've turned up at the station and had nowhere to go.
E: Mmm. So are you going to try and get your money back, then?
D: Too right I am. I mean, it wasn't just the return journey – on the way out, the train left late and then we were all ordered off at the next stop to catch a connecting train that was supposed to make up the lost time. But when we got off, no-one had the faintest idea what was going on. There was no connecting train and we had to wait almost an hour for the next one to come along. And of course, when it arrived it was packed, so the kids had to stand most of the way.
E: What a nightmare! It must've spoilt your weekend a bit.

Unit 11

2 While you listen (page 64)

L: Honestly, I just wanted the ground to open up.
D: Poor you! Trying to make an impression and then it all goes horribly wrong.

C: It's always the way, isn't it? It reminds me of that time we were with Michelle in that restaurant in Portugal. Do you remember Amy?
A: Yeah, yeah.
C: We were with these lads and she was trying to impress them with her sophistication and knowledge of food and she was ordering for them. She ordered what she thought was this egg dish and then the waiter brought these things. They were horrible. Do you remember?
A: Yeah.
C: They were like blue-veined golf balls. And these lads just looked at them and the colour just drained from their faces.
L: Oh no!
C: Honestly, Michelle just didn't know what to say. It was so funny. She went bright red.
D: Where is Michelle? I thought she was coming. Amy, did you speak to her?
A: Why should I?
D: Well, just you two usually…
A: Usually what?
D: Just – you know – you're the one who normally rings her.
A: Yeah well, there's nothing to stop any of you.
C: OK. Don't get in a mood. Have you two had some kind of falling out?
A: Just drop it, Caitlin. I don't want to talk about it.
C: OK. I just …
A: Well don't. … I think I'll get another drink. Does anyone else want one?
D: I'm fine, thanks.
L: Yeah, I'll just have a Coke, if you don't mind.
A: Caitlin?
C: No, it's OK. I haven't finished this yet.
A: OK.
L: What was THAT all about?
D: I have no idea. Those two have always been so close.
C: Yeah, but they HAVE had their arguments in the past. I mean, Michelle's got a bit of a temper and, you know, Amy's not exactly the most tolerant person I've ever met.
L: Well, that's true. She's nearly bitten my head off in the past for fairly petty things.
D: I know, but they've always got over any arguments they had before now. It must've been something fairly major for them not to be speaking. Caitlin, haven't you spoken to Michelle?
C: No, I was hoping to see her tonight – like you. I haven't seen her for ages.
D: No?
C: No, to be honest, she was always Amy's friend more than mine. I sometimes felt a bit left out when I was with them – you know – not quite part of their gang – and then since Michelle's been with Paul and I got my job, we've just drifted apart really.
D: I know what you mean. Still, have you got her number? Maybe you should give her a ring – find out what's happened. Amy's obviously not going to say anything else.
C: She's coming back.
L: Well, maybe we should just change the subject anyway – unless we want to ruin the whole evening.

1 Listening (page 66)

A: Oh, that's great, that is!
B: What's up?
A: Look at this mess! It's revolting! What's wrong with him? He's like an animal! I suppose he thinks we're just going to clear everything up after him! Honestly, I've had it up to here with him! What does he think we are? His servants or something? He never lifts a finger round the house!
B: Look who's talking!
A: What's THAT supposed to mean?
B: Well, talk about the pot calling the kettle black. I mean, you're not exactly the tidiest person in the world yourself, are you? And you wonder where Kenny gets it from!
A: Oh, so it's all MY fault he's turned out like this, is it?
B: OK, OK. There's no need to bite my head off about it. I'm not saying it's anyone's fault, am I? And anyway, he hasn't turned out that bad. He's just a perfectly normal 19-year old.
A: Normal? You call THIS normal? He's a complete and utter slob.
B: Look, just leave it, will you? I'll clean this up if it's bothering you THAT much.
A: That's not the point, is it? He's just so selfish. He's constantly leaving stuff lying around all over the place. It's got to change, it really has. I just wish he'd think about us a bit more. That's all.
B: Yeah – and I wish YOU wouldn't get so worked up about petty little things all the time! But we live in an imperfect world, don't we?
A: We obviously do, my sweet! But I'll tell you one thing – if he doesn't sort himself out soon, he'll find himself out on the street and looking for his own place to live!

Unit 12

4 While you listen (1) (page 69)

According to a recent survey carried out by *The Economist* magazine, Ireland is by far and away the best country in the world to live in. Now, whilst this may surprise many living in the United Kingdom, which incidentally came in at 29th, it will surely be of no surprise to the tens of thousands of Irish people who have been busy reversing the trend of a century and moving back to the land of their roots. For over a 150 years, emigration had been part of the Irish way of life, a point emphasised by the fact that there are approximately three and a half million people living in the Irish republic itself – but over 70 million people of Irish descent scattered around the globe. The terrible potato famines of the 19th century were followed by the poverty and chronic unemployment of the 20th.

However, once Ireland joined the EU in 1973, the foundations for economic growth started to be put into place. The 1990s saw the economic miracle finally arrive – a total and utter transformation in Ireland's economic fortunes as the so-called 'Celtic tiger' was born. The country experienced consistent year-on-year growth of almost ten per cent and now has the fourth-highest GDP per head in the world – a massive 36 and a half thousand dollars per person. Coupled with this has been a huge drop in unemployment from 20 per cent 15 years ago to around four per cent today, all of which has meant Dublin's newspapers now come with ever-expanding job sections and the country is looking to import up to 300 thousand new workers in the next few years.

In many ways, Ireland is the perfect advertisement for the policies of the IMF and the World Bank as it is one of the few economies that has opened itself up to free trade, foreign investment and unregulated business activity, cut welfare spending and checked wage increases and yet still managed to boom. It is this, coupled with the traditional values of family and community life, which have pulled so many emigrants back to the old country. We were curious about how they've found the switch and so set out to interview some recent returnees. Here's what they had to say.

6 While you listen (2) (page 69)

I: I'm originally from a small town in the west of Ireland and I moved to the States when I was 21. I think most of my school class emigrated, to be honest, as there just didn't seem to be any job prospects for us back then. But that was nearly twenty years ago and a lot's changed since then. I had a couple of kids and it'd got to the point where I really had to decide if I wanted them to be American or not. I also found myself getting a bit cheesed off with elements of the expatriate community in Boston, where I was living. I am Irish and proud to be so, but some of these guys were more Irish than the Irish, you know. Emigration just seemed to have resulted in a really over-the-top, stereotyped idea of Irishness and I couldn't really handle that. Anyway, I upped and moved a year ago now and it's been the best thing I've ever done. I walked straight into a great job as a software engineer and I'm making great money. Dublin's a real boom town at the moment – new buildings springing up everywhere, hi-tech industries going crazy – and it's a lot more cosmopolitan than it ever used to be as well. There's a real buzz about the place and I'm pleased to be part of that.

J: I'd been working as a nurse in London for years, but had been hearing a lot about the boom back home. What really swung it for me was one day I heard a radio ad looking for English construction workers to go and work in Ireland! I just couldn't believe it. I mean, my dad came to England to work as a bricklayer and half of London was built by the Irish, so it just seemed to be a real sign that the tide had turned the other way. I moved back three years ago to Tullamore, as I've got relatives there and it's been OK so far, I suppose. There are lots of lovely things about living here – it's much safer for kids and there's still a real sense of community. That said, though, there is a real gap between Dublin and the provinces. A lot of the boom mainly hit the capital and it's only very slowly filtering down to the rest of the country, so there's still a big town versus country – rich and poor – divide. On a more personal level, I'm finding the lack of privacy a bit of an issue myself. I mean, it's nice that everyone watches out for everyone else, but it does sometimes feel a bit like they're just poking their noses in as well! Still, I do love the fact that we've got the English building our roads! We don't even pick our own potatoes anymore, you know. We've got the Latvians to do that for us!

M: I lived abroad for nigh-on fifty years and now I'm back I have to say it's been a bit of an anti-climax. I can't see what all the fuss is about, to be honest. I think things have been hyped-up more than perhaps they should've been. The Ireland I grew up in is dead and gone, I feel. The Catholic Church has lost a lot of its pull and power and in its place, well, the young folk just go shopping, don't they? Sure, they may be better off, but that's not everything in life, you know. There's a kind of cynicism and selfishness and individualism that comes with the capitalist dream and oldies like me do worry about the community spirit dying out. Divorce is on the increase, the traffic is terrible and we've got suicide figures like you wouldn't believe. Folk like me who've been around the block a couple of times know to take a lot of the talk with a pinch of salt, you know.

Unit 13

2 Listening (page 78)

Conversation 2

A: Wow, what a great film.

B: Brilliant, brilliant!

A: That scene where they were sitting in the bar and the Joe Pesci character pretends he's going to kill him …

B: Oh yeah, fantastic. It was just so tense because you don't know if he's going to end up shooting him or not – and the guy's so obviously on the edge.

A: Yeah, he was great, Joe Pesci.

B: Brilliant. And just that opening, when he opens the boot and shoots the guy and then the frame freezes and he goes "I always wanted to be a gangster."

A: Yeah, fantastic. But it was brilliant because it really did give you a feel for what must've been so great about it. I mean, I loved that scene as well where the camera just follows them through the kitchens and back rooms when they go to the Copacabana club.

B: Yeah, yeah, no, there were just so many good scenes. It was brilliant. Great film.

Conversation 3

A: So did you go and see that film in the end?

B: Yeah, although I kind of wish I hadn't.

A: Oh, really? Wasn't it very good?

B: No, it was all right. It's really quite moving, but it's just that there was this couple sitting behind me. Honestly, if they weren't rustling a bag, they were talking! It was incredible. They didn't even pretend to whisper. It ruined the film really.

A: Oh, that's a shame. Did you say anything?

B: If I'd been in Britain, I would've. But, I don't know, I just felt a bit awkward. I wasn't absolutely sure of saying the right thing – you know – and I didn't really want to get caught up in some huge scene.

A: No, I know what you mean.

B: I'm glad actually, because this woman next to me said something and the guy just really slagged her off.

A: Oh, really? So do you reckon it's worth seeing? I mean could you follow it all right?

B: Yeah, pretty much. I'm sure I missed stuff, but I got most of it. The film itself is pretty good, though – it certainly brought tears to my eyes.

Conversation 4

A: So what are you up to later?

B: I've vaguely arranged with Hans to go and see the latest Harry Potter film.

A: Harry Potter? Are you serious?

B: Yeah. Why? Are you one of these people who gets all snobby about films?

A: No, no, but it's a kids' film. I mean, how old are you?

B: Listen, it's just like any other big-budget action movie – it's just a bit of escapism.

A: Well, it doesn't do anything for me. It's just all hype and no substance.

B: Oh, no substance! There you go, that's typical of you film snobs. Not everything has to be deep and meaningful, you know.

A: I didn't say it did. It's just not the kind of film I would go and see.

6 Listening (page 81)

(T = Tracy, R = Rod)

T: So what're you up to tonight? Any plans?

R: Well, I'm supposed to be going out with some people from work later, but I'm kind of looking for an excuse to get out of it. I just don't really feel like it, to be honest. It's just a bit much after seeing everyone all week in the office, you know.

T: Yeah, I can imagine.

R: Why? What about you? What've you got on?

T: Well, I was toying with the idea of going out somewhere. There's this play on called *Carl and Carla* that I read a review of and it sounded quite interesting. It's about identity and desire and that kind of thing.

R: Yeah? It sounds a bit arty-farty to me.

T: Yeah, maybe. But would you be up for going out, then?

R: Yeah, if there's something good on, I'd love to. Go on. Give me a look at the listings mag. Here, how about this? *Revenge*. That sounds OK, don't you think?

T: You're joking, aren't you? I can't stand those kind of Hollywood action flicks. Too over-the-top for me, I'm afraid.

R: OK, well, how about checking out a comedy club? That could be good.

T: Yeah, OK. Which one did you have in mind? I think this one sounds good, the *Big Night Out*.
R: Yeah, that sounds great. And then if you feel like it, we could go on to a club after that. I thought this place *Larger* looks good.
T: Where? Let me read it. Oh, it sounds a bit full-on to me, to be honest. I'm too old for that kind of place. This one sounds a bit more like my cup of tea, *Blow Up*.
R: What is it? Oh, OK. Retro stuff, so 60s and 70s. That might be all right, I suppose. I wouldn't mind giving that a go.
T: Brilliant. That's that sorted, then.
R: Yeah, great. I'd best just give the guys from work a call and let them know I can't make it.

Unit 14

3 Listening (page 83)

J: I went to see this amazing film the other night – *Hotel Rwanda*. Have you ever seen it?
D: No, but I've heard about it. What was it like?
J: It was incredible. Very powerful, but pretty harrowing too, I have to say. I mean, it had me in floods of tears a couple of times. There's this one horrific scene where the main guy, this hotel owner, is driving and it's really foggy and he keeps hitting all these bumps and so he gets out to see what's going on and he suddenly realises he's been driving over all these mutilated corpses. It's just horrendous!
B: So what's the story, then? I must admit, I don't really know much about what went on over there. It was the 80s, wasn't it?
J: No, mid-nineties. '94. Basically, the president got killed and that sparked this ethnic tension between these two different groups, the Hutus and the Tutsis, and the Hutu extremists went mad and killed over three quarters of a million Tutsis in just a few months. They basically just hacked people to death with these huge machetes – while the rest of the world sat back and watched it unfold.
B: God, it sounds like a pretty heavy film.
J: It was. I felt awful about it afterwards. I mean, we all just sat back and let it happen. We should've intervened, we really should.
B: It sounds like it, yeah.
D: But hold on a second, Jackie. Last time we talked about this kind of thing, you were rabidly anti-war, weren't you? In fact, I distinctly remember you saying that war was never justified.
J: You're twisting what I said, Don. All I meant was that it's pointless trying to bomb countries into democracy – and I don't agree with attacking other countries just because you're scared that they might attack you.
D: Oh, so it's all right to invade a country to stop them killing each other, but not because there's a chance they might end up killing you. Is that what you're saying? Where's the sense in that?
J: I'm not saying that at all. What I'm saying is I don't think it does us any good to invade countries and then tell them we're liberating them when they probably see us as aggressors.
D: Hardly! Most people living in repressive regimes would be glad to see us marching in. You've seen the TV pictures of the celebrations before, haven't you?
B: Ah well, I do have to say, Don, I'd take what you see on TV with a pinch of salt, to be honest. I mean, there's always a degree to which they just show us what they want us to see, isn't there? You're never going to get the whole picture of what's really going on.
J: Exactly! There's a lot of propaganda and brain-washing that goes on. They turn war into some 24-hour-a-day entertainment show and bring us loads of so-called experts just to distract us from what's really going on. They don't show you the innocent civilians killed in all our bombing raids, do they? And then with things like Rwanda, they only give us the story after it's all too late.
D: Yeah, but from what you said, it was all over quite quickly there. All the killing, I mean. It doesn't sound like we would've had time to go over there and sort it all out even if we'd wanted to.
J: Well, that's the cosy way to look at it, but I've come to think that probably we let those poor people die just because it wasn't in our economic interest to help them. If there'd been oil in Rwanda, we'd have been over there like a shot.
B: Oh, come on, Jackie! It's never as black and white as that. All kinds of factors come into play.
J: Maybe, but money's the most important one.
D: Well, all I can say is you've changed your tune, Jackie.

Unit 15

2 Listening (page 88)

Conversation 1

A: I can't believe it. You?
B: Why are you so surprised? It wasn't exactly a shotgun wedding. We HAVE been together for almost ten years.
A: Well, exactly. I mean, why now? It's not as though you really needed a public statement of your commitment. I mean, you've got three kids!
B: Well, that's mainly it, actually. There were just all these legal complications if we weren't. Joan didn't have any rights to my pension if I died and I had no rights on the children if she did.
A: Is that right? So it was just for the bit of paper then, really.
B: Yeah, well, that's why we didn't really tell anyone about it – just our immediate families. We didn't want to make a big thing of it. We didn't even really get dressed up or anything. We were in and out of the registry office in about ten minutes flat. Mind you, when we actually exchanged our vows, I did get a bit emotional. It was weird. I thought I was going to burst into tears.
A: I don't know. It's not that surprising. It's a big thing, however long you've been together. I think it's a shame. You should've had some kind of party, made more of it.
B: Maybe. We were talking about it. We might have a do later in the year for our tenth anniversary. A kind of double celebration.

Conversation 2

A: So how was it?
B: Oh, a bit of a drag, to be honest. I mean, the whole ceremony must've taken about three hours. You have to sit through all these endless speeches – some old academic droning on about something or other. I nodded off a couple of times. Then it was about an hour and a half of watching people file on and off the stage to shake the Chancellor's hand and collect their scrolls. And needless to say, being zoologists, we were the last ones up.
A: Oh God, yeah! Of course! So did you have to dress up in a gown and everything?
B: Oh yes, gown, mortar board, suit, the lot. I looked a right idiot.
A: I can imagine. Doesn't exactly go with the green hair and grunge image!
B: No! Still, my parents were happy and I only really did it for them. They'd been nagging me about it for ages. You know, like they had to get the photos of their clever son.

A: Ah yes, the photos, I'll look forward to seeing those.

B: I bet you will! I might have to burn them before you get the chance!

Conversation 3

A: How was it then?

B: Oh, it was great in one way, but I did feel a bit uncomfortable.

A: Yeah? How come?

B: Well, God knows how much the whole thing cost. We were served champagne before we even sat down for the meal and the food was incredible. And then they had Bill Simms compèring the actual ceremony and he was hilarious.

A: Yeah, so what's wrong with that? It sounds great.

B: It was, it was. It's just that I couldn't help thinking it was all at the taxpayers' expense and considering the whole thing was meant to be celebrating achievements in helping the needy, it just seemed a bit hypocritical. We could've spent the money on more important things, like – you know – helping the needy!

A: Oh, for goodness sake! Don't take things so seriously all the time. Consider it a perk of the job! It's not as if you're being paid vast amounts of money or getting company cars or anything.

B: Yeah, I know. It was just a passing thought really. You know.

A: Yeah, I do know what you mean, it's just as I said, …

B: Yeah.

Conversation 4

B: So how was it?

A: It was amazing, really – almost a party atmosphere. I mean, when they brought the coffin out, they played *Movin' On Up* by Primal Scream and people were almost dancing.

B: Really?

A: Yeah. Apparently, he'd specifically requested it in his will. The other slightly bizarre thing was that when they tried to lower him into the grave, the coffin wouldn't fit.

B: You're joking? I knew he was big, but I didn't realise he was quite that big.

A: Oh yeah, he was a big man, a big character. Oh God, I think I'm going to cry. Have you got a tissue?

Unit 16

4 Listening (page 93)

Conversation 1

A: So how did you get into that line of work, then?

B: Well, it was strange, really, because I used to be a dental nurse and I'd started to find it all a bit repetitive and predictable and wanted to kind of stretch myself a bit and then one day I was chatting to this old friend of the family and she suggested that I quit and retrain – so I did. And I haven't looked back since.

A: Oh, that's great. You're lucky that you enjoy your job so much.

B: I am, I know. I set up on my own about two years ago now and the practice has just been growing and growing. People come along for a massage or some shiatsu or aromatherapy or whatever and they leave feeling all calm and chilled-out and then they tell their friends and word of mouth does the rest. It's been brilliant.

A: Oh, that's great. So what's this course you're doing, then?

B: Oh, the acupuncture course? Yeah, that's great. I'll have finished by September and then I'll be a fully-qualified practitioner, so, you know, another string to my bow.

Conversation 2

A: So when did you first find out?

B: Well, I was diagnosed about four years ago. I had this mole on my leg and it'd got all red and itchy and had this strange kind of crust on it and I knew I should really get it looked at, but I put it off and put it off and then eventually I went in and the doctors didn't seem to think there was anything much wrong with it. They just removed it and sent it away to be analysed. I went in a few weeks later just for a routine check-up, and that's when they broke the news to me. It just came completely out of the blue. I was devastated, I really was. You just never really think that kind of thing can happen to you, you know.

A: No, I can imagine. God!

B: And then they put me on this experimental drugs trial, which was a blessing in disguise in a way. It meant I avoided having to go through chemo and it's all turned out OK, really, because it went into remission a year or so ago and I've been feeling much better since then.

A: That's amazing! So being a guinea pig really worked, then.

B: So far it has done, yeah. Fingers crossed. But I'm not taking anything for granted. I mean, you never know when you might have a relapse.

Conversation 3

A: Did you hear that thing on the news this morning about dieting?

B: No, what was that?

A: Oh, it was great news for me. They said it's actually really bad for you if you're a bit on the plump side and then you lose too much weight. It can really do you in.

B: Uh? How did they work that out?

A: Well, apparently, it puts a real strain on your heart, the sudden change. And to think, I've been killing myself trying to get rid of this belly for weeks now!

B: No, you must've misheard it, mate. It can't be right. Are you sure they didn't just say it's GOOD for you?

A: I'm positive. I'm going for another burger to celebrate. Do you want anything?

Conversation 4

A: So how did it go the other day? The dinner with Dan's parents.

B: Oh no! I haven't spoken to you since then, have I? God, what a night THAT was!

A: That sounds a bit ominous. What happened?

B: Oh, it was all a bit of a nightmare, to be honest. His mum was totally weird. She seemed really hyper and odd when we arrived and she was fussing round all the time, but then she suddenly started screaming at Dan when he said he didn't want any dessert and then she burst into tears! It was all pretty heavy.

A: It sounds it! So what was all that about?

B: Well, apparently, she's only just managed to get off sleeping tablets. She'd been hooked on them for years and she'd been taking more and more and more and then about three months ago she decided to quit and she just stopped cold and has been struggling to cope ever since.

A: So she's going through cold turkey, then.

B: Yeah, yeah. It's horrible to see, though. I felt awful for her.

3 Listening (page 94)

C: Did you see this story about the designer babies?

J: Oh yeah, I saw it on the news last night. I don't know where I stand on that really, to be honest. The whole thing's a bit of a minefield, if you ask me.

C: It can't be good, can it?

J: You don't think so?

C: No. It's a slippery slope, isn't it? They let this couple select their baby for a certain type of tissue, the next thing is, people will be selecting them to have blue eyes or be more intelligent.

J: I don't know about that. I think that's a long way off, don't you?

C: Well, that's another thing, isn't it? I mean, I think it's creating false hopes for these parents. The whole procedure's totally untested, you know. It'll probably come to nothing.

J: So what are you worried about then? You're kind of contradicting yourself, aren't you?
C: No, I think they should just let nature take its course. It'd be better for all concerned. When it comes down to it, we all die. That's life!
J: Sure, but that's just an argument against any medical intervention, isn't it? And it's very easy to say that when it's not your son dying. From what I've heard, the doctors were pretty up-front about the chances of success. It's got to be worth a try, though, hasn't it?
C: Even when it's going to cost so much?
J: Well, that's a different issue, but as far as I understand it, the couple are going to pay for the treatment themselves.
C: Yeah, they are, but if it IS successful, there'll be pressure to make it available more widely and for different problems and it'll drain money away from other areas. As I say, I just think the whole thing is just asking for trouble.
J: Mmm, I DO know what you mean, but I'm just really not that sure. It'd just seem harsh not to allow it in this particular case.

Unit 17

2 Listening (page 98)

Conversation 1
A: I saw the most disgusting thing on the bus this morning.
B: Yeah? I'm not sure I want to know.
A: No, it was kind of funny.
B: Go on, then.
A: So I was on the bus and this old guy gets on and he hobbles on and sits just opposite me and the guy's got this really horrible cough and he just starts coughing, you know, really loudly (demonstrates) …
B: OK, I get the picture.
A: And then suddenly he sneezes and out comes this set of false teeth and they drop onto the floor.
B: Oh, oh …
A: Yeah, but get this. He then just picks them up off the floor and pops them back in his mouth, without even wiping them or anything!
B: Oh, you're joking! That's horrible!
A: I know. I just had to turn away, and as I turned my head, I looked straight at the woman next to me who was doing exactly the same, just turning away, with this look on her face. And I must've looked the same – you know, just squirming. And we both just cracked up.
B: Poor bloke!
A: I know. We shouldn't have laughed really, but it was just the way me and this woman looked at each other. We were both just going 'Woahhh'. It was just really funny.
B: Yeah.

Conversation 2
A: How was the class?
B: It was a complete farce.
A: Why? What happened?
B: Well, first the teacher turned up late and then he was obviously completely unprepared. He kept on forgetting what he was supposed to be saying. It was terrible.
A: Really?
B: Yeah. I mean, he tried to laugh it off – you know, just make a joke of it – but it was just embarrassing really. I was fuming by the end.
A: I bet. I mean, it's not the cheapest business school there is.
B: Tell me about it! The place is a joke. I'm actually thinking of demanding my fees back.

Conversation 3
A: How was the lecture?
B: It was fine – although it was a bit embarrassing.
A: Yeah? How come?
B: Well, we just got the giggles in the middle of it and we were sitting right in the front.
A: What brought that on?
B: I don't know. It wasn't that funny. I just passed a note to Tim saying the guy doing the lecture looked like a fat David Beckham and he just set me off and then the two of us were just giggling uncontrollably, and of course, because we were in the front row, we were desperately trying to keep a straight face, which just made things worse. I just had tears rolling down my face … And I just let out this snort at one point and the guy giving the lecture just gave me the filthiest look.
A: I'm not surprised. Honestly, anyone would think you were 12 carrying on like that!
B: I know. It was a bit like being back at school again.

Conversation 4
A: So what happened?
B: They played this horrible practical joke on me. They filled my desk drawers with porridge.
A: No! With porridge? When? How?
B: I don't know. I guess they must've done it last night after I left the office. Anyway, I knew they'd done something because I saw a couple of them sniggering when I came in. Anyway, I sat down and I was there most of the morning without noticing and people kept asking me if I'd had breakfast and talking to me in a Scottish accent. Stop smiling! It was really irritating.
A: I'm sorry. I shouldn't, so when did you realise?
B: Oh, I needed a stapler and I just looked in the drawer and there's just this horrible sludge there – and all my stuff.
A: You're joking! They didn't empty it first?
B: No!
A: I can see why you didn't see the funny side now.

2 Listening (page 100)

A: Did I tell you I saw Will the other day?
B: No. How was he?
A: Great. He was in really good form. He got into full joke-telling mode. You know how he does.
B: Yeah, he had us in stitches the last time I saw him. I don't know how he does it. I'm terrible at remembering jokes.
A: I know. Me too. I do remember one from the other day, though.
B: Oh yeah? Go on then.
A: Well, this woman accompanies her husband to the doctor's office. After his check-up, the doctor calls the wife into his office – on her own. He says to her, 'Your husband is suffering from a very severe stress disorder, so if you don't follow my instructions carefully, he's bound to die.' And the wife says 'That's terrible! Is there nothing you can do?' So the doctor says, 'Well, there's something YOU can do, actually. Every morning, you should fix him a healthy breakfast. Be nice to him all the time. Make him a nutritious meal for lunch and for dinner make him something especially nice – whatever he wants that day. The other thing is, you mustn't burden him with chores or discuss any of your problems with him and don't nag him as it'll only make his stress worse. But most importantly of all, you should make love to him at least once a day. If you can do this for the next ten months to a year, I think your husband should regain his health completely.' The woman says 'I see. Well, thank you very much doctor.'

On the way home, the husband asks his wife, 'So what did the doctor say?'

And she goes, 'Oh … he said you're going to die!'

Unit 18

2 Listening (page 104)

Conversation 1

A: Did I tell you we were held up at gunpoint while we were on holiday?

B: No! My God! When? What happened?

A: It was three or four days before we came back. We were at a cash point and this guy came up to us on a moped and just pulled out a gun and told us to give him the money. And I just handed it over and he rode off down the street.

B: Bloody hell! You must've been terrified.

A: Not really. We didn't really have time to be. It happened so quickly. I mean, we were both a bit shaken-up afterwards, but actually while it was happening …

B: Yeah, still, … dreadful, dreadful. It must've spoilt your holiday completely.

Conversation 2

A: Did I tell you I got a ticket while we were away?

B: No? Already? You've only been driving six months!

A: I know, but it's not fair. I was only just over the speed limit and the road was virtually deserted, so it's not as if I was doing anyone any harm.

B: Really? The police must've just been having a bad day. What did they say when they stopped you?

A: That's just it. I didn't speak to anyone. I was caught on camera. I just got the fine through the post – sixty quid, three points on my licence and no right to appeal. Honestly, it's like living in a police state. If they spent half as much time and money tracking down real criminals …

Conversation 3

A: Did you hear about Adrian?

B: No, what?

A: Oh, he got done for drink driving, didn't he?

B: Oh, you're joking! Mind you, he had it coming. The number of times I've been to the pub with him and he's driven home.

A: Yeah, I know. I guess it serves him right.

B: So, has he been banned?

A: Yeah, one year and on top of that he got a £2000-fine.

B: Ooph, nasty! Still, as you say, I guess it serves him right. And in other circumstances he could've gone to prison.

Conversation 4

A: Did you see that thing about that lad who was murdered in Manchester?

B: Oh yeah, it was dreadful. What makes someone do something like that? What goes through their heads, people who do that kind of thing?

A: I know. I know. It just seemed totally unprovoked.

B: And it was in broad daylight in a crowded street! I can't believe no-one intervened.

A: I know. Mind you, would you have? The guy who did it was obviously a maniac.

B: Maybe, although it's an impulse thing, isn't it? I've chased a mugger before now. I didn't catch him, but you know … you would've thought someone would've.

A: Hmm, maybe. It's hardly the same thing.

B: No, I suppose not. Anyway, let's hope they get him soon.

Conversation 5

A: I was speaking to Ricki the other day. Did you know she takes her kids to school every day and picks them up?

B: Really? But they're quite old, aren't they?

A: Yeah, I think the oldest one's 16 and the other's 14. But she said she's worried they'll get mugged or abducted or something.

B: That's a bit over-the-top, isn't it? I mean, it's not as though they live in the roughest part of town.

A: I know, but she claims there's been a spate of attacks on teenage girls and she doesn't want to take the risk.

B: Right. I don't know, though. How long's she going to do that for? She's got to let go eventually – or is she going to drive them everywhere till they're 20? She just smothers those kids. It can't be good for them.

Unit 19

2 Listening (page 114)

L: Hah! Hey, great game on Saturday.

T: Yeah, yeah, yeah.

L: What was it you said, Terry? We're going to thrash you?

T: Yeah, OK. You were just lucky. We were all over you.

L: Uh? I think we must've been watching a different game. You hardly had a shot on target.

T: Apart from that one which hit the bar.

L: OK, apart from that, but that was only a long-range effort. They didn't really create any clear-cut chances, did they?

T: And what about your goal? It was miles offside.

L: Dream on! Just because that donkey you signed for a centre back hasn't got any pace, it doesn't make everyone who gets past him offside. How much did you pay for him? £18 million? Talk about a waste of money. The guy can't even tackle!

T: He just needs a few games to settle in. I'd rather have him than that lot you've got. All they do is boot it up the field. There's no style about it.

L: That's such crap! We play some really good football. Look at Mariner – he's very under-rated. He controlled the whole game and I bet he gets paid half of what your lot earn.

T: I have to admit he did play well, but can he keep it up for a whole season? Basically, we had a bit of an off-day and you played at the top of your game, but you still only scraped a win.

L: Scraped! I don't think so. All that money, and you still couldn't win. What's the betting you'll end up outside the top three and then go bankrupt when your sugar daddy leaves you?

T: Dream on! We'll see who wins the title and I think I can say with absolute certainty that your lot don't stand a chance, Lee. In fact, the likelihood is you'll get relegated.

L: Get out of here! We'll be pushing for a top six spot.

G: Oh, for goodness sake! Can't you two just give it a rest? It's August! It's not even supposed to be the football season. Do I have to put up with this all year round now?

L: All right, all right, keep your hair on! It's just a bit of friendly banter.

G: Banter? Huh! Is that what you call it? Shouting at each other, more like. What is it about football that makes people scream at each other and start fights?

L: Hey, don't compare us to hooligans! It's not the same at all.

T: Yeah, it's a bit harsh. Just because we're passionate about it.

G: Oh God, that old chestnut! Listen, there are plenty of people who are 'passionate' about sport, but (a) – they don't go on about it 24 / 7 and (b) – they don't go round beating each other up when they lose. You don't see tennis supporters screaming at each other or golf supporters or rugby or cricket fans. What is it about football? It's so tribal.

L: Well, it's a better game for starters.

G: Well, that's a matter of opinion. Personally, tennis is the only sport I really like watching.

T: Well, that lot are not exactly models of good behaviour, are they? Always throwing their rackets around.

G: That doesn't happen that often, and it doesn't transfer to the crowd either. I mean, when did you last see a tennis crowd spitting at the players or hurling racist abuse at the black players?

L: It's just because tennis crowds are more middle-class.

G: Hah, that's got to be the most feeble argument I've ever heard! Quite apart from the fact that it's quite insulting to working-class people, do you really think football crowds are that working class, given the prices football clubs charge these days?

T: No, but I bet there's just as much racism in tennis as in football, you know …

Unit 20

4 Listening (page 117)

A: So what're you up to over the holidays, Gary? You got any plans?

G: Oh, you know, the usual. I've got the in-laws coming down for a week to see Michelle and the kids, so she's already started freaking out because she's never had to do Christmas dinner for her folks before and she's petrified it's all going to be a disaster and she'll get a telling-off and a lecture from her mum, and then the kids are both getting really hyper because they're expecting more presents than ever. Michelle's old man will probably end up passing out in front of the telly after a few too many sherries and cold turkey sandwiches – and I'm just praying I'll be able to sneak out on occasion and get away from it all for a while, you know, leave them all to it!

A: It sounds like more stress than it's worth to me. Makes me glad we're going away.

G: Oh really? Where are you off to, then?

A: Oh, we've booked a little villa in the Dordogne and we're going to be there over Christmas and the New Year, just the two of us, so that should be really nice and chilled.

G: Ooh! Sounds very romantic. What about you, Jamelia? You doing anything special?

J: I don't celebrate Christmas, do I?

G: Oh, I didn't know. Don't you? How come? What's all that about? Is that a religious thing or something?

J: I'm a Jehovah's Witness.

G: Oh, OK. So that means you don't celebrate Christmas, does it? I didn't realise.

A: No, me neither. I have to say, I'm pretty ignorant about what being a Jehovah's Witness involves. I'd always just assumed it was basically the same as Christianity.

J: It is in some ways, but we don't celebrate Christmas or Easter because they're pagan.

G: What do you mean they're pagan?

J: They're not proper Christian holidays. The early church just tacked them onto festivals which were already being celebrated by the heathens – Christmas is basically a pagan mid-winter ceremony, the winter solstice, and anyway, I don't believe Jesus was born then. He was born on October 1st and He never commanded anyone to celebrate his birth. Which makes sense really. I mean, to me it's just weird remembering someone when they were just a tiny little baby. It's like when you see photos of yourself as a child. It's not how you see yourself now and not how you'd wish to be remembered. Do you get me? So we see celebrating His birth as disrespectful.

G: Um, yeah. I see where you're coming from, but I've just never really thought about it. It just seems a bit extreme to me, all that.

A: Yeah, though when you hear YOUR plans for the holidays, you can see that paganism is still alive and well.

G: Oh, thanks a lot! So is that the main difference, then? Just that you don't celebrate Christmas and Easter?

J: Or birthdays or anything like that – Mother's Day, Father's Day, Valentine's Day. They're all pagan.

G: Wow! That's a lot of not celebrating you do, then!

J: There's no need to take the mickey, you know!

G: No, sorry, I didn't mean to offend you or anything. It's just that it's quite hard for me to get my head round, that's all. So do you go round from door to door as well, then?

J: Yes, me and my kids do that at the weekend. We're duty bound to warn people about the end days. It's part of the religion.

A: Phwoar! Sounds like hard work to me.

G: I know. Rather you than me, really.

J: Yeah, well. You make your choices – and you have to live with the consequences.

G: Yeah, I guess so.

Writing: Making requests and enquiries

4 Listening (page 120)

1. A: I was wondering if you'd like to go to the cinema later.
   B: Sounds great. What were you thinking of seeing?
2. A: Could you do me a favour and go to the shops for me?
   B: If I have to! What do you want me to get?
3. A: Excuse me. Sorry. You wouldn't happen to know where the toilets are, would you?
   B: Yeah sure. They're just down the corridor on the left.
4. A: You couldn't help me carry these things to my car, could you?
   B: Listen, I would, but I've done my back in. I'm not allowed to lift anything.
5. A: Is there any way you could ask your sister if she'd think about it?
   B: Oh, tricky question … let me think. Um … No! Not a chance! Ask her yourself!
6. A: Would it be at all possible to get the report back to me by Friday?
   B: Sorry. I would if I could, but we're completely snowed under this week.
7. A: Would you mind helping me with this essay?
   B: Oh sure, I'd love to. It's not as though I have a life of my own to worry about, is it?
8. A: Do you know if there's a good place to eat round here, by any chance?
   B: I haven't the faintest. Sorry. I'm new here.

Unit 21

5 Listening (page 123)

Julie: We got in well after midnight and he was the only cabbie around, so we were obviously completely at his mercy. He didn't speak a word of English, so we just showed him the hotel address and he nodded like he knew it, so in we hopped, and off we went – and he then proceeded to completely fleece us! To say we took the scenic route is putting it mildly! We must've passed every single monument and historic building in the whole city – and then some! And all the time, he kept looking nervously at me in his mirror, checking me out. I had a gut feeling something was up, but what can you do? As we arrived at the hotel, he announced it was a hundred thousand, and we were just so wiped-out, I just paid it! I did the maths the next morning once I'd remembered the exchange rate – and nearly had a heart attack. But, anyway, we're here now – and we're determined to make the most of it!

Mandy: It was awful! I was such a bag of nerves, I just completely botched it up. I started off OK and did the first couple of junctions OK, but then I stalled going round a corner on a hill and that just completely threw me. My concentration went to pieces and I then proceeded to clip a parked car and nearly knocked their wing mirror off. To top it all off, I failed to notice a guy reversing towards me and the examiner had to make an emergency stop to stop him going right into us! It was a complete nightmare, honestly!

John: Honestly, I really thought we were goners! It must've been about half past eleven at night and there were seven of us packed into this tiny little hatchback. It can't have been legal, but no-one seemed that fazed by it all, so I just kind of went with the flow. Anyway, we were driving round the outskirts of town looking for this mythical seafood restaurant and we went this way and that and it was all starting to look ever more like a wild goose chase when the woman driving suddenly said "Oh, I know. It's up here on the right. I'm sure it is" and we veered off to the right. Then all of a sudden, there were all these headlights coming towards us and everyone was beeping their horns at us and I realised we were going the wrong way down a one-way stretch of motorway! Don't ask me how, but she somehow managed to dodge all the oncoming cars, do a super-quick U-turn and go back the way we'd come! Plus, we never did find the restaurant, so I ended up back at my hotel shaken, tired AND absolutely ravenous!

James: We hired this car while we were over there and everything was fine for the first few days. It was much posher than our old heap. You know, power steering, air con, sat nav, all that jazz. Later on in the holiday, though, I needed to fill up, so we pulled in at a garage and I then proceeded to spend about half an hour desperately trying to figure out how to get the cap off the petrol tank! No matter how I twisted it or pulled it, it just wouldn't come off. It was a total nightmare, but luckily the garage was manned so eventually the assistant bloke came over and he put me out of my misery and showed me how to do it. Mind you, he'd had a good laugh at my expense first. The thing was, though, that even after all that, I still didn't really get how it worked – and had pretty much the same palaver the next time we had to fill up!

Unit 22

2 Listening (1) (page 126)

M: So go on, then. Have you got a picture?

E: Of course! Actually, I've got his passport picture – it's so ridiculous having to get him a separate one. Here.

M: Oh, he's so cute. How old is he here?

E: Three weeks.

M: Oh, that's so sweet. So when was he actually born?

E: 8th of December – at 3 o'clock in the morning.

M: They always seem to arrive in the middle of the night.

E: I know. I wonder why that is?

M: I don't know. Probably just want to be awkward. Start as they mean to go on! So how was it, the birth?

E: Oh, don't ask! I was in labour for almost 18 hours.

M: Oh no, that's awful!

E: I can't begin to tell you! It was just so painful!

M: Didn't they give you any drugs or anything?

E: Yeah, I mean, I ended up having to have an epidural in the end, but up till then it was pretty excruciating. Honestly, I can see why some women go straight for a caesarean.

M: Yeah, I guess. But the baby was all right, wasn't he?

E: Yeah, yeah, absolutely. He was just big.

M: Right, so how much did he weigh?

E: Almost five kilos.

M: Gosh! No wonder it took so long!

E: I know!

M: So is he sleeping all right?

E: Well, he is now he's on a bottle. The last couple of weeks he's been pretty much sleeping right through till about six, six thirty, but when I was breastfeeding he seemed to wake up about every three hours. It was really wearing, and of course Keith couldn't feed him, so it was pretty bad. I can see why sleep-deprivation is used as a form of torture. It really sends you a bit loopy.

M: I bet, but he's all right now.

E: Fingers crossed.

M: So who's looking after him while you're at work?

E: Oh, I was really lucky. I found a childminder who lives on our street and she's really nice, so he stays with her.

M: Oh that's great. So is he OK? Has he settled in all right?

E: Yeah, he seems to have. I was pretty worried, because he's has been a bit clingy, you know. Sometimes I can't put him down without him screaming, so I thought he would be really awful there, but actually he really seemed to take to her. There were a few tears the first day, but more from me than him, to be honest!

M: Yeah, it must be a wrench.

E: Yeah, but I'll get used to it.

4 Listening (2) (page 127)

Conversation 1

A: The whole weekend was a nightmare, to be honest, thanks to my darling nephew!

B: Oh yeah, he's a bit of a brat, isn't he?

A: To put it mildly! Honestly, he just runs circles round my brother and his girlfriend. It's like one great big constant battle about everything – and they always end up giving in. We went to do a bit of shopping for dinner and we were in the supermarket and Jordan saw these chocolate biscuits – his favourite, apparently – you know, in the shape of Tellytubbies or something – and my brother says to him, we've got some of those at home so we don't need any more, and Jordan starts saying he wants them now, and so my brother says no again, but then before you know it, Jordan's thrown himself on the floor in a full-blown tantrum, screaming blue murder, kicking and punching my brother, and everyone's staring at us and my brother's not really doing anything. Then after about ten minutes – by which point I've just tried to melt away into the background and pretend I'm nothing to do with them – Simon just says, 'Oh, for God's sake! Have the bloody biscuits then', and we move on.

B: No wonder the kid's such a brat! Sounds like he needs a good slap!

A: I don't know about that, but his parents certainly do. My brother's girlfriend is just as bad, if not worse. It's all 'Oh leave him be! Let him have what he wants, he's only three, my little prince.'

B: Oh yuck! That's so nauseating! I tell you, I am NEVER going to become a parent! It just seems to turn your mind to mush!

A: Tell me about it!

Conversation 2

A: Man, it's just so annoying the way she talks to us. She says things like 'it's wicked', you know, like trying to be down with the kids and it just comes across as stupid and patronising.

B: Fair enough, but that's no excuse to answer back the way that you did. I thought we'd brought you up to show a little more respect.

A: Yeah, and you always say you shouldn't just take people at face value, you know – question authority, challenge assumptions and all that – and what I'm telling you is that woman says she respects us, but it's all just show. She's just a bitch!

B: Listen, that's enough! If you ask me, you were lucky just getting detention after what you said – and any more of that language and you're going to be grounded.

A: What? That's so unfair. I thought you'd be more supportive.

B: I am. I know where you're coming from. I just think you can express your anger in more constructive ways.

A: Yeah, right!

2 Listening (page 128)

M: Are your grandparents still alive?

R: My mum's parents are, yeah, but my dad's folks passed away a few years ago.

M: Oh, I'm sorry.

R: No, that's OK. We were never that close anyway.

M: What about on your mum's side? Do you see them much?

R: Yeah, a fair bit, I suppose, but they're both getting on a bit now, so you know what it's like.

M: Yeah, not much fun usually, is it?

R: No, not really. My gran's lovely, but her memory's not what it used to be, so she sometimes forgets who I am and she drifts off quite a bit in the middle of sentences and things, and my granddad's health isn't that great. He's quite hard of hearing, so you always have to say everything three times.

M: Oh no. What a shame!

R: Yeah, and he had a stroke a few years back, so he can't really talk properly or anything.

M: Oh, that's terrible! I'm really not looking forward to getting old.

R: No, me neither. Mind you, at least I don't have to listen to him going on anymore. He used to spend hours reminiscing about the war and the good old days and everything. It used to drive me mad, all that.

M: That's not a very nice way of looking at it!

R: Yeah, well … it's true. Don't your grandparents ever bug you with all those stories?

M: No, not at all. They're all lovely. My dad's folks are really with it, actually. They're both still really sharp. They've kept up to date with things, so I get little e-mails from them from time to time, which is great. And my mum's mum, she's, I don't know, 85 or something, but she's still pretty sprightly. She still gets around on her own, so that's good too.

R: Wow! Well, you're lucky. I wish my grandparents had been a bit more like that.

Unit 23

3 While you listen (page 132)

K: So how was your holiday? How were the in-laws?

E: Not too bad, all things considered. They could've been worse, you know. They seem to be gradually coming to terms with the fact that their darling son has dared to marry a foreigner!

K: I should hope so too after all the time you two have been together. What is it now? Four years? Five?

E: Getting on for six now, actually. Yeah, no. They're kind of getting used to me, I think, though Olivier's mum does still sometimes have this really annoying habit of pretending not to understand me when I talk to her in English.

K: That'd drive me nuts, that would.

E: Yeah, it can be pretty infuriating, I can tell you, and she also sometimes talks about me in the third person like I'm not even there, but apart from that it's pretty good now. Olivier's sisters and his big brother seem to have taken me into the fold and I'm slowly getting my head round the way the family works, what the pecking order is, that kind of thing.

K: So that's good, then.

E: Yeah, it is … but … um … I did manage to commit a major faux pas one day over dinner, though!

K: Come on then! Spill the beans!

E: Oh God! It was awful. Me and my big mouth! Really! What happened was we all went out for dinner one night to this really nice little restaurant in the village where they live and half the family were there, all these uncles and aunts and cousins and I was stuck down one end of this great big long table with my mother-in-law and Olivier and one of his sisters and they were all explaining to me who everyone was, you know, and I was trying to keep up and try to match names to faces when suddenly Olivier said, "Oh and that's my uncle Didier", and I'd heard about this guy because he was always talking about him on the phone every time he phoned his sisters, you know, the running soap opera that's their family …

K: Yeah.

E: And so I knew he'd got divorced recently and left his wife of twenty something years and run off with one of his students from the university where he works, right, so I innocently said, "Oh, so he's the divorced one, right?", and no sooner had I finished the sentence than this awkward silence fell and everyone starts shifting uncomfortably in their seats. Olivier starts kicking me under the table and I'm kind of silently mouthing "What?" to him. Then his mum gives me this really icy look. It was horrible.

K: Oh no! You poor thing! You must've been mortified. So what was the deal? Why all the tension?

E: Well, that was the thing. I had no idea at this stage. We all just sat there for what seemed like an eternity and then one of the brothers changed the subject and started making small talk about the menu and that was that. It was only later that Olivier bothered to tell me that talking about the divorce in public was a real no-no and that his mum couldn't bear to hear about it. I mean, how was I supposed to know? His whole family's a real minefield, honestly. I should just never have opened my mouth! Anyway, enough about all that. How was YOUR holiday? Didn't you go to Morocco with that new bloke of yours? What was his name again?

K: Jack. Yeah, we were supposed to, but … um … (starts snivelling)

E: What? Kirsten. What? Oh no! I've put my foot in it again, haven't I?

K: It's OK. I'll be all right in a minute. Sorry. I'm just being stupid about it. I never liked him that much anyway, really.

Unit 24

2 Listening (page 138)

A: You're not actually reading that magazine, are you?

B: I was just having a flick through, just keeping myself up to date with the latest celebrity gossip, you know.

A: So you actually buy that rubbish?

B: No! No, they just have it here to read. I wouldn't buy it, but, you know, if it's there.

C: That's what they all say. I bet you've got a full annual subscription.

B: I haven't, but I'd tell you if I did. It doesn't bother me – it's entertaining, isn't it? I mean, check out these photos of Lemar Le Saux and Kate Pride's wedding. Have you ever seen anything so tacky? Look at that carriage! It's so over-the-top – and the tiara and dress! Talk about revealing!

A: It's all hideous. Who are they, though?

B: Oh, come on. You must've heard of them. There's been so much in the papers about them. He's in some boy band and dumped his last girlfriend to go out with her. And then she was, I don't know – some reality TV wannabe actress or something – completely talentless. In fact, her only talent seems to be bedding B-list celebrities and getting photographed snorting coke.

C: Didn't she admit herself into that rehab clinic?

B: Yeah? Probably. I lose track. There always seems to be one celeb or other getting treatment for some addiction. Anyway, you've changed your tune. I thought you said you weren't interested.

C: No, I didn't. I'm with you. I'm a sucker for any of those glossy gossip mags and trashy tabloids. What I was implying was that most people are actually into it too, but just won't admit it. It's like these people who pretend not to like crap TV. It's always 'I don't normally watch Big Brother, I just happened to switch over and caught the end of it'.

B: Yeah, but they never happen to turn back!

C: Exactly.

A: Well, I don't think you two should be drawn in by it. We're just becoming obsessed with celebrities and it's dumbing down our whole media culture.

B: Don't be such an old fogey! It's just a bit of harmless fun. And it doesn't stop me taking an interest in politics or things like that.

A: No, I know, but don't you think it's just all a bit cruel? You know, we build these people up and say how wonderful they are just so we can knock them down. I just think the invasion of privacy has become totally overwhelming.

C: Oh, I think that's a bit naïve. When it comes down to it, most of these celebs manipulate all the publicity. They all employ publicists and take out injunctions and libel actions at the first whiff of scandal. You know, live by the sword, die by the sword.

A: I don't know about that. I don't think that just because you want to become, say, an actor, you want your whole life laid bare. If you ask me, now we've got rid of bear-baiting and public executions, we've developed celebrities as an alternative form of public abuse.

B: Oh, come on, Howard! That's going a bit far! Public execution and gossip magazines are hardly the same thing! And it didn't stop you laughing at Kate Pride's wedding dress.

A: It IS the same kind of thing. It just appeals to the lowest common denominator. All these things are based on public humiliation and cruelty and I just think it cheapens everyone involved.

C: You are just winding us up, aren't you? It's got to be a joke. You don't really believe that, do you?

Writing: Giving presentations

4 Listening (page 140)

I give a lot of papers at conferences to all kinds of different audiences, with different levels of English and different levels of experience. Sometimes the audience will all be incredibly fluent, very well-qualified and very knowledgeable, other times they'll be slightly less familiar with the field. I usually talk for between 45 minutes and an hour and it's hard to keep people's attention for that long, so I make sure I know what I'm going to say like the back of my hand! I write the whole talk out on my computer first, word for word, as I'm going to say it. Then I re-write it onto little postcards, cutting a few bits out. Then finally, in the run-up to actually giving the talk, I read these cards over and over and over again to fix the thing in my mind. I still refer to the cards when I'm talking, but only as a guide. Knowing the talk this well is the key to it all, really. It means I can improvise a bit and respond more to the audience, adapt things as I feel fit. I think it's really important to tailor things to suit the audience, to make sure they can relate to what you're saying. It's also good to inject a few laughs into the talk if you can, keep it light. Some people seem to forget that you can be serious, but still have fun!

I guess kind of connected to this is actually just getting into the right of frame of mind to present. In a way, it's good to just be natural and do your own thing, but it's also important to keep the audience on-side, to stop them nodding off, so you need to make it a bit of a performance as well, give it a bit of oomph, a bit of energy! That helps. I'll use Powerpoint if I have to – I know some people find it useful to see visual summaries – but I prefer not to. I find I get sidetracked and end up worrying more about the technology than about the actual talk. Plus, I hate watching presentations where it looks like they've just discovered Powerpoint and have about a thousand slides and images zooming in and all that kind of thing! It's such a distraction.

I've actually had to give presentations in a foreign language a few times too, and then I taped myself and listened to it, making sure I sounded OK and was stressing the right words and linking words together well. It was quite a nerve-wracking experience, though, I can tell you!

Grammar commentary

G1 Modifying nouns and adjectives (page 11)

Look at the following ways of modifying nouns.

She's a complete snob.
He's a real laugh.
He's an absolute nightmare!
You're a right whinger.
You're such a hypocrite!
He's a total alcoholic!
She's a bit of a fashion victim.

We usually use *a bit of a / an* to soften negative nouns. It makes the negative noun sound slightly less strong.

We often follow clauses containing *such a / an* with a result clause.

It was such a boring film (that) we walked out halfway through.
He was such a bully (that) his wife left him after a couple of years!

Look at the following ways of modifying adjectives.

She's really smart.
He's very bright.
She's so selfish.
He's completely useless.
She's quite funny.
It's rather cold today, isn't it?
He's a bit strange.

We usually use *a bit* to soften negative adjectives. It makes the negative adjective sound slightly less strong.

My boss is a bit dictatorial at times.

We often follow clauses containing *so* with a result clause.

He's so weird (that) nobody ever wants to sit next to him in class.
He was so unhealthy (that) he had a heart attack when he was 31.

In spoken English, we don't usually say *that* in these clauses.

Look at the following ways of modifying positive adjectives with *not very / not that* to politely express something negative.

He's not very nice to his kids.
She's not that clever.
He's not really all that good with money.

G2 Comparisons (page 21)

We often emphasise positive comparisons like this:

He was miles better in that other film we saw him in.
It's about a hundred times more expensive than it used to be.
There's no comparison! This one's about a million times nicer.

We often emphasise negative comparisons like this:

It's nice, but nowhere near as nice as that Thai thing you cooked last time.
I do like chess, but I'm nothing like as good at it as you are.
It's not even close to being their best CD. I think it's pretty average.
I'm useless at it! I'm not even in the same league as you!
I'm from China, so I find the food here in England a bit bland by comparison.

If we want to say two things are quite similar, we can say:

Vince Taylor was the English equivalent of Elvis.
There are definite parallels between the two players. They play a very similar kind of game.

G3 Modal verbs (page 24)

Must and can't for guessing

We often use *must* to make guesses about things we're 95% sure are true based on the evidence available to us.

He must be rolling in money if he's the head of the school.
You must've been really annoyed with him after he did that.
She must really hate him to talk about him like that!

In this context, the opposite of *must* is *can't*. We use *can't* to guess about things that we're 95% sure aren't true.

A: He said he's going to move to Rye.
B: Rye? He can't be serious! Why on earth would he do that?

A: I spent most of the holiday in hospital.
B: That can't have been much fun.
A: No, it wasn't. Believe me.

We use *can't / must have* + a past participle to guess about things in the past.

For more information on this, see G13.

Can

We use *can* to talk about things that are usually or generally possible

You can always talk to me if you need to get things off your chest.
The police can make life really difficult for you if they want to.
She can be very thoughtless sometimes.

Could

We often talk about things that we think were possible – or impossible – in the past using *could've* – or *couldn't have* – and a past participle.

I was really lucky! I could've died up there in the mountains!
Why didn't you tell me you were moving? I could've helped you.
It's not my fault. There was nothing I could've done about it.

We also use *could* to talk about other kinds of possibility:

(a) to make offers:

I could lend you some money if you really need some.

(b) to make guesses about things we're only 50% sure of:

I'm not sure where they are. They could be in the garage or somewhere.

(c) to talk about ability in the past:

It was so hot I could hardly breathe.

For more information on this, see G13.

Won't

We use *won't* to make promises about now and the future.

I won't be long.
It won't be very expensive.
I won't bore you with all the details now.

We also use *won't* to talk about other kinds of certainty about now and the future:

(a) to talk about things we think are certain not to happen:

He won't remember. He always forgets my birthday!

(b) to talk about opinions or decisions about the future made at the time of speaking:

Well, if you do decide to quit, I won't try to stop you.

(c) to talk about the repeated refusal of things to do what we want them to do:

The car won't start again. Can you help me push it?
I don't know what's wrong. The file won't open for some reason.

(d) to talk about likely consequences in first conditionals:

You won't be able to sleep if you don't talk to him about it!

(e) to predict things about the present based on the evidence available to you:

They won't be there yet. The journey usually takes at least an hour.
It's only 6.30. He won't be up yet. We'd best wait.

Shouldn't

We use *shouldn't* to talk about things now or in the past that we don't think are desirable or correct.

A: Do you want another piece of this?
B: I shouldn't really, but what the hell! It's so delicious!

I shouldn't really be talking to you about it! Janie asked me not to!
I shouldn't have eaten so much earlier. I feel dreadful now.
It's his own fault he crashed. He shouldn't have been driving so fast!

We also use *shouldn't* to talk about the future to mean 'I don't think it will':

It shouldn't take too long. I'm sure I'll be back by this afternoon.
It shouldn't be that expensive.

Would

We use *would* and *wouldn't* to talk about imaginary situations in the past or present.

I would've kicked up a right fuss if that had happened to me.
It's a good job you weren't there. You wouldn't have enjoyed it.
I would help you if I was free, but I've got a lot on today.

For more information on this, see G13.

We also use *would*:

(a) to make polite requests and to ask for permission:

Would you mind passing me that book there?
Would you mind if I left early today?

Notice the verb patterns we use with these structures.

(b) to make polite offers and invitations:

A: Would you like something to eat?
B: Oh yes, please. I'd love a sandwich or something.

(c) to talk about things that happened regularly in the past:

We used to go to Borneo every summer. We'd stay with my grandparents and we'd go out for dinner every evening. It was great!

(d) We use *wouldn't* to talk about the repeated refusal of people or things to do what we wanted them to do in the past:

When he was a child, he wouldn't eat any vegetables.

For more information on this, see G23.

Bound to

Bound to is often called a semi-modal. It works in a similar way to modal verbs: it's followed by the base form of a verb and it's a way of expressing your own personal point of view about something. We use it to talk about things we're 99% sure of in the future, particularly when we have previous experience that makes us think this.

Why don't you just come clean and tell her. She's bound to find out about it sooner or later.

A: Look at those clouds! Do you think it'll rain later?
B: It's bound to. It always does when we've organised a picnic!

G4 *-ing* clauses (page 29)

In written English, we often introduce an explanation using *-ing* clauses. These examples are about the present results of things that happened in the past. They both use *having* + past participle.

Having been elected, he was granted immunity to criminal prosecution.
Having lost my father to lung cancer, I am very conscious of the risks of smoking.

If we were saying these things, they'd probably be more like this:

After he was elected, he was given immunity to prosecution.
My dad died of lung cancer, so I'm quite conscious of the risks of smoking.

These examples are about the results of things that are true at the time of writing. They all just use an *-ing* form of the verb.

Having no experience, I am looking for a trainee position.
Not having sufficient qualifications, I was rejected by every university I applied to.
Being English, he was just far too polite!

Again we don't tend to use these forms when speaking.

In all *-ing* clauses like this, the subject of the clause and the subject of the main verb have to be the same.

G5 Reporting speech (page 35)

We use lots of different verbs to report the gist of what people have said to us. It's important to notice the patterns that follow each verb – prepositions, verb forms, etc. Several different patterns are possible with most of these verbs! Here are some common patterns:

I couldn't believe it! She accused me of being a film snob!
I tried to persuade him to change his plans, but he wouldn't listen.
Don't complain to me about it! I did warn you not to do it!
It's OK. Nick's offered to look after the house while we're away.
Stefan's invited us round to theirs for dinner on Sunday.
She was a great teacher. She really encouraged us to make the most of our time at school.
I've asked them to move it three times now, but they've refused to do it every time!
He denied having ever been anywhere near the place.
He just wouldn't stop moaning about his wife. It was embarrassing!
Mickey suggested (that) we try / suggested trying a different courier service.
The government was quick to condemn the move.

The verbs *condemn* and *reject* are almost always followed by nouns. Governments or organisations can *condemn* attacks, proposals, behaviour, statements and people. You can *reject* an offer, a proposal, an argument, a suggestion, an appeal or a person.

It's important to remember that usually we only use these verbs when we report what other people have said. When we actually want to moan or persuade people or deny things, we tend not to use these actual words.

G6 Using auxiliaries (page 45)

Tags

We use auxiliaries to make tag questions.

You can speak a bit of German, can't you?
She thinks I'm an idiot, does she? Well I'll show her.

For more information on this, see G25.

Showing interest and responding

We also use auxiliaries to respond to things people have said and to show interest.

A: I went to Bangladesh for three weeks.
B: Oh, did you? That must've been interesting.

A: I speak pretty good Chinese.
B: Do you? Where did you pick that up? Have you lived in China?

A: I've got her number on my mobile.
B: Have you? That's brilliant! You've saved my life!

Showing agreement

We can use auxiliaries to show agreement with something someone has just said.

A: I can't stand this kind of music.
B: No, neither can I.

A: I hate opera.
B: So do I.

Avoiding repetition

Auxiliaries help us to avoid repeating verbs which have just been used.

I don't really like golf, but my husband does.
He says he's got a Master's, but I'm not so sure he has.

Notice we may need to change the tense, but we still only use the auxiliary if it avoids repeating the same verb:

A: I'm not going on the trip tomorrow.
B: Aren't you? I thought you were.
A: Yeah, I thought I might, but I really need to study for my exam.

A: You've bought your ticket already, haven't you?
B: I wish I had. It's much more expensive now.

Emphasising

We can also use auxiliaries to add emphasis. In this case, we usually stress the auxiliary. If there's no auxiliary, we add *do* or *did*.

Excuse me. I'm next. I HAVE been waiting longer than him!
I DID try to phone you, but I just couldn't get through.
I DO like Sundays!
What HAVE you done to your hair? It looks ridiculous!
I'm not stupid. I DO know how to do it!

We often use auxiliaries like this as a 'soft' introduction to a negative comment or a contrasting idea.

I HAVE tried English food before. I just didn't like it that much.
Don't get me wrong. I DO like her – just not in the way you think.
I DID like the film. I just didn't think it was great, that's all.

G7 *have done something* (page 45)

Look at these two examples:

My bag was stolen.
I had my bag stolen.

Both sentences are passive constructions which are used because we don't know the doer of the verb *steal* and because the object of the verb *steal* is more important to us. We use the *have it done* passive when we want to emphasise not only the object of the verb, but the person the object belongs to. *Have it done* structures are very common when we know the type of person who has done the action (thief, hairdresser, mechanic, dentist, etc.), but the precise individual is unknown or irrelevant:

You need to have your eyes tested!
I need to have this jacket dry-cleaned before I wear it again.
I don't have a car, so I had the TV delivered.
Our dog was really old and we had to have him put down.
Have you seen Karen? She's had her hair permed! It looks nice.
I'm afraid you're going to have to have your kidney removed.
It was horrible! He had to have his stomach pumped!
I had my wallet stolen on the tube the last time I was in London!

In informal spoken English, it's also common to say *get something done*.

I usually get my car serviced about once a year.
Can I get this photocopied, please? I'll need about 40 copies.
We got the whole place redecorated last winter.
You should get that arm looked at. It might be broken, you know.

G8 Adverbs that modify adjectives (page 46)

We often add an adverb before an adjective to modify its meaning in some way. Many adverb + adjective collocations are quite fixed and it's a good idea to learn them as chunks of commonly used language. Here are some examples:

badly mistaken / damaged
bitterly cold / disappointed
carefully chosen
delicately balanced
eagerly anticipated
enormously influential
enthusiastically received
highly controversial
highly qualified
heavily influenced by
ideally situated
lavishly rewarded
perfectly acceptable
severely restricted / weakened
completely incompetent
virtually impossible / identical
vitally important
widely available

With extreme / absolute adjectives – adjectives that already mean 'very very' something – we can use *absolutely* or *really*, but we don't usually use *very*. Similarly, we don't use *absolutely* with normal adjectives, but we can use *very* and *really*.

A: Was it hot there?
B: Yeah, absolutely boiling.

A: Was the food good there?
B: Yeah, it was really delicious.

Notice that we don't usually use extreme adjectives in questions. They're much more common in answers. Nor do we usually use them with *too*.

It was too hot.
~~It was too boiling~~.

Other extreme adjectives include: appalling, crucial, devastating, disgusting, exorbitant, filthy, freezing, gorgeous, horrendous, horrific, petrified, ravenous, terrifying. We also use *completely* and *utterly* to emphasise some extreme adjectives – but not normal adjectives.

I was completely ravenous by the time I got home.

G9 *Not only … / At no time* (page 63)

In more formal kinds of writing as well as in formal kinds of spoken English – political speeches, journalese, etc. – it is quite common to use inversion in order to add emphasis. To do this, we often start a sentence or clause with *not only* or *at no time* and then invert the subject and the auxiliary. If there is no auxiliary, we add *do / does / did*. Look at these examples with *not only*:

Not only do I have to read all the reports carefully, but I also have to consider how best to start discussions about them.
Not only was I getting further behind, but I was also coming into work earlier and leaving later.
Not only was I losing money, but now I also risked forfeiting my vehicle as well.

These are more common in written than spoken English.
For example we might say the first sentence like this:

It's a real pain! I have to read all the reports through really thoroughly and then on top of all that, I have to think about how to discuss them all!

Examples with *at no time*

At no time did I make any sexual advances toward the plaintiff.
At no time during the exam are candidates allowed to move from their designated places.
At no time whatsoever will we accept responsibility for any loss or damage.

If we were saying the first sentence, it'd probably be more like this:

I never made any sexual advances towards her whatsoever!

Inversion after *only* and *no*

In formal language, it is also quite common to invert after other expressions using *only* and *no*.

Only when I finally managed to speak to the assistant manager was I given a proper response.
Only after the vaccine has been lab tested can we comment further on its development.
In no way did our company fund any of the violent protests in the area that we have been accused of involvement in.
On no account are you to discuss any aspect of the interviews with other candidates applying for the same post.

G10 Speculating using *must, might* and *can't* (page 64)

We often speculate / guess about things based on the evidence available to us. We use *must* to talk about things we're 95% sure are true; *can't* to talk about things we're 95% sure aren't true; and *might* to talk about things we think are possibly true.

To make guesses about the past, we use one of these modal verbs + *have* + past participle or *been* + *-ing*.

He might've called while we were out, I guess. (= I think that possibly he called.)
He can't have been driving very fast. Otherwise, he would've been more seriously injured. (= I'm pretty sure he wasn't driving fast when he had his accident.)

To make guesses about the present, we use one of these modal verbs + the base form of the verb or be + *-ing*.

He can't like you very much. Otherwise, he would've sent you a card or something, wouldn't he? (= I don't think he likes you very much.)
He must be feeling dreadful about it. I know I would be if I was him. (= I'm pretty sure he's feeling dreadful now.)

When we speculate, we often follow up our guesses with a sentence using *otherwise*. We use *otherwise* instead of the *if*-part of a conditional sentence.

She must be having a great time. Otherwise, she would've told us, wouldn't she? (= If she wasn't having a great time, I think she would've told us about it.)
She can't have seen us. She would've waved otherwise. (= I think that if she had seen us, she would've waved.)

G11 *I wish you wouldn't!* (page 67)

We use this structure to complain about annoying things people regularly do – or don't do.

I wish you wouldn't say things like that! I hate it when you do. (= You often say horrible things like that and you've just done it again and it annoys me!)
I wish he'd just call me when he's going to be late. It'd stop me worrying so much. (= He often forgets to call me and he's done it again recently and I hate it!)

It's unusual to say *I wish* *<u>I</u> wouldn't* – because we can control the things we do ourselves!

Note that we don't usually use the verb *be* with *I wish you wouldn't* because it describes a general state rather than a habit. For example:

I wish you wouldn't ~~be~~ get so angry all the time.
I wish my nose ~~wouldn't be~~ wasn't so big!
I just wish you ~~wouldn't be~~ weren't so thoughtless sometimes!

We also use the structure *If only* to talk about things that annoy us about other people – or things we'd like to be different.

If only he'd call me when he's late! It'd stop me worrying so much.
If only my nose was a bit smaller! I'd be much better-looking!

For more information on using *wish*, see G12.

G12 Using auxiliaries and modals with *wish* (page 71)

We often use *wish* to talk about things we regret doing – or not doing – in the past, or to talk about ways in which we would like the present to be different. When we are talking about things we regret about the past, we use *wish* + past perfect. Notice how we use auxiliaries to respond to or add to these wishes.

A: I wish I'd never said anything about it!
B: Yeah, well, you did, so it's too late to go on about it now!

I wish I'd taken him up on the offer when I had the chance, but I didn't – and there's no point regretting it now!

When we talk about things we feel bad about or disappointed about in the present, we use *wish* + past simple verb. Again, notice how we use auxiliaries to respond to or add to these wishes.

I wish I had a bit more time to stop and talk, but I really don't.
I wish I could drive. It's bad that I can't after all these lessons!
I wish I could tell you I was enjoying the course, but I'm not.

A: I wish he'd stop smoking! The whole house stinks of stale cigarette smoke.
B: He will when he's ready.

For more information on using auxiliaries, see G6.
For more information on using *wish*, see G11.

G13 Unreal conditionals (page 79)

We use second conditionals to talk about ways in which we imagine the present or future could be different. Notice the way we use the past simple or past continuous to talk about imaginary / hypothetical ideas here:

I'd feel better if I didn't have to constantly worry about how I'm going to pay the doctor's fees!

A: Why don't you come with us?
B: I would if I wasn't working tonight, but there's no way I can get out of it. Maybe next time, though, yeah?

We use third conditionals to talk about imaginary pasts – ways in which the past could have been different, if the situation had been different. Notice the way we use the past perfect simple or past perfect continuous to talk about imaginary / hypothetical ideas here:

You should've complained. I would've done if that had happened to me.

If you hadn't been talking to Mina, you might've heard me the first time I told you!

For both second and third conditionals, the result part of the sentence can use *would* (to talk about things we imagine as likely results), *might* and *could* (to talk about possible results), *could* (to talk about results that someone was able to do) and *wouldn't* (to talk about things we imagine as very unlikely results).

Past events, however, don't only have past results; they also often have present results. If we want to talk about the imaginary present results of a past event, we use a mixed conditional. Often, this is half of a third conditional – to talk about the past – and half a second conditional – to talk about the imaginary present.

If my parents hadn't decided to move, I'd probably still be working in a convenience store in Hastings!

If you hadn't been driving past, I'd probably still be waiting there!

Note that in the second conditional part of these sentences, we often use the continuous form. We do this when we want to talk about an imaginary action that we think might already be in progress if the first half of the sentence had actually been true.

Mixed conditionals are very common in both spoken and written English. They don't all fit the patterns above. The best way to deal with them when you meet them is to try to understand when each half of the sentence is referring to and to try to work out if it's talking about an imaginary or a real condition. Here are some more mixed conditionals:

If he's coming, I'll ask him.
Well, if you want to leave, then leave!
If it'll help, I'd be happy to lend you the money.
If only you'd listen more carefully, then you'd understand!
If she's there, I go!
If you feel that way, I'd support you.
If that's what you're expecting, you must be mad!
If she's been there before, why didn't she know her way round?

There are several other words that we use instead of *if* in conditional sentences. Here are the most common:

Supposing you failed the exam, yeah? What would your parents say?
Well, provided / providing / as long as / so long as you think you can pay it back tomorrow, I suppose I could lend you a few pounds.
Assuming I get the rise I've asked for, I'll probably buy a new car next year.
Unless he asks me to marry him, I'm going to move back home sometime soon.

If we think the person we are talking to understands the conditions we are referring to, we don't need to make full conditional sentences with *if*.

(If you) Do that again and I'll slap you!
(If you) Get a Barclaycard and your troubles will be over.
He can't have seen us. (If he had seen us) I'm sure he would've said hello.

G14 Relative clauses (page 87)

Defining relative clauses

There are two kinds of relative clauses – defining and non-defining. If we have to add extra information about a noun in order to make it clear which person or thing we mean, we use a defining clause. We don't use commas between defining relative clauses and the nouns they define.

The guy who / that works behind the till told me they got robbed last week.
I just jumped in the first cab that / which went past.

When the noun we're defining is the object of a relative clause – not the subject – we don't need to add a relative pronoun.

The guys (who / that) I play football with have invited me to a party tomorrow.
I saw that film (that / which) you were going on about. It was amazing!

We rarely use *whom* as a relative pronoun in spoken English. It sounds too formal and old-fashioned. It is usually only used after a preposition and in more formal kinds of writing.

To whom it may concern.
Students for whom English is a second language should have achieved an advanced level before beginning the course.

We use *whose* to show possession.

That's the woman whose party I went to last week.
Learning English is particularly difficult for people whose first language doesn't have a Roman script.

Non-defining relative clauses

When we add extra information about a noun and this information is not part of an explanation of which thing or person we mean, we use a non-defining clause. We use *which* for things, *who* for people, and *whose* for possession. Notice that we don't use *that* as a relative pronoun in non-defining relative clauses. We put a comma at the beginning of a non-defining relative clause and a comma or full-stop at the end.

One of the people injured was Clarence Darkins, who had also been hurt in the earthquake last year.
They invested the money in a new printing machine, which speeded up their operation a lot.
The DTEFLA course, which I took way back in 1995, has now changed to the DELTA course.
Michael Thomas, whose last-minute goal sealed the title back in 1989, has announced his retirement.

Of whom / of which

We use *of whom* to give information about just one part of a group of people that we have just mentioned.

Only 800 escaped from the prison camps, of whom 650 were recaptured.

We use *of which* in the same way, but referring to a group of things or an uncountable noun.

There has been a sharp increase in crime over the last twelve months, a considerable amount of which was juvenile crime.

We often use them with words like *some, all, none, a large percentage, the bulk, a tiny minority, half*, etc. These words can come before or after the relative pronouns.

There has been a sharp increase in crime over the last twelve months, of which a large percentage was juvenile crime.

Only 800 escaped from the camps, most of whom were recaptured.

G15 *-ever* (page 89)

When we use *however* to mean *it doesn't matter how*, we can also use *in whatever way* or *no matter how*.

However / It doesn't matter how / In whatever way / No matter how you look at it, it's basically been a bit of a disaster.

We use *whoever* to mean the person / group of people who.

Whoever told you that knows nothing about music!
Whoever wins this game will meet Brazil in the semi-final.

We use *whatever* to mean *it doesn't matter what*.

Whatever happens, I'll back you up, OK.
Whatever else you can say about him, I'll tell you one thing. He doesn't mince his words!

We also use *whatever* in informal situations to mean anything or everything.

A: What do you want to do tonight?
B: Whatever. I'm easy.

Whatever is also used in some common fixed expressions.

He cancelled the show because of 'health problems', whatever that's supposed to mean. (= I'm not sure what that means exactly)

A: Can you just put that down over there, please?
B: Whatever you say, boss. (= If you say it, I'll do it, because you must be right!)

Don't go in there, whatever you do! (= it's really important you don't!)

Wherever means in or to any or every place.

Just sit wherever you want.
I keep hearing this song wherever I go. It's driving me mad!

Whenever means any or every time.

Just bring the sofa round whenever. I'll be in all day.
Whenever she's around, I just get all tongue-tied and lost for words!

G16 *Considering* (page 91)

We use *considering* to introduce a particular fact – usually a negative one – that is important when we are judging something else. It often has the meaning of *when you think*. We sometimes use *when you consider* instead. It has the same meaning.

You did OK, considering you'd only played once before.
It's amazing I passed, when you consider how little revision I did!
I'm not the best cook in the world, so I think the dinner was pretty good, considering / all things considered.

G17 Perfect tenses (page 93)

Perfect tenses are always used to look back from a particular point in time – from now (present perfect), from a point in the past that is clearly understood (the past perfect), or from a point in the future (the future perfect).

Present perfect

The present perfect simple is used to talk about things in the past that we see as somehow being connected to the present. There may be a present result of a past action.

A: Are you OK?
B: No, I'm not, actually. I've just had a blazing row with my boyfriend.

Have you dyed your hair? It looks different.

Alternatively, we may simply want to stress that we have had an experience in the past and can talk about it now, if the listener wants us to.

Oh, you're from Estonia, are you? I've been there. It's lovely.

We can also use the present perfect to talk about how many times something happened from the past to now.

This is the third time this week that has happened!
I've tried it three or four times now, but I still can't get into it.

In British English, we never use the present perfect with a finished past time reference – *last week*, *two years ago*, *when I was a kid*, etc.

Present perfect continuous

We use the present perfect continuous to show that an action that started in the past is still continuing now.

I've been trying to get through to her all morning, but her phone is just constantly engaged.
I haven't been feeling good about us for quite a while now, so I think we need to have a talk.

The present perfect continuous is often used to suggest that the action described will continue happening in the future.

I started a couple of years ago, and the business has just been growing and growing ever since.

The present perfect continuous is also used to emphasise that we see the past action described as having been extended over a period of time or that we see it as having happened again and again and again. Once more, there will be a present result.

Have you been running or something? You sound really out of breath!
It's been snowing overnight. Come and have a look out the window!

Lots of verbs don't work well with the present perfect continuous.

I've always loved it here. ✓
I've always been loving it here. ✗

You either love something or you don't. You can't love it over and over again. In the same way, we tend to make negatives with the present perfect simple more than with the present perfect continuous.

She suggested that I quit and retrain – so I did. And I haven't looked back since. ✓
She suggested that I quit and retrain – so I did. And I haven't been looking back since. ✗

You can't *not look back* over and over again. You either don't do it – or you do.

Past perfect

We use the past perfect simple to talk about single events that formed the background to an event in the past or that explain why this event happened. It is usually used with other past tenses and enables us to jump back further into the past from the main point in time we're talking about.

I felt OK about it, actually, because I'd had a similar operation before, when I was a kid.
I'd started finding the job a bit repetitive and predictable, so I quit.

Past perfect continuous

We also use the past perfect continuous to talk about the background to an event or to explain why this event happened. It usually describes the events or actions leading up to something which is the main focus of what we are talking about.

We'd been arguing a lot, so we just decided it was time for a break.
My knee had been causing me problems for ages, so I decided to go and get it looked at.

Future perfect

We use the future perfect simple to talk about an action we think will be finished by another point in the future. We often use a time expression starting with *by* with the future perfect.

I'll have left for Peru by the time you get back from Paris.

Notice that we sometimes use *should* and *might* instead of *will* to show less certainty.

I'm not done yet. Call me around six. I should have finished it all off by then. (= will almost certainly)
Take a key with you. I might've gone out by the time you get back. (= will possibly)

Future perfect continuous

We use the future perfect continuous to talk about how long something will have been happening by a point in the future.

Next January I'll have been living here ten years.
We'll have been going out together for three years next Monday!

G18 Adjectival clauses (page 97)

In written English, we often use an *-ing* clause instead of a non-defining relative clause with an active verb.

Tackling the thorny issues of love and fear of rejection, this book is perhaps Coelho's masterpiece.
(= This book, which tackles the thorny issues of fear and rejection, is perhaps Coelho's masterpiece)

We often use a past participle instead of a non-defining relative clause with a passive verb.

Separated in their teens, the couple meet again eleven years later.
(= The couple, who were separated in their teens, meet again eleven years later)

Reasons, results and time

Clauses like this may give information about reasons, results or time.

Faced with a long stretch in jail, Johnson decided to jump bail.
(= because he was faced with)
Not wanting to disappoint his audience, McArthur penned a bloody end to this thriller. (= because he didn't want to disappoint)
The snow fell for hours, completely covering the streets outside. (= so that it completely covered the streets)
Looking across the road, he could see a child wading in the water. (= when he looked across the road)

Where time clauses begin with words like *after*, *by*, *while*, *when* and *on*, they are often followed by *-ing* clauses.

On entering the country, he was detained at customs for a whole day.
After discussing it with my wife, I've decided not to take the job.

The subject of clauses like these is usually the same as the subject of the main clause – Johnson, McArthur, the snow, he, I, etc. Using *-ed* / *-ing* clauses instead of clauses which begin with conjunctions like *because*, *when*, etc. makes the writing sound more formal and is especially common in literary writing.

G19 Passives (page 105)

We use passive structures for a variety of reasons. It could be that we don't know who the doer of an action was:

My bike got stolen last week.
The baby was just left outside a church.

Or perhaps the action was done by a large group of people:

The cathedral was finally completed in the 1940s. (obviously by workmen)

If we want to make sentences like this one active, we have to use they as a 'dummy subject'.

They finally finished the cathedral in the 1940s.

The most common reason for using the passive, though, is to focus on the object of the sentence – when the doer of the action is known, but is unimportant at the moment of speaking.

Two men have been arrested in relation to the bombing.

Passives are more common in formal written English.

Some verbs are not usually used in the passive – verbs which don't usually have an object, like *arrive*, *leave*, *happen*, *come*, *go*, *fall*, *collapse*, etc. – and verbs describing states, like *have*, *belong*, *be*, *seem*, *exist*, etc.

Make sure you know the forms the passive takes in different tenses.

The rubbish is usually collected on a Wednesday.
My car's being repaired at the moment.
That bank near me has closed down and been converted into flats.
It was stolen from right outside where I work!
The hotel was being renovated while we were there.
Personally, I wouldn't eat steak if I thought it had been grown in a laboratory!
Of course, it will have been properly tested by the time it reaches the market!

It's rare to use passives with either the present perfect continuous or past perfect continuous. Try saying some – they're a real mouthful! For example,

That house has been being renovated for the last two years!

We prefer to use *they*

They've been renovating that house for the last two years.

Passive structures also follow modal verbs and prepositions.

I'm not sure whether you'd be allowed to wear that, actually.
It should've been done by now.
I can only assume something must be being done about it as we speak.
How did you feel about being / getting finger-printed at the airport?
Would you be interested in being employed as an interpreter?

G20 Giving advice (page 107)

There are lots of different structures used to ask for and give advice. Here are some of the most common:

A: Do you think I should take the Cambridge Advanced exam?
B: If I were you, I'd wait and improve your English a bit more. You're probably best taking it next year.
A: Yeah, you're probably right.

A: Do you know any good restaurants round here?
B: Well, you could check out that Greek place up the road. That's well worth a try.
A: OK. Thanks for the tip.

Have you tried having a word with the head of department about it?
Why don't you try doing a web search and seeing what comes up?

When we want to NOT recommend something – to say something isn't very good, we often use sentences starting with *I'd* or *I wouldn't*:

I wouldn't bother going there – unless you're particularly keen on modern art.
To be honest, I wouldn't really recommend that place. It wasn't that good when we went there.
I'd give the local pizzeria a miss (if I were you). It's not that good.

G21 Degrees of certainty (page 115)

When we are fairly sure about something, we often use *I bet*. It can be used to talk about the past, present or future.

I bet you were surprised when that happened, weren't you?
I bet you haven't even read it, have you?
I bet it gets hot there in the summer, doesn't it?
I bet the whole thing will blow over sooner rather than later!

We use *I hope* to talk about things we want to be true in the present – or want to happen in the future. It's usually followed by a verb in the present simple.

I hope you and the kids are all well.
I hope you enjoy the trip.

If we want to talk about things we think are highly possible in the future, we can use any one of several different structures:

I think we stand a fairly good chance of getting the contract.
There's a definite / distinct possibility that fuel prices will go up soon.
I think the likelihood / probability is that the number of dead will turn out to be far higher than they're currently estimating.
The economy's bad and more applicants are chasing fewer jobs, so the odds / chances are you'll have to interview more times to get the job you're after.
In all probability / likelihood, you'll stop craving cigarettes after a couple of weeks.
They're bound / certain / sure to want to have a look through all the accounts.

To talk about things we think are slightly less possible in the future, we can use these structures:

I think we've got a reasonable chance of stopping them.
We've got an even chance of making a small profit this year (= a 50/50 chance)
I guess we might manage to break even this year.

Here are some structures often used to talk about things we think are unlikely to happen:

The chances of her ever saying 'yes' to a guy like me are pretty slim / slender.
The odds / chances are that only 25% or so will actually stick out the whole 12 months!
The odds of him ever actually finding it are pretty low / slim.
I don't have a hope (in hell) of getting it published.
He doesn't stand a chance of getting that job he's applied for.

A: I hope you pass.
B: Fat / No chance! I'm absolutely convinced I'm going to fail!

In all probability / likelihood, we won't be together for that much longer.
There's absolutely no way they'll let you take all that as hand luggage.

G22 Verb patterns (page 117)

Several verbs used to report speech are frequently followed by *to* + verb. Here are some examples:

He just completely refuses to even consider it.
I felt so guilty that in the end I confessed to lying on my application form.
I really object to having to pay extra to park my car here.
I'll see if I can persuade her to show her face tonight.
A voice in his head commanded him to do it.
They urged them to rethink their decision.
I did warn you to be careful round there!

However, plenty of other patterns are also possible. For example, some of the verbs above can be followed by certain nouns:

The prince refused all privileges and worked like anybody else.
He confessed to a string of robberies in the capital.
I really object to his arrogance and self-promotion.

Other verbs are often followed by a preposition and an *-ing* form.

My brother nagged me into doing my own web log.
She absolutely insisted on trying every single pair of shoes on!

For more information on reporting speech, see G5.

G23 *Wouldn't* (page 123)

We use *wouldn't* in several different ways.

Imaginary situations in the past or present

It wouldn't have happened if you hadn't opened your big mouth!
You wouldn't be saying that if you knew what I know!

Refusal to do things

We can use *wouldn't* to talk about the repeated refusal of people or things to do what we wanted them to do – in the past.

It was scary. She just wouldn't stop crying.
Sorry I'm late. My car wouldn't start, so I had to get the bus.
No matter what I tried, the bloody thing just wouldn't work!

In reported speech / thoughts

He promised me he wouldn't say anything to anyone about it.
I told you I wouldn't be able to come.

The direct speech that these sentences report would be something like this:

I won't tell a soul, I promise.
I won't be able to make it, I'm afraid.

Creating distance

We can use *wouldn't* to make a sentence sound more tentative, less certain.

I wouldn't want to get into a fight with him!
I wouldn't think it was that hard to organise.

You can make this second example even more tentative like this:

I wouldn't have thought it'd be that hard to organise.

For more information on *wouldn't*, see G3 and G11.

G24 *No sooner had … than …* (page 133)

Inverting a sentence by putting the adverb and auxiliary before the subject is a way of adding emphasis to certain pieces of information in a sentence. Inversion is more a feature of literary or journalistic writing than spoken English, but the *No sooner … than …* structure is sometimes used in conversation to make descriptions more dramatic.

No sooner had one lot of guests left than the next arrived!
No sooner do you feel safe turning on your computer than you hear on the news about a new kind of Internet security threat.

Here are some other ways of inverting sentences that are rarely used in informal spoken English, but are more common in writing and very formal speech.

Never before had anyone ever called his feet beautiful!
Nowhere else in the country will you find such an array of great restaurants.
Not until the end of the film do you realise what's really going on.

For more information on inversion, see G9.

G25 Question tags (page 139)

We often use question tags to check things we think are true – or simply to help push conversations along. The intonation often goes down at the end of the sentence, making them sound more like statements than questions.

In positive sentences containing an auxiliary verb, the question tag is made by making the auxiliary negative and adding the relevant pronoun.

You have ridden one of these before, haven't you?
You can play the guitar, Leo, can't you?

In negative sentences, a positive auxiliary is used.

He's never been to the States, has he?
You couldn't do me a favour, could you?

When there is no auxiliary verb in the sentence, we use the 'dummy auxiliaries' *don't* or *didn't* to make the tags.

You like hip-hop, don't you, Jian?
He worked for Pentagram before, didn't he?

If we want to express surprise or annoyance, we can use a positive tag with a positive sentence.

Oh, she's Japanese, is she? I don't know why, but I'd always thought she was Korean.
So you think it's funny, do you, Dellar? We'll soon see about that!
So it's all my fault, is it? That's so typical of you to think that!

Here are some grammatically unusual – but common – question tags.

Close the door, will you?
Just put it over there, will you?
I'm a club member, aren't I?
Let's take a break now, shall we?

Groupwork

Student A: Unit 6, page 36, activity 3

Text 1

A report by the OECD (Organisation for Economic Co-operation and Development) has revealed that Norway heads the table of countries that provide foreign aid – with the United States in last place of all the developed countries in the survey. The report is an embarrassment to the US government, coming in the wake of criticism at its perceived mean response to recent disasters. The States is in fact by far the biggest donor of aid in absolute terms, providing over $7bn more than any other country. However, when this is expressed as a percentage of GDP, the government spends a mere 0.14 per cent compared to Norway's 0.92 per cent.

Text 2

A cancer survivor from Britain has just completed the New York Marathon nearly five days after the rest of the field. Lloyd Scott, a former fireman, 'ran' the course in a 58kg vintage diving suit in order to raise money for cancer charities. Mr Scott had previously completed the London Marathon in the suit and this time improved on his time by some eight hours.

Text 3

Governments have no place in providing charity. Giving should be a private matter. As one commentator said, government-led foreign aid is the process by which money is taken from poor people in rich countries and given to rich people in poor countries, where it is a cushion for corrupt and oppressive ruling classes. The role of governments should be to simply encourage free trade and break down protective tariffs in Europe and America that so damage economic development in Africa and the developing world.

Student B: Unit 16, page 95, activity 5

Text 1

Scientists in Newcastle have successfully cloned a human embryo from eggs collected from women undergoing IVF treatment. The cloned cells formed into the beginnings of an embryo no bigger than the head of a pin and did not survive beyond five days. However, the researchers claim the experiment proves that cloning can be done, although they revealed that one crucial factor is that the eggs need to be extremely fresh – less than an hour old. Supporters of the research claim it could pave the way to creating treatments for spinal cord injuries and genetic diseases such as Type 1 diabetes.

Text 2

A 66-year-old Romanian woman, who has undergone nine years of fertility treatment, has given birth to a baby girl. The baby was born prematurely, weighing a mere 1.4kg, and is in intensive care.

The doctor who provided the IVF treatment defended the decision, saying the woman – a retired university professor and children's author – was in a good state of health, and he had been impressed by her faith in God.

Text 3

Researchers from the University of Manchester have claimed that three oils used in aromatherapy can destroy antibiotic-resistant bacteria such as MRSA and E.coli in just two minutes. An estimated 5,000 people a year are killed by these bugs when they contract them in hospital. The researchers believe the discovery could revolutionise the way we combat the problem of superbugs, although they said they were currently unable to reveal which oils exactly carry the benefits because of commercial sensitivities.

Student A: Unit 4, page 25, activity 7

You've had your car stolen.

Think about the answers to these questions.

- When / where did it happen?
- How did you feel when you found out?
- What did you do?
- Have the police recovered it?
- If so, where did they find it? What kind of state is it in?
- If not, what are you going to do?
- Who do you think might've stolen it and how?
- Are you insured for theft?
- How long will it take to get a new car or your old one back or repaired?

When you have thought about these answers, have a conversation with Student B. Begin like this:

A: How was your holiday?

Listen to what Student B says. Give sympathy and ask questions to find out more. When Student B asks you *So how're things with you?*, say how you're feeling and that you've had your car stolen. Wait for Student B to give you sympathy and ask you questions before you continue with any further details. Only answer the questions Student B asks.

Student C: Unit 16, page 95, activity 5

Text 1

A recent study into the long-term effects on children born very prematurely has renewed the debate over expensive medical interventions. The study revealed that of 1289 babies born under 26 weeks, only 308 survived into childhood. Of those survivors, nearly half develop a severe disability or learning difficulty, another third have impairments such as short-sightedness and only 20% were free from any disability. Some people have suggested that Britain should follow the example of the Netherlands, where no effort is made to save babies before 25 weeks.

Text 2

Scientists in Newcastle have successfully cloned a human embryo from eggs collected from women undergoing IVF treatment. The cloned cells formed into the beginnings of an embryo no bigger than the head of a pin and did not survive beyond five days. However, the researchers claim the experiment proves that cloning can be done, although they revealed that one crucial factor is that the eggs need to be extremely fresh – less than an hour old. Supporters of the research claim it could pave the way to creating treatments for spinal cord injuries and genetic diseases such as Type 1 diabetes.

Text 3

The scientist who grew a human ear on the back of a mouse has suggested it may be possible one day to grow a liver. If successful, the technique would solve the shortage of livers required for transplants.

Student B: Unit 6, page 36, activity 3

Text 1

Experts have revealed that some charities saw a drop in donations and came to the brink of closure because of the millions that were given to the Asian tsunami appeal.

Sid Barrett, director of the charity Relief Aid, drew comparisons with other well-publicised disaster appeals. 'Following the attack on the twin towers, the appeal for the victims attracted 1 per cent of all the charitable donations given worldwide that year. That was a big percentage when you think about it and far more than was actually needed. On the other hand, appeals for money in places like Cote d'Ivoire and Liberia, which attracted much less media attention, received only half the amount that was required.'

Another prominent charity said 'there is only a finite amount that the public give each year, so it's inevitable that if they give to one good cause, they don't give to another'.

Text 2

Governments have no place in providing charity. Giving should be a private matter. As one commentator said, government-led foreign aid is the process by which money is taken from poor people in rich countries and given to rich people in poor countries, where it is a cushion for corrupt and oppressive ruling classes. The role of governments should be to simply encourage free trade and break down protective tariffs in Europe and America that so damages economic development in Africa and the developing world.

Text 3

Dear Sir,
John Spiral is right when he says in his article *Charity's come cold-calling* that charities' fundraising methods need to be better controlled. I have collectors for charity approaching me in the street and on my doorstep nearly every day of the week. They frequently harass me and try to make me feel guilty for saying no. These kinds of marketing techniques have no place in charitable organisations and they should be banned.
Kevin Flett

Unit 11, page 67, activity 7

You are Martin Green. You've been studying hard all day and you've just come home and found the front room in a terrible mess. Toby is sleeping on the sofa. You decide to wake him up and have a word with him about things.

Make sure you mention the problems discussed in the text you read. Try to use some of the grammar from Activities 4 and 5 and some of the expressions from Activity 2 as well. Spend five minutes planning exactly what you want to say.

Student A: Unit 17, page 100, activity 4

Joke 1

A man asked his doctor if he thought he'd live to be a hundred. The doctor asked the man, "Do you smoke or drink?"

"No," he replied. "I've never done either."

"Do you gamble, drive fast cars, or fool around with women?" inquired the doctor.

"No, I've never done any of those things either."

"Well, then," said the doctor, "what do you want to live to be a hundred for?"

Joke 2

There was once a very prim and proper older lady who had a problem with wind. Since she came from a generation that didn't even talk about this kind of problem, it took a long time for her to seek help. Finally, however, she was persuaded to consult her family doctor.

After she'd filled out all the proper forms and had waited about 20 minutes in the waiting room, the doctor called her into his office, leaned back in his chair, folded his hands and asked how he could help.

"Doctor," she said, "I have a very bad gas problem."

"A gas problem?" went the doctor.

"Yes. Yesterday afternoon, I had lunch with the Secretary of State and his wife and had six, um, er, ah . . . silent gas emissions. Last night, I had dinner with the governor and his wife and had" – at this point, she started blushing – "four silent gas emissions. Then, while sitting in your waiting room, I had five silent gas emissions! Doctor, you've got to help me! What can we do?"

"Well," said the doctor thoughtfully, "I think the first thing we'll need to do is give you a hearing test."

Joke 3

A man and a woman who had never met before found themselves in the same sleeping carriage of a train. After the initial embarrassment, they both went to sleep, the woman on the top bunk, the man on the lower.

In the middle of the night, the woman leaned over, woke the man and said, "I'm sorry to bother you, but I'm awfully cold and I was wondering if you could possibly get me another blanket."

The man leaned out and, with a glint in his eye, went, "I've got a better idea – just for tonight, let's pretend we're married."

The woman thought for a moment. "Why not?" she giggled.

"Great," he replied. "Then get your own damn blanket!"

Student B: Unit 5, page 30, activity 3

The West Beach Diet Spinach Salad

Serves 4 people.

INGREDIENTS

6 oranges
4 cups spinach, stalks removed
1 cup watercress, stalks removed
1 tablespoon pine nuts
1/3 cup finely chopped shallots (2–3 large shallots)
2 garlic cloves, finely chopped
5 tablespoons balsamic vinegar
2 teaspoons sherry vinegar
ground pepper to taste

DIRECTIONS

1. Peel five of the oranges and remove the white pith. Over a bowl positioned to catch the juice, cut the oranges up into chunks, using a sharp knife. Remove the pips and set the chunks to one side. Squeeze the juice from the remaining orange into a bowl and reserve.
2. Mix the spinach and the watercress in a mixing bowl. Put the pine nuts in a small frying pan and cook over medium heat for about 6 minutes, shaking the pan occasionally until the nuts turn a light golden brown. Transfer the nuts to a small bowl.
3. Put the shallots, garlic, vinegars and reserved orange juice in a pan. Bring to the boil over a low heat. Stir in the pepper, and then pour the dressing over the spinach and watercress. Toss until everything is fully coated.
4. Arrange the mixture on salad plates, spoon the orange segments on top and then garnish with pine nuts.

Student B: Unit 11, page 67, activity 6

He needs to learn to chill out!

Toby Jenkins-Jones, 19, is studying Medicine at London University and shares a house with three other students.

I started my degree last September and I've had the best time ever since then. London is party central and I fully intend to take advantage of all that it has to offer! I share with three other guys and, by and large, we have a real laugh and get on pretty well. David and Jez are great guys and we're quite close, I suppose. The only problem is Martin. We found him through an ad we placed in a student paper and he seemed OK when we interviewed him for the room, but boy, did we get that wrong! He's so uptight! He really needs to lighten up and let his hair down from time to time. It's not healthy to be so serious about your studies! Someone needs to tell him that all work and no play makes you a very, very dull boy! He'll get old before his time if he's not careful. He wants to get his head out of his books for a night or two, and go out and get a life!

He's a couple of years older than the rest of us in the house, so maybe that's got something to do with it, but he's also got this thing about how he's from a poor background and how his dad worked down a mine. He seems to think that the whole world is against him and he's forever going on about how he's had to struggle to get where he is today! It's so tedious, it really is! I wish he'd just accept that people are people and that where you're from is relatively unimportant. Personally, I just think the real problem is he's not happy about who he is.

Another thing that really bugs me about Martin is his hypocrisy. He's constantly nagging the rest of us about the state of the house and what a tip it's turning into, but to be honest, it's a bit hypocritical coming from him! I mean, he's not exactly the tidiest person in the world himself. He's so quick to find fault with others that perhaps he misses failings a bit closer to home! He graduates later on this year and we're all really looking forward to that! The sooner he's gone, the better! Then the partying can really begin!

Student C: Unit 6, page 36, activity 3

Text 1

A high-profile charity has been accused by *The Tribune* newspaper of financial mismanagement and corruption, which has left millions of pounds unaccounted for and led to the resignation of its leader. The charity, which can't be named for legal reasons, passed on less than 60 per cent of the money it raised to the people it was supposed to be supporting. The founder of the organisation has also been accused of accepting bribes related to one of the charity's building projects in Africa.

Text 2

Dear Sir,
John Spiral is right when he says in his article *Charity's come cold-calling* that charities' fundraising methods need to be better controlled. I have collectors for charity approaching me in the street and on my doorstep nearly every day of the week. They frequently harass me and try to make me feel guilty for saying no. These kinds of marketing techniques have no place in charitable organisations and they should be banned.
Kevin Flett

Text 3

A report by the OECD (Organisation for Economic Co-operation and Development) has revealed that Norway heads the table of countries that provide foreign aid – with the United States in last place of all the developed countries in the survey. The report is an embarrassment to the US government, coming in the wake of criticism at its perceived mean response to recent disasters. The States is in fact by far the biggest donor of aid in absolute terms, providing over $7bn more than any other country. However, when this is expressed as a percentage of GDP, the government spends a mere 0.14 per cent compared to Norway's 0.92 per cent.

Student B: Unit 4, page 25, activity 7

You were arrested on holiday.

Think about the answers to these questions.

- Where did you go on holiday?
- What were you arrested for?
- Did you know what was going on? If not, how did you find out?
- How long did they hold you for?
- How did it resolve itself?
- Did you find out why they thought you were guilty of something?
- At what point in the holiday did it happen?
- How did you feel afterwards?
- What did you do for the rest of your holiday?

Student A will start the conversation by asking you *So how was your holiday?* Say how you felt about it and that you were arrested while you were there. Wait for Student A to give you sympathy and ask you questions before you continue with any further details. Only answer the questions Student A asks. When you feel you have said enough, say *Anyway, listen, enough about me. How're things with you?* Listen to what Student A says. Give sympathy and ask questions to find out more.

Student A: Unit 16, page 95, activity 5

Text 1

The scientist who grew a human ear on the back of a mouse has suggested it may be possible one day to grow a liver. If successful, the technique would solve the shortage of livers required for transplants.

Text 2

Global efforts to tackle the spiralling problem of HIV/AIDS in Africa and the Third World are being undermined by the continual migration of doctors and other healthcare workers to developed countries. A recent report condemned Britain and other governments for their reliance on overseas doctors and nurses to cope with the increased demands on their health services as a result of ageing populations in the western world.

The report stated that while Sub-Saharan Africa currently needed one million more healthcare workers to deal with its own problems, in many countries numbers were actually going down. This was in spite of those countries increasing the number of doctors they were training.

Text 3

A 66-year-old Romanian woman, who has undergone nine years of fertility treatment, has given birth to a baby girl. The baby was born prematurely, weighing a mere 1.4kg, and is in intensive care.

The doctor who provided the IVF treatment defended the decision, saying the woman – a retired university professor and children's author – was in a good state of health, and he had been impressed by her faith in God.

Student B: Unit 17, page 100, activity 4

Joke 1

After marrying a sweet young woman he'd met on the Internet, this 90-year-old guy told his doctor that they were expecting a baby.

"Let me tell you a story," said the doctor. "One day, an absent-minded chap went hunting, but instead of a gun, he picked up an umbrella. Suddenly a bear charged at him. Pointing his umbrella at the bear, he shot and killed it on the spot."

"That's impossible!" the old guy exclaimed. "Somebody else must have shot that bear."

"Exactly," replied the doctor.

Joke 2

A man had placed some flowers on the grave of his dearly departed mother and was walking back towards his car when his attention was diverted to a woman kneeling by the side of a grave.

The woman seemed to be praying and she kept repeating, "Why did you have to die? Why did you have to die?"

The man went up to her and said, "I'm awfully sorry to disturb you. I don't wish to intrude upon your private grief, but I've never seen anyone in such obvious pain before. Who is it that you mourn so deeply? Is it one of your children? One of your parents?"

The female mourner took a moment to collect herself and then replied, "No – it's my husband's first wife."

Joke 3

Two elderly women – Marge and Ethel – were out driving in a big old car. Neither could really see over the dashboard properly and as they were cruising along, they suddenly went through a red light. Marge, who was sitting in the passenger seat, thought to herself, "I must be losing my mind. I could've sworn we just went through a red light back there". A few minutes later, they came up to another crossroads and went through another red light. This time, Marge was 99% sure the light was red, but was worried she might somehow be wrong. At the next crossroads, they went sailing through yet another red. At this point, Marge turned to Ethel and said, "That's three red lights in a row we've gone through now! You could've killed us!" "Oh", said Ethel, looking around, "am I driving?"

Group 2: Unit 24, page 137, activity 5

Where are they now?

Andy Warhol once claimed that everybody will get their fifteen minutes of fame – and it is certainly starting to look that way! We now have celebrity chefs and celebrity gardeners, fly-on-the-wall TV shows about celebrity love islands and celebrity detox camps, and countless celebrity gossip magazines and web sites. Celebrity scandal is splashed all over the tabloids on a daily basis, and in our subsequent conversations many of us talk as if we are on first-name terms with the Justins, Kylies, Leonardos and Christinas of this world.

And yet what happens when the limelight fades and the crowds move on to the next new sensation? Here, we track the twists and turns in the lives of four ex-celebs now residing in the 'where are they now?' file.

Monica Lewinsky

Once just a humble intern in the White House, Monica Lewinsky was thrust into the limelight when it emerged – courtesy of leaked recordings of phone conversations between Lewinsky and her one-time confidante, Linda Tripp – that she had had a series of sexual encounters with the then President, Bill Clinton. This scandal became known as Monicagate and led to Clinton being impeached. He was acquitted of all charges and, ironically, even saw his popularity ratings subsequently rise.

Lewinsky claims she survived the harsh glare of the media spotlight by developing an enthusiasm for knitting. She went on to endorse a brand of diet products, set up her own line of handbags and host a short-lived reality TV dating show. She authorised an official biography in 1999 and is currently studying psychology in London!

Laurence Tureaud

Better known as Mr. T, Tureaud started out as a bodyguard, working for the likes of Mohammed Ali, and then did stints as a military policeman and a bouncer before landing a role in 'Rocky III'. His real claim to fame, though, lies in the character known as BA (short for Bad Attitude) that he played in the smash US series, 'The A team'. He actually changed his name by deed poll in 1980 to Mr. T, apparently claiming it would ensure everybody paid him sufficient respect when addressing him!

Instantly recognisable due to his trademark mohican haircut and love of chunky, flashy jewellery, Mr. T pursued a sideline career as a rapper and maker of motivational videos aimed at keeping young kids on the straight and narrow.

He was diagnosed with lymphoma in 1995 and underwent major chemotherapy. Eventually, however, he beat the disease and got back to work as a jobbing actor. Tureaud is a born-again Christian and makes frequent appearances on various religious TV networks and, like many ageing stars, has also been involved in litigation, suing a company for the illegal use of his image in their advertising.

Mr. T lives in California and remains single to this day.

Unit 11, page 67, activity 7

You are Toby Jenkins-Jones. Up until about a minute ago, you were having a nice sleep on the sofa in your front room. Martin has just woken you up and is shouting at you about the state the room is in. You're not in the mood to discuss things. Tell him how you feel about him.

Make sure you mention the problems discussed in the text you read. Try to use some of the grammar from Activities 4 and 5 and some of the expressions from Activity 2 as well. Spend five minutes planning exactly what you want to say.

Student C: Unit 5, page 30, activity 3

Spicy Asian Chicken Livers

Serves 4 people.

INGREDIENTS

500g chicken livers – approximately 12 pieces
salt and freshly-ground black pepper
1 cup peanut or soy oil
1 cup cornstarch
1 teaspoon Chinese five-spice blend (available at Asian supermarkets)
3 spring onions, cut into diagonal pieces about 2cm long

The marinade

3 tablespoons soy sauce
2 tablespoons Japanese mirin – or sweet sherry
1 tablespoon sake wine (sweet rice wine) – or sweet white wine
3 tablespoons sugar
1 tablespoon fresh ginger, finely chopped

DIRECTIONS

1. To make the marinade, mix the soy sauce, mirin, sake, sugar and ginger in a small, deep bowl. Stir well to dissolve the sugar and add in the ginger. Cover the chicken livers in the marinade. Refrigerate and leave for 30–45 minutes.
2. Remove the livers from the marinade and dry with a paper towel. Lay them flat on a large plate and season well with salt and pepper. Discard the marinade.
3. Heat the oil in a large non-stick pan over medium-high heat. Cover each piece of liver in cornstarch. In batches, fry each piece of liver on both sides until golden and crispy. Do not put too many pieces into the pan at the same time. Remove the livers from the oil and drain on a paper towel. While on the paper towel, sprinkle both sides of the livers with the Chinese Five Spice.
4. Top each piece of liver with a length of spring onion and skewer into place with a toothpick. Serve with a Teriyaki Dipping Sauce. Serve immediately.